"This book has stirred [illegible] ...troit Metropolitan area. A cur[illegible] ... the chapter headings will provide the explanation as to why."

Amyre Makupson, News Anchor
WKBD UPN50

"This book is written in an easy-to-read format. There is hope for those seeking to better themselves through well paying jobs. Al has acknowledged several biblical principles that cannot be ignored. Many of the antidotes certainly ring true."

Rev. Edgar Vann , Senior Pastor
Second Ebenezer Baptist Church

"Some people look at a problem and wring their hands. Al Stokes has looked at the problem of unemployment and rolled up his sleeves. His fact-filled book should be of great benefit to both the unemployed and the under-employed"

Mort Crim
Broadcast Journalist

"One goal of the Detroit Regional Chamber is to provide guidance and ideas that can help foster prosperity in the entire region that comprises Metroploitan Detroit. This book offers sound guidance and ideas as to how individuals may prosper through securing better employment."

Ann H. Hoag, Director
Detroit Regional Chamber

"Employment levels are indeed cyclic. But the best performers are always employable. The suggestions provided and guidance given in Al's book are based upon some known truths, with reasonable evidence that they work."

L. Brooks Patterson
Oakland County Michigan Executive

"Al has captured the essence of what we as management search for in our quest to train and promote employees. The chapter, Attitude and Performance is very good."

Melanie J. Myers, V. P.
Bank 1 One

"There is a definite need for skilled, knowledgeable people in the High-Tech industries of this country. Employers are constantly looking for people with the proper skills, education, and attitude. Al Stokes has noted in his book, the good jobs that pay well, are reserved for those that meet the criterion."

Joseph L. Petrosky
Center for Advanced Technologies

"The contract employment industry provides a valuable service. You Can Get A Better Job, has pinpointed and highlighted not only the value of work, but how to remain gainfully employed."

Robert J. Pfeffer III, Account Manager
Epcom Corporation

"I highly recommend the reading of this book. I find it to be accurate and realistic in its description of and resolution of situations in the workplace. You'll be hard-pressed to find a book on employment that is more helpful."

James A. Hall
Writer, Educator, Lecturer

"A book on employment that is not only practical, it makes sense. You will no doubt find yourself somewhere within these pages."

Tom Schroder, President
Traditions Residential Group

"Contract employment firms do indeed offer outstanding employment opportunities. 'You Can Get A Better Job' has highlighted this fact."

Jeff Lindemann, Area Manager
TechniPower Contract Staffing

"A superior, well written manual in which Mr. Stokes draws from his vast experiences and personal mentorships. Fantastic!"

Beverly Jean White
Author, Editor, Lecturer

"It's abundantly clear that a book on employment such as this is needed. Every business owner wishes their employees to embrace the lessons of A Job Well Done."

Jon L. Pepper, Associate Business Editor
The Detroit News

"A thoughtful discourse on the subject of employment. For young people, new to the workplace, this book offers eminently practical advice that can direct and influence them with affirmation"

Sandra Combs Birdiett
Freelance Journalist

"The building and construction industry provides equal opportunity for men and women to find gainful employment. You Can Get A Better Job, has highlighted this fact and offers vital training information."

Ken Jordan, President
C & J Construction

You Can Get A Better Job

A Sensible Approach To Employment

Albert H. Stokes

Edited by

Linda Simpson
Beverly Jean White

Hallawood & Company, Publications, Inc.
Southfield, Michigan

This book is available for special purchases in bulk by organizations and institutions, not for resale at special discounts. Please direct your inquiries to the Publisher. Published by Hallawood & Company Publications, Inc., 29209 Northwestern Highway PMB 566, Southfield, Michigan 48034-1006. Visit our Website at www.hallawood.com.

Library of Congress Cataloging-in-Publication Data
Stokes, Albert H.

Library of Congress Catalog Card Number 99-72115
CIP
ISBN 0-9663386-0-X TXL 842-402
Self-Help, Motivational, Reference

For permission to reprint copyrighted material, grateful acknowledgement is made to the following sources:

The Resume Handbook by Arthur D. Rosenberg & David V. Hizer. Copyright © 1996, Arthur D. Rosenberg and David V. Hizer. Published by Adams Media Corporation.

Directory of Contract Service Firms, 1997-28th Edition, Copyright © 1997, Published by Jerry Erickson, C.E. Publications, Inc.

Second Thoughts by Mort Crim, Copyright © 1997, Mort Crim Communications, Published by Health Communications, Inc.

Windows Guide To The Internet, Second Edition by Michael Fraase, Copyright © 1994, The Coriolis Group

Covers designed by **L. T. Graphics Studio**
Logo designed by **Tech-Art**
Proof Edited by **Linda Simpson**
Line Edited by **Beverly Jean White**
Typesetting by **Letter Perfect Graphics**

Dedication

This book is dedicated to the two people who helped God to mold and shape my character, the late Rev. Charles O. Miles and his loving wife, Luvenia Miles.

Acknowledgments

This work could not have been accomplished without the help of the following people: My loving and faithful wife Yvonne, Dr. Maurice Wheeler and the entire staff of the Detroit Public Library, the four men of God in my life: Kim Evans, Bishop Keith A. Butler, Rev. Timothy Gambino, and Rev. Aldolphus Cast. Special thanks to G. Richie Gardner and Alex Cusenza, for their support.

FOREWORD

When considering whether or not to write a foreword for this book, the first question that came to mind was, "Why me?" Being the CEO and publisher of The Michigan Front Page, and responsible for its daily operations, time is always at a premium. Before making any contribution, it was incumbent upon me to determine the purpose of this book. After reading the 'Overview' of the book, my interest was sparked. It addressed several key elements that I espouse: education, technology and attitude. Knowing the importance of these elements in obtaining employment, I was led to a further examination of the text.

I have long been an advocate of embracing new technologies as a means of remaining on the cutting edge of education. Education is a process. A life-long process. We must all strive to continually educate ourselves. It is ultimately our responsibility. Al Recognized that an entire segment of the public had been neglected and wrote a book designed specifically for them. A unique perspective on the subject of employment is being offered. That is the essence of what any writer does on any subject written about, provide their perspective. Al draws upon his many years of technical and managerial experiences and is able to articulate their relevance to everyday situations. I also detect a passion in his oral communications. He truly believes in the idea of forming sensible strategies for employment.

Influence can be defined as the ability to effect a change in beliefs, attitudes, or behaviors. Al desires to have an influence on the beliefs, attitudes and behaviors of his readers. You, as the reader, are required to think about the central themes of each chapter. Your assignment is to determine how they can apply to you in your quest for more meaningful employment. This is a book that can be permanently placed on your bookshelf. It is comprehensive, stimulating, entertaining and thought provoking. Many of the lessons are timeless.Through it, readers can improve their own wellbeing. It is hoped that 'You Can Get A Better Job, A Sensible Approach To Employment,' will become a powerful influence in the lives of those who would come to understand the value of gainful employment.

Samuel Logan, Publisher & CEO
The Michigan Front Page

TABLE OF CONTENTS

INTRODUCTION

"When you think you have exhausted possibilities, remember this, you haven't."
Robert H. Schuler

Life, liberty, and the pursuit of happiness all can be achieved by fulfilling one state: being gainfully employed. Being employed empowers us. It has been said that if you feed a person a fish, you have only fed him one meal. However, if you teach a person to fish, you have helped to feed him for a lifetime. To take it a step further, the person you have assisted in teaching how to fish can relay what he has learned to others, and on down the line. This book teaches you not only how to fish, but from which pond to cast off. This is the central theme of the book, **You Can Get A Better Job,** ***A Sensible Approach To Employment.*** There are no mysteries to becoming gainfully employed. All that is needed is guidance. The guidance provided in this book is proven, sound and understandable doctrine that has withstood the test of time. The message is clear. You can help yourself by investing time to learn a skill, preferably, one that is in demand. Everyone has worth and value and can be productive.

The first chapter, **"The Merits Of Work,"** establishes why working is vitally important to individuals and to the generations they may foster. We all have dreams. We can dream of prosperity and see ourselves in its grasp. We must set out to discover where we can excel in order to make our dreams come true. Such is the theme of the chapter **"Dreaming And Discovery."** Other chapters all relating to self improvement are **"The Comfort Zone," "A Job Well Done," "Getting Along With People," "Presentation" and "Attitude And Performance."** These chapters provide instruction and information on where to get training for the jobs of the present and future. As the title suggests, the chapter called **"Preparation,"** has to do with preparing for employment. The days of good paying industrial jobs, for those with less than a high school education, have long since passed. Things will never be the way they were. The global economy has seen to that. America, as well as the other industrialized nations, must be competitive.

You Can Get A Better Job, ***A Sensible Approach To Employment,*** contains chapters that provide insight into the real "goings on" in business, corporations, and small companies. What type of people are they looking for? How will the choices be made? The reader can devise a plan to accomplish goals based on information that is contained in the chapters **"Politics," "Strategies For Employment," "Opportunities And Possibilities."**

Southeastern Michigan, where I live, like many other states, has undergone a very painful awakening. They have come to understand what is meant by the **"global economy."** It affects everyone, from the average citizen to the politicians who confiscate our dollars in the form of taxes. The message is clear. Accept change, adapt to it, and continue on until the next change occurs. Those living in Metropolitan Detroit have not had to adhere to this message until now. With the influx of foreign competition in the automobile market and its suppliers, many people have lost their jobs. Some unfortunately have no hope of regaining them. However, they do have the hope of becoming retrained for other jobs. They have to believe the words, "Yes, you can get a better job." Detroit and the auto industry are not unique in their loss of jobs due to international competition. The textile mills of the South, the coal mines of the Midwest, and the steel mills of the East have all undergone drastic reductions in their work forces. Less expensive products from overseas have brought this on. Why sit around reminiscing about the way things use to be? Go forward and embrace tomorrow with the expectation of good things happening.

It is a fact that many households in this country are headed by single parents. Usually this parent is the mother of the child or children. There are many reasons why women find themselves alone as guardians. The reasons why are not the subject of this book. We do know this, that depending upon the generosity of strangers and government services is not only humiliating, it is unreliable. In addition, the wrong message is sent to children, one of dependency. Some of these women have hidden talents. They have the ability to learn skills and become productive. What they need is information, guidance, and encouragement. They need to know what are the good paying jobs, where they are located, and what training is needed to secure them.

We all, at some time or another, have paid to see a sporting event. We are willing to pay high prices to see those who are very good at what they do. They make it look easy. They have prepared long and hard to reach that level of performance. They practiced doing the right things. You will become good at what you practice. When you practice doing the right things, they become easy to do. When you practice the wrong things, they too become easy. You can reach a point where you do not know how to do things the right way. Individuals new to the job market need to know that they are building an employment history. That history could be a trail of jobs done well or of employers who cannot give them good recommendations. Such is the theme of **"A Job Well Done,"** a chapter in the book.

Administrative assistants, and similar workers all over the country, can attest to the fact that they are underpaid and overworked. Such is the position they have. Market forces dictate what they will be paid. The same market forces convey a message that they can easily be replaced because the knowledge and skills they have are common. Does this mean there is no hope of them getting a better job? No, it does not. With guidance, a more marketable vocation can be chosen, one that can allow them not only to negotiate how much they will make but where in the country they will work.

Within the corporate setting, one can be lost in the sea of humanity. To use a crude metaphor, everyone gets potatoes. What are potatoes? That is your compensation, your paycheck, given out twice a month or on some other interval. Then there are those that are not satisfied with just the potatoes. They want gravy on their potatoes and they get it. The gravy is composed of the perks that accompany positions of status. You do not get gravy just by being a good employee. You must first have the desire to move up the corporate ladder and play the political games. There is much to know, but where do you get that kind of inside knowledge that is practical and written in intelligible English?

You Can Get A Better Job is written for the semi-educated, moderately educated, the young person new to the job market, the semi-professional, and the professional, seeking to better themselves in the work place. There are some down-to-earth, sensible things that each individual can do to enhance their marketability. Becoming more marketable enhances a person's employability. Thus the subtitle, ***A Sensible***

Approach To Employment was created. Some people know that they can do better, but they are in that area called **"the comfort zone,"** which is akin to wearing a pair of broken-in shoes. They may not be aesthetically pleasing but they feel good. When you are headed somewhere important, you shed those worn, broken-in shoes. That comfortable job is the pair of broken-in shoes. That job must be replaced with a new one. It is easy to talk about but a difficult thing to do.

In my youth, when returning from a grueling day of lawn-cutting in Grosse Pointe, I would ride in the back of my dad's truck, weather permitting. The truck had removable gates on all sides. It could then become a flat bed if desired. Our journey into Grosse Pointe was always along Lake Shore Road, and we would branch out from there. The estates overlooking Lake St. Clair were all breath taking. I vowed that I would one day live in a similar home. I was never told by my parents that some things were off limits to me. I attributed all the comforts of a luxurious life to hard work. My dad certainly worked hard and instilled in all of us the principle of working for a living. "Do not look for someone to hand you something," he always said.

America is the land of opportunity, where a people are free to exploit their natural abilities for profit. One of the hardest things to overcome when living in a new country is the language. You can learn to count the currency and decipher the international street signs. To speak, read and write the language of a new country is quite an accomplishment. This happens with astounding frequency to immigrants who come to America from every third world country on the globe. They come here for the freedom to earn their way and keep most of what they have earned. Their goal is to live for their own sake, not for the sake of the government or their fellow man. They will gather together as a family, pool what little resources they have and begin to produce something. This is especially true of the immigrants migrating from such places as Vietnam, China,

Indonesia, India, etc. The work ethic is instilled in them from an early age. They know that they will either work or die. Some of the people that come from these second and third world nations endure real hardships in their native lands. What's more, there are no social services in place to help.

You cannot guarantee someone's outcome in life. You cannot guarantee an opportunity either. If you steadfastly believe that your misfortune is caused by someone else's gain, you will continually be in bondage. That is a true slave mentality, no desire for freedom. You fail in life because you didn't take advantage of the opportunities that were set before you, not because someone has kept you down. You are told by some that it is not your fault. Consider this, there is a great deal of money to be made by those who communicate this notion. It is also easy for individuals to believe that they are in their predicaments because of the mystical person called the "MAN." Forget the fact the you are a high school drop out, an alcoholic, or a drug addict.

When class was in session, you wanted to be cool and skip school with Joe Dokes. Now you and Joe have to work in a car wash because you cannot read. The work is honorable and better than a life of crime, but you will not have an abundant existence. Consequently, the speech of the social panderers that lay all of your failures at the feet of other people sounds good to you. These social panderers earn their living from your misery. They will not do a thing to put an end to the cycle of poverty and dependence. If that were to happen, you would not need them and they would have to get a real job. You must take advantage of the opportunities when they are set before you. When you do not, it is no one's fault but your own.

You have talent and are willing to work hard. The traditional type of schooling just does not fit you. The signs have been there, that you work well with your hands. It brings you satisfaction and a sense of accomplishment. You see other people prospering, even the ones who are out there breaking the law. That is not for you though. You want to make your money honestly and not have to look over your shoulder at every turn for trouble. There is that lotto commercial again. "They say that all it takes is one dollar and I could be a millionaire." Then again, you have seen the reality of the situation. All those people on public assistance chasing that same pipe dream. They are the ones who can least afford it, taking a five dollar food coupon and redeeming it for a one dollar lotto ticket. It is always someone in the suburbs who wins the big jackpot.

Your job at the fast food eatery pays you just enough to sustain you. You're only two steps above the minimum wage. After you subtract the money you spend on public transportation and your personal needs, there is not a sufficient amount left to make any real progress. If it were not for the fact that you still live at home with your parent(s), you would be destitute. You have thought about working two jobs, but the logistics of traveling would be a nightmare, especially in the winter months.

****

You may find a case similar to yours in these next examples of people wanting to do something better with their lives. It is 4:00 a.m. and the alarm clock has just awakened you. You have one hour to get yourself prepared and travel to your job that starts at 5:00 a.m. Traffic is light at that time of the morning. Your travel should be free from congestion. However, once you arrive at your place of employment, you begin another eight hours of monotony and drudgery. You have stood in front of that machine for so long, you can determine whether it is running properly from its sound. Push the green button and the red light comes on. When the red light goes out, the green light comes on. Then you push the green button again. Back and forth you go until your 20-minute break comes. After the 20-minute break will be the 30-minute lunch period allotted to all of the factory's hourly personnel. Where can you go and eat in a civil manner in 30 minutes? Not far, so you bring your lunch and eat in your car when the weather is pleasant.

The end of your eight-hour shift has arrived and all you're doing is counting the minutes until you are permitted to run your pass through the magnetic reader. What is on your mind? Getting home as quickly as possible so you can take a shower. You want to wash the smell of machine oil out of your hair. You will have a good dinner, then perhaps a little television afterwards. You need a little quiet time to reflect on the events of the day. Time is spent pondering what you would do if given the opportunity to do something else. Then it is off to bed so that the scenario can be repeated the next day. There is not much to look forward to except payday. You are smart enough to recognize your vulnerability as far as job security is concerned. There is no such thing! Whether it's a union shop or non-union shop, your job could disappear tomorrow.

In addition, you took this job right out of high school and were glad to get it at the time. You have no special skills or training other than what is required for your present job. However, you feel deep within yourself that you will be able to follow through if pointed in the right direction. You would like to be trained to do something else, but what would you do and where would you do it? You know and have heard of other people who are doing what they love to do and are getting paid to do it. What is so special about them? Why not you? Are you destined to spend the rest of your life in a dead end job? Sure, it is honest work and you are grateful to have a job, but you cannot avoid the feeling that there is something better for you out there. Somewhere there is a job just made for you with your name on it. One problem, you are here and the job is there. How do you get there? This book was written for you, because the fact is, **You Can Get A Better Job.**

****

The new job-posting was placed on the bulletin board by the coffee station. The routine is one that you have experienced before. Those working in large corporate settings know the routine. It is the one where you submit your name for consideration for the new position. You have the experience in all practical terms because you have been performing that job in that capacity ever since the opening arose. Once again, the letter of rejection hits your mailbox. When the new person is hired, a formal introduction takes place. It gets worse. You are expected to train this new person for the position that you applied for and were rejected. How do you do that and maintain the proper attitude? It has become easier to entertain thoughts of gender discrimination because you happen to be a female. Your thoughts are, "All of the good positions are being filled by males." You have let your boss know of your desire to move on to something new many times. However, it is in his best interest to maintain things as they are because of the proficiency with which you perform your daily tasks. Well how about a raise in pay commensurate with your performance? Forget about that. Your boss has told you that they cannot pay you any more because you are already at the top of your classification. What's the big deal? Why don't they have your classification changed? Fear not. **You Can Get A Better Job.**

****

In your mind, you have paid your dues. The corporation, though still very large, has reduced it numbers considerably since you joined it. There have been several mergers of divisions. They brought no significant change to your career. That is to say, your career was not hurt by the mergers. This time it is different. The salaried ranks have been reduced, as well as the hourly ranks. You are not afraid of losing your job. What does concern you is that the merger gets rid of all the old bosses and executives who know you. They will no longer be able to watch over your career to see that you get some gravy on your potatoes. They can't even help themselves because they have lost their coverings too. All of the hard work you did is now for naught. You are one among many now competing for even fewer spots. Your promotion was within sight and almost cast in stone. Now, it is but a vision of what could have been.

There is that graph staring you in the face. It is the graph that has age along the bottom and classification level along the side. You can see the correlation line clearly. It is interpreted this way. If you are not at a certain level by a certain age, you won't get there. This is not written down in human resource manuals but you know it to be true nonetheless. You were on track; not anymore. The merger has hurt your career. Now you have got to make a choice. You can sit around for several more years and hope to get noticed, or you can launch out into the deep and blaze a trail somewhere else. But that means leaving the nest, and a comfortable nest it is. However, you are confident that you can do better somewhere else. Somewhere, you will be allowed to exercise all of the talents that you have. It is not over for you. **You Can Get A Better Job.**

****

You have been a check-out clerk for two years and would like to move up to something better. You know that the company you work for has a program for managers in training. You would like to get into one of those programs. You feel as though you have just as much on the ball as those who are managers now. Why shouldn't you have an opportunity to better your standing with the company? Are there things that you can do to make the pendulum of opportunity swing your way? Of course. It starts with an effort to make things happen for you.

****

Your company has just gone through a merger with one of its larger divisions. It has happened to you once before, but the outcome before was just a name change. This time would be much different. All of the executives that knew you are scrambling for jobs themselves. They are no longer in a position to help you. Some of them will have to retire because no other division will employ them in the same capacity. They already have their executives in place. All of the previous work and "politicking" you did is now for naught. The promotion you so valiantly sought was within your sights prior to the merger. To the management of the new division, you are just a name filling a position. The promotion pool has grown significantly and you have nothing going in your favor.

You are not content with just being employed with the company. You want status and the perks that come with it. It's time to make a decision because reality has struck. There is that reality curve staring you in the face. You know the one. The curve has two axis's. On the vertical leg is your job level or classification. On the horizontal leg is your age. The rule of thumb is that if you didn't reach a certain level by age 40, chances are you are not going to get there. You were right on track prior to the merger, following the diagonal line where the two lines meet. Now your promotion is seriously in doubt. It will take you years to re-establish yourself. Do you want to play those games all over again and not be certain of the outcome? Or, do you want to find your place with a new company, forfeiting your seniority with the company, but taking your valuable experience with you? You could get an immediate pay increase along with a job closer to home. That has to be worth a few bucks, too.

You are not being mistreated by your present employer. You just want some of the gravy for your potatoes. Everybody gets potatoes. a potato is the paycheck you receive. The gravy is the perks on top of the paycheck. When you truthfully evaluate the situation, there are individuals equally and even more qualified than you who want to get promoted. But you have been around long enough to know that politics play a large part in the promotional decisions. Some of your colleagues have never worked anywhere else, unlike you who have held many previous jobs. Those poor souls do not have a clue as to what is out there in the job market and are afraid to find out. What are you going to do? Hand in your resignation and find another job, or stay and hope for the best, scrambling with the rest for fewer positions in a much larger company?

****

Your quality of life is sustained and determined by how much money is at your disposal. The amount of money at your disposal is determined by the type of job you have. Liking what you do also has a great deal to do with your quality of life. Your quality of life is important because all you really have on this earth is time. Time is the sand in the hour glass of life. There is a finite amount of sand in the hour glass. You cannot place more in it, you can only hasten its departure. When all of the sand runs out, your life is completed. What your employer is buying is some of the time allotted to you. That is why it is important to be doing what you really want to do. Time passes so quickly. Isiah Thomas, one of the most skillful persons to ever touch a basketball, said this of himself: "I am the most blessed person in the world. I am doing something that I love to do and I am getting paid to do it. I would be doing it for free if I were not getting paid." Wouldn't we all like to be able to make this claim? It does not happen by accident. It is a journey with steps that are methodically taken. Author Marsha Sinetar wrote a book entitled, *"Do What You Love, The Money Will Follow."* That is fine if you can support yourself using that premise. I have a saying that is more practical. It is, "Do what you have to do until you can do what you really want to do." This book was written to inspire and give direction to those who really want to do something else with their lives.

You cannot live better than your means of support will allow. Your means of support is your job. Attempts are made to circumvent this rule, but they are rarely successful. This explains the success of legalized gambling and lotteries across this country. There are great numbers of people trying to attain wealth without working for it. It is seldom the case that one has enough money. Even billionaires continue to amass wealth. By what method are we to gain wealth? We must work for it. Because all jobs have a different wage scale, the goal must be to place yourself in the stream of a good job that pays well, and one that you like. Sound impossible? It isn't. All it takes is some sweat-equity and perseverance to bring this dream into reality.

****

All humans have worth. It is my belief that we can demonstrate our value through work. It brings me joy to help people. The knowledge that we have did not come by spontaneous generation. There were always people there, willing to help us. Why can't we help others to attain their goals and fulfill their dreams? Many metaphors will be used to describe real life situations in this book. They will also be used to convey certain messages and lessons.

There are many self-help books written for those with college and graduate degrees. These books are telling them something they already know. They are marketable. The degree gives them the opportunity to work just about wherever they choose. What about people who are not acclimated to the classroom but are skillful with their hands? They should not be considered castaways. They can and should be productive members of our society. Others need to be encouraged to enter special training, to go back to school and learn computer skills. Some of these individuals have ideas that could make them independently wealthy citizens. Shouldn't they be encouraged to discover what America has to offer? They are the people this book is written for. These individuals number in the hundreds of thousands across the country. Will all take heed to this message? Most likely they will not. That does not negate its soundness, timeliness, and validity.

This book is not written in lofty speech using technical, terse terms that only a linguist can understand. Instead, I have elected to keep it simple, providing the information in an easy-to-read format. As you read this book, you'll discover that a wide spectrum of employment senarios are being addressed. This was done in an attempt to meet the needs of a wider readership, rather than focus on a single group of individuals. What is really being offered in this book is a perspective on employment. It is the perspective of the author.

The number of books published on the subject of Thomas Jefferson number around 558. Seven hundred sixty nine books have been published on Abraham Lincoln. Even more astounding, 7,868 books have been published on greatest of American conflicts, the Civil War. What do all of these have in common with this book? In every case, the authors are providing their perspectives on events that occurred. In addition, they are offering commentary on the speeches and political gestures.

How did they begin their missions? What qualified them to write these books? Their missions began by researching the events, checking and re-checking. What qualified them is a more difficult question to answer. I believe they wrote out of passion for the subjects. I have followed this same pattern. I have written on a subject that I have a wealth of knowledge and experience on, employment. My passion and mission with this book is to enhance the lives of the readers.

In this manner, they too can acquire a piece of the pie called, "the American dream."

THE MERITS OF WORK

"This we command you, that if any would not work, neither should he eat."
II Thessalonians 3:10

We have come to understand that work has a greater significance than just as a means to support ourselves. "Work is applied effort. It is whatever we put ourselves into, whatever we expend our energy on for the sake of accomplishing or achieving something. Work in this fundamental sense is not what we do for a living but what we do with our living." These words were written by one of America's greatest human treasures, William J. Bennet, in his book, *The Book of Virtues.* Your quality of life is governed by the type of job you have. You cannot live better than the ability you have to earn money. If one does not work, one's existence and well being will be determined by some agency administering welfare. It matters not what theorists expound. It is just that, theory. I have seen first hand what welfare fosters in people.

Welfare enslaves everyone it can without discrimination. The slavery is not physical, but mental, and produces a generation of people who feel angry and slothful; who feel entitled to something that is not theirs. It robs people of their dignity. Their ability to envision a positive image of themselves is totally snuffed out. Their self-worth is now determined by the state in which they live. There are very few people with such principles as to not want the hard earned funds of others. How many people would work if they could receive equivalent money in unemployment without working? When you lose your inspiration to work, you lose your desire to press your way forward. When you no longer desire to move forward, you stand still. When you stand still, you are finished.

There was a period in which the politicians arranged for unemployed auto workers to receive extended benefits. They were called Trade Readjustment Allowances (TRA). It was thought to be a safety net for those who had no other means of support. In reality, it took away the incentive to retrain for the future. There was no need. They were getting money now. Why worry about the future? Work has virtue in itself and everyone should come to understand this fact. As these individuals collected their checks, they failed to notice what was happening. The majority of them sat around and did nothing. The money being paid to them was that good. However, the money that they thought was free was not. The price they paid was the loss of time. This loss of time was significant because it was time that could have been spent training for something else. There were no requirements that the individuals receiving TRA become involved in any re-training programs.

Compassion should be the measure by which we empower people to help themselves. It has been said over and over again, "Give a person a fish and you have fed him a single meal. Teach a person how to fish and you have fed him for a lifetime." Teaching a person to fish is analogous to helping him acquire the skills to get a job. There are those among us who have no intention of ever working. Instead, they will depend upon the generosity of the public for their sustenance. They become entrapped in a cycle of poverty and discouragement. Begging on the streets is no way to survive in a country that boasts being the richest in the world. At various street corners in and around metropolitan areas, it is common to find men and women displaying signs saying, "I Will Work For Food." If you were to take them up on their offer to work for food, your indulgence would be met with fierce resistance. What they really want is for you to reach into your pocket and give them some of your money. What they'll do with the money is debatable.

This is not what I would call a cleverly devised scam. It is very obvious that most of these individuals would rather depend upon the generosity of the public than work. Isn't it conceivable that if you were a manager of a fast food eatery you would oblige a person who said he would work for food? Only the most cold-hearted among us would resist allowing this person to take the garbage out, mop a floor, or even pick up the trash in the parking lot in exchange for a meal. What is the value of a hamburger, an order of fries, and a soft drink to the manager compared to tasks that the rest of the employees would rather not do?

Think about all the food that hits the floor during a normal workday and must be discarded. It adds up to a great deal more than what would be used for barter. I have seen this very thing many times while awaiting the changing of traffic lights. Unemployed individuals post themselves at these corners because it accomplished two things. It provided them with an opportunity to approach vehicles that are stopped. Secondly, the location acts as a mechanism to garner sympathy because they are in the immediate vicinity of food that can be purchased. These freeloaders, both men and women, are hoping to shape your thoughts. The impression is given that once some money is in their hands, they'll go right over to the eatery and purchase a meal. That is not going to happen.

Living in the Detroit metropolitan area, we are fortunate enough to have the Canadian Broadcasting Company (CBC) come over our television air waves. A documentary was aired on the street beggars of the city of Toronto. The individuals that were recorded revealed all of the techniques they used to cajole funds out of people passing by. The premise of the story was that these people did not want to work. They earned a fair living by begging, while the money was tax free.

The individuals were not smart enough to know not to reveal the fact that they were perpetrating a scam. These antics are not peculiar to Toronto. The scenario is repeated with great frequency in many urban areas. If you do not work for your own sake, what else can you do? One has to believe in his own self worth. Politicians and bureaucrats cannot be relied upon to deliver you from the bondage of this slavery. It is in their best interest to see to it that you remain where you are, thus continuing their employment. Government programs abound, but your best hope will be in the private sector.

I, like many others, have been told that I have no compassion and lack a basic understanding of the plight of the unemployed. What I have is a belief that all people can be productive and make a contribution to society. If there are no impediments, physical or mental, every individual is capable of contributing to their own well being. I refuse to do anything that will allow people to remain in a "do nothing" state of mind. The generational cycle of poverty is a frame of mind more than a condition of state. True compassion is helping people help themselves so that they no longer need help. They in turn, can be an example to others and bring hope to them in the same manner. I am mindful that there can be events in the lives of some that necessitate some sort of general assistance. This assistance should not be a way of life. In return for this assistance, the recipients should render some sort of public service to the community. I can imagine that there would be at least a moment's feeling of pride from this activity.

Many states now have strict guidelines to determine which of its citizens are eligible for public assistance. These guidelines have been enacted in an attempt to curb the cycle of poverty and expectations of something for nothing. When it was announced that government assistance to certain able bodied people was ending, these individuals were forced to find work. Some may have started out as minimum wage earners at fast food eateries or similar jobs. What happened was predictable. They began to gain pride in working for their money. The residual effects included learning good work habits, the importance of presentation, and doing jobs well. These individuals moved on to better jobs. The cycle of poverty was broken.

TRUE STORY

The events depicted in the aforementioned documentary was not surprising to me. Growing up in an urban environment, you had a feel for what was commonly called "scams." Many years prior to viewing the CBC documentary, I was walking along one of the streets of downtown Detroit and noticed a man perched near a Hardee's restaurant. I was impeccably dressed, as always when I conduct business. I was the perfect mark, or so he thought. As I was walking by he uttered that familiar phrase, "Hey, Mister, can you spare a quarter for a cup of coffee?"

Because he was polite enough to call me mister, instead of a myriad of other titles like, Mac, Bud, Brotherman, etc., I engaged him. I wanted to affirm my belief that it was a scam. I said to him, "I'll do better than that. Let's go into this Hardee's and I'll buy you a complete breakfast." His reply was predictable "That's okay, man, go on down the road." The look of sincere desperation had now been replaced by a scowl. I had called his bluff. Was I right or what? If you were down and out and hungry, and food was all that you really desired, would you turn down a gratuitous meal? I think not. However, if you had planned on abusing the exploiting of the public for selfish gain, to use the money to buy drugs or alcohol, the last thing you would want is for some do-gooder to buy you food.

****

Perform your own test. For homeowners, it will be easy enough. There is an abundance of chores that need to be performed around the house, chiefly, yard work. It seems that there is always more work to do than there is time to do it. Ask one of the bearers of a sign displaying "I Will Work For Food" for a minute of their time. Make them an offer to feed them, as well as pay them $10 an hour, for performing some yard work. You may think that an offer like that would be their dream come true. In fact, it could develop into something larger than just your yard. Those who live around you most likely have a similar problem, not enough time to get things done. The neighbors, seeing that you have someone assisting you with your yard work, would inquire as to the particulars. A request would be made to have the person come and work on their yard when he finished with yours. Guess what? This person is now on his way to feeding himself for a lifetime. Getting people to do that kind of work is difficult unless you are willing to pay a professional landscaping company the rate that it would charge. I am confident that you will not be successful in employing the sign-carrier.

In urban metropolitan areas, job postings are abundant. Any Sunday news classified advertising section will prove this to be true. The wages paid may be in the vicinity of what has been established as the minimum wage, but the minimum wage was not to be that which a head of household would earn. Instead, it was intended to act as a base minimum that would entice employers to hire young, inexperienced workers. In addition, those new to the workplace would be introduced to good work habits such as punctuality. This can only be accomplished if it is a profitable proposition for the employers.

After all, they are not in business to employ people, but to make money. After a sufficient amount of time has passed, it is assumed that the person starting out at the minimum wage moves on to another job to make more money. I have seen help wanted signs plastered on the sides of busses, trucks, and buildings. Many of those jobs pay well above the minimum wage. That is because the free market, when allowed to work, does just that, it works. If employers cannot get people to work for a set wage to perform a specific task, the wages will have to be raised to a level where it will attract workers.

There will always be problems associated with where one works versus where one lives. I have talked to many who dwell in the inner cities who say all the jobs are in the suburbs and there is no means of public transportation to get there. Who said that it was going to be easy? What is easy to do is to make an excuse as to why you can not succeed. Perhaps getting to where the jobs are requires a little creativity. Every situation is different and its iterations cannot be solved within the pages of this book. I discovered a truth long ago. It is that people find a way to do what they really want to do. They also search for and find a way to avoid that which they would rather not do. Therein lies the challenge, to go against the grain of one's own self-defeating desires.

Working is the key that unlocks the door to the American dream. Things are not always as they are portrayed. Where did our nation's rich get their wealth? They worked for it. Sure, individuals such as Donald Trump were not born destitute. However, if one were to read his book, *The Art of The Deal*, one could come away with a different perspective of this very affluent man. He stated in his book that he usually only sleeps four hours a day. That leaves him with a four-hour advantage to make phone calls because his competitors are sleeping for eight hours. The man is a tireless worker. The same can be said for many other celebrities. What captivates the mind of many is the idea that there is some easy money to be made. Swindlers use this ploy to their advantage. They capitalize on our selfish desires to get something for little, or nothing. Get-rich-quick schemes abound, taking advantage of those who can least afford to lose what little money they have.

Politics always comes into play when there are discussions involving the unemployed. Surveys are taken and the data that is used will reflect one position or another, depending on who has initiated the survey. What is overlooked are those in our society who are unemployable because of their abuse of legal and illegal substances. Alcoholism and drug addition take their toll in the form of lost jobs and productivity. The solution to this problem is not the subject of this book. However, there are some jobs that are so boring and monotonous that drugs and alcohol are used to add some excitement to the task. In reality, a person who drinks or uses drugs on the job not only endangers their own life, but the lives of others as well.

If you are a person who is entangled with substance abuse of any type, your ability to better yourself in the job market is seriously hindered. To put it simply, you cannot be high on the job. If you are found out, you will not have a job much longer. One theme that I try to continually stress is that you are constantly looking for a better job. You must guard against doing things that will hinder you at some future date. How would it look on your resume, “fired for substance abuse?”

****

The elderly are people who, figuratively speaking, are of a dying breed. They have work ethics that were instilled in them from their youth. My grandmother was 92 when she died, and was full of worldly wisdom. She was a woman whose entire family picked cotton in the broiling summer sun of Alabama. One of her favorite sayings was “If a man doesn’t work, he’s going to steal. If he steals, he’s going to jail.” This message is still in the hearts of our nation’s elderly. There are a group of elderly people who work to keep themselves busy. They understand that it is far better to remain active in the twilight years of their lives by working. As one of them said to me, “You can either be worn out when you die from doing things or rusted out when you die from doing nothing.”

Then there are the elderly who must work in order to take care of themselves. Often, these jobs are taken to supplement meager pension checks. This is an unfortunate situation to be at such a point in one’s life. What working does is provide them with a sense of self-worth. Not having to depend upon government assistance or the generosity of strangers has to heighten one’s self esteem. What we have today is a conundrum. On the one hand, we have the elderly who have the wisdom of their years, the experience and the will to work. On the other hand, we have the young that have the energy but lack the desire and the dedication. If a person could graft traits of the young into the old, what a winner he would be.

****

Those who are in rural settings, and are seeking employment, have to go to where the jobs are. I make reference to the section of this book entitled **"Opportunities and Possibilities."** The task of finding employment elsewhere can be simplified by acquiring a classified advertising section from a newspaper. If the immediate area is not large enough to contain a classified advertising section, one of the larger neighboring communities will.

Waiting for some company to set up a factory in their rural surroundings may happen, but I would not count on it. Companies use many factors to decide where they will locate a brand new facility. We only hear about the location after the decision has been made. There is work. What is needed are people who are willing to do the work. It may not be exactly the kind of work that is desired but I adhere to the philosophy of "doing what you have to do until you are able to do what you would like to do."

DREAMING AND DISCOVERY

"Stir up the gift of God that is in thee."
II Timothy 1:6

What the mind of man (or woman) can conceive, the ingenuity of man can achieve. That fact has been demnstrated time and time again through the ages. Look at the most marvelous creature on the face of the earth, man. No two of us are exactly alike. Each of us is created with unique talents and abilities. The object is to discover what those talents and abilities are and exploit them. Exploit in this sense is not intended to signify misuse, but to take advantage of the gifts that God gave us. The exemplification of these talents can be found in various individuals. The great pyramids of Egypt are an example from ancient times. I have marveled at all of the experts who lay claim to having the definitive answer as to how these great wonders were constructed. Their theories on the methods of construction differ, but they all are in agreement that the pyramids are a magnificent achievement.

One of the most gifted, brilliant men to have ever lived was sculptor and artist, Michelangelo. What a glorious vision of the possibilities, to take an 18-foot block of marble and carve out the statue of David. Even more remarkable was the mural painted on the ceiling of the Sistine Chapel. The life of Michelangelo is graphically depicted in a movie entitled, "David," starring Charleston Heston. This a movie well worth renting, if the attributes of a dreamer are important to you.

By far, man's greatest achievement is flight. Why flight? Because it is both natural and unnatural. Flight occurs naturally for the creatures of the earth that were meant to fly. When it comes to man, it is an entirely different story. Man willed himself to fly. It was in the heart of many a dreamer to fly as the birds. Machines were created to allow him to do so. In our modern day setting, I find the space shuttle to be the culmination of someone's dream. Imagine a vessel that enters the outer atmosphere of earth as a rocket does, re-enters and lands like an airplane.

What is so unique about the space shuttle? Unlike a plane that can abort an imperfect landing and retry, the space shuttle cannot. It is nothing more than a gliding rock when it spirals back into the earth's atmosphere. It has no second chance to get the landing right. A perfect landing must be made the first time around. These are all testaments to man's ability to dream and make that dream a reality. There are men and women who have taken concepts that exist only in their imagination and nursed them until there was a manifestation. What of those who said it couldn't be done? Did the doubters and unbelievers detour these dreamers? Of course not. They were ignored and the dreamers carried on.

Almost every household in this country has at least one of these in the kitchen. It saves a tremendous amount of time by shortening the length of time required to cook food. You guessed it. I speak of none other than the microwave oven. The microwave oven was invented by a gentleman by the name of Percy Spencer. Mr. Spencer dropped out of school in the eighth grade. His lack of formal education did not prevent him from dreaming of solutions to many of life's problems.

Mr. Spencer's perfection of the microwave oven stemmed from work that was being done on radiowave energy during World War II. While working for Raytheon, Percy Spencer was given the task of making radar more compact, reliable, and the components cheaper. That would enable more units to be built and deployed in the defense of Europe. Radar was initially an invention of the British government. They, however, were at a stalemate. This new secret weapon was cumbersome, expensive and unreliable. If a way could be found to mass produce radar units, it would give those fighting against the Nazis a distinct advantage.

An envoy was dispatched from England to petition the Raytheon company for help. Raytheon's best thinker and inventor was Percy Spencer. Percy told the representatives of the British government, "Let me take the unit home and think about it." They reluctantly submitted to his request. A few days later, their indulgence was rewarded. Percy Spencer had taken the massive radar unit completely apart. He spent time dreaming of how each component could be simplified and mass produced. It was through the use of on board radar that planes flying over the Atlantic Ocean were able to spot enemy submarines. The German submarines had a stranglehold on merchant marine shipments to England. Something had to be done to prevent the triumph of evil. The rest of the story is contained in our history books. However, the history books will not tell you that Percy Spencer was a dreamer.

The name Michael Flatley may not be well known, but his artistry is known throughout the world. He is the dancer and choreographer who originated the Irish folk dance production, "River Dance." He is a person who gave up everything to follow his dream of producing a one-of-a-kind dance tour. He owned a successful dance studio in Ireland but left it in his pursuit. "I was getting into trouble as early as six years old for dreaming. They would tell me, 'quit looking out the window, Michael, there's nothing out there.' I wasn't staring at 'nothing.' I was dreaming of what could be. If you can visualize yourself doing what it is you want to do, you can have it. I wasn't going to quit dreaming, even at a young age. Dreaming took me from digging ditches one year to being on stage in front of 18,000 people the next year." Michael Flatley is indeed a dance visionary. He later went on to produce a second Irish folk dance production called, "Lord of the Dance."

While viewing a Public Broadcasting System offering, I came across a lecture by Tom Peters. Tom Peters is the author of the monumental best seller, *In Search Of Excellence.* Tom Peters is one of the individuals who inspired a revolution in the direction and design of American corporate management. In this PBS show, he provided detailed information on three companies that were the best at what they did and why they were the best. One of them was the 3M Corporation. 3M is a corporation that requires that their employees spend time dreaming.

The question may rightfully be asked, "What does all this have to do with getting a better job?" It all has to do with a vision of where you want to be, not where you are presently. When there is a vision and the motivation is properly based, you should not be deterred. A vision changes over time. As you carry on, the full vision comes into sight as how to achieve the goal. Ask anyone who has become successful about their original vision. They will invariably tell you that it did not occur exactly the way they had envisioned it. What they saw was not what they received. What they received was much greater. In order to succeed in the face of opposition, one has to have determination and vigilance. The attitude must be taken that the way things are now is temporary.

When you dream, you become a "what if'er." "What if I were to try this or what if I were to try that?" Chances are you could fail. Chances are that you could succeed also. History is filled with the tales of individuals who had failures. However, they refused to allow those setbacks to deter them from obtaining the prize. It takes courage to dream and discover what it is that you are good at. One of the most successful automobile dealerships in the country is owned and headed by Mel Farr, President of the Mel Farr Group. Some may not be familiar with who Mr. Farr is. We in the Detroit metropolitan area and football enthusiasts most certainly are. He is a former running back for the Detroit Lions football team. The team has been owned by the descendants of the auto magnate, Henry Ford, for decades.

It was a dream of Mel Farr to own an automobile dealership. During the times when he was not playing football, Mel Farr worked as a car salesman for Ford dealers. When asked by his colleagues why he didn't just take it easy in the off season and party, his reply was, "I already know how to dance. What I don't know how to do is run a dealership." What Mel Farr was waiting and hoping for was an **"opportunity."** The opportunity came when Mel's football days came to an end. Henry Ford II sponsored Mel in Ford's school for new car dealers. It was a great deal of hard work, but the hard work paid off a thousand fold. Mel Farr now owns five dealerships as well as car leasing and rental companies. He is a prime example of what hard work and dedication can accomplish.

A few years ago, Mel Farr addressed an assembly of MBA's in Chicago. It was a lecture to encourage those attending to become the very best in their chosen vocations. Becoming the best at what you do does not always require one to be the smartest, but the most courageous. He told them, "Every one of you in here is smarter than me. You all have your MBA and that speaks for itself. I have something you don't. What

I have is courage. It took courage to do what I did. I started out not knowing what the end would be, but I stepped out anyway. I bet everyone of you is content to work for someone else. That does not take courage." Mr. Farr is indeed a courageous and smart man. He has the kind of smarts that most successful entrepreneurs have, "street smarts."

Is it possible to be afraid of success and failure at the same time? You bet it is. That is why most people do nothing and allow others to determine their future. For one thing, it is easier for them not to have to think for themselves. So what if you fail on several attempts in pursuit of your dream. There is no harm in trying and failing. The reverse is not true if you fail to try. Failure is the price you'll pay for success. Look at every rejection as a learning experience towards perfection. It is like turning your English essay in to the teacher. She marks it up in red ink and tells you to do it over until you get it right. The experience is painful while going through it. Afterwards, you are grateful for having been rejected because it forced you to hone the skill of writing properly.

"Drill another hole." Men and women who do oil exploration are prime examples of individuals with pit bull tenacity. They know that they are in the midst of an oil field. All the tests indicate that it is so. They give the order to begin drilling. After reaching the prescribed depth, they find that the well is barren. What is the order given by them? "Drill another hole." They are confident that the black gold is lying there, waiting to be siphoned. Guess what, another dry hole. "Drill another hole." Every prudent calculation and preparation has been made to justify this exploration. The point being, if you continue to drill holes, you may eventually achieve success, although there is no guarantee of success. One thing is for certain, if they do not continue to drill, they are guaranteed not to become successful in their quest. In the case of the reader, the reward is employment, exceedingly fulfilling employment.

There are important lessons that can be learned from these examples. Stay at it. Be persistent and as tenacious as a pit bull. Be willing to endure the hardships of temporary failures and disappointments. The decision has been cast in stone. There is no going back. You must be immovable and steadfast in your passion towards that which you hope to accomplish. Do not give up your dream.

Non-professional women in the work place have been swimming upstream for decades. What is meant by upstream? Going against the normal flow and having a difficult time because of it. Although there have been marked improvements in the rate of compensation that women have been receiving with respect to men, some gender bias still exists. As a whole, the cases of women doing the exact same jobs as men and being paid less are diminishing. I have not declared that all is well and that there is peace in the world. I am saying that marked improvements have been made during the last 10 or 15 years. What we have now are wage disparities based upon occupation. Women feel that there is still a lack of equality. Those jobs that were and still are traditionally filled by women are lower paying occupations. Nothing is going to change this trend as long as the skills demanded for those jobs are low and the supply of persons to fill the positions are plentiful. I have not erred and said that the secretary's job was not important. Indeed, a good secretary is invaluable. The fact remains that it is easier to learn the skills required for becoming a secretary than it is to becoming an accountant. So what is the answer? Place yourself in a position to get a better paying job.

Some Good Advice

"And his brethren said to him, 'shall you indeed rule over us?' And they hated him yet the more for his dreams, and for his words."
Genesis 37:8

Do not tell unbelievers your dreams. It will most certainly get you into trouble. You can share your dream with those who support you, but be prepared to fulfill it yourself. The friends and relatives who do not encourage you will cause a spirit of discouragement to come over you instead. Some of those closest to you will laugh, scoff and basically tell you that you cannot accomplish that which you have set out to do. Misery loves company. As long as you are not fairing well, you will have company. Set out to pick yourself out of the doldrums and you will be surprised at what people really think about you. "Who do you think you are, trying to be better than us?"

It is certainly not a good thing to let your ambition be known to your colleagues who have a vested interested in you not succeeding. Your gain may be their loss. All of you are striving for the same thing, the promotion to the next level. Only one of you is going to get it. If there is cooperation needed between you and your colleagues to perform your daily functions, it will be rendered at a snail's pace or not at all. When you reveal that you want to be above them, obstacles will invariably be placed in your path. You will find out about meetings at the very last minute. This will be done so as to prevent you from having enough time to prepare your documentation. The worst kind of meetings are those for which there wasn't time for a formal meeting notice to be sent out. There you sit, wondering why it is so hard to get some things done.

Why We Don't Get What We Want

When we were young, our desires and wants were limited to what we could comprehend attaining. Maybe what we wanted most was a new Schwinn bicycle, a two-wheeled scooter, a Red Flyer wagon, or something as simple as a baseball glove. When we became adults, we put away childlike things and our wants and desires took on a more mature nature. The dilemma is, how do we get what we want and if we don't, why not? This is another subject full of endless individual reasons why something didn't happen in our favor. It is impossible to expound on and cover every reason. However, there are some generalizations that can be made.

I am a firm believer in this statement, "What man can conceive, he can achieve." The question then is, what are you willing to give up to get what you want? How hard are you willing to work to get it? I adhere to an adage that declares that "you can get what you want but it will cost you what you have got." What do you have? Time. Time is sand in an hourglass. You cannot add any sand to the hourglass. All you can do is hasten the departure of the sand from the glass. What most people try to do is slow down the rate that the sand flows through the orifice in the middle of the hourglass. When the sand runs out, we're dead. What are companies buying besides your labor? They're buying your time.

We don't get what we want because for the most part, we are not willing to pay the price to get it. Not only are most people not willing to pay the price, they are not willing to endure momentary failures. They want to gain the success without having to suffer. All weight lifters know this to be a fact. There is no gain in muscle without the pain that accompanies it. Hence the saying, "No pain, no gain." Abraham Lincoln withstood a litany of failures before he became President of the United

States. If there is a model for the phrase "No pain, no gain," it has to be him.

- At age 23, he lost his job for reasons unknown. In the same year, Lincoln was defeated in a bid for the State Legislature.
- At age 27, Lincoln was defeated in a bid to be Speaker of the House of Representatives.
- At age 34, Lincoln was defeated in a bid for Congress. At age 37, he was elected to Congress and he lost his bid for re-nomination at age 39.
- At age 40, he was defeated in his bid for director for the land office in his home state of Illinois.
- At age 45, he was defeated in his bid for the U.S. Senate.
- At age 47, he was defeated for nomination to be Vice President of the United States.
- At age 49, he was again defeated in his bid for a U.S. Senate seat.
- At age 51, Mr. Lincoln was elected President of the United States. Mr. Lincoln consistently put forth the effort required to get what he wanted although he did not always get it. Eventually he did get the ultimate prize.

****

The vast majority of people will always choose the easy way to do things instead of the best way, especially if the best way involves more effort. They fail to realize that there is virtue in hard work and the struggle to succeed. Even when faced with what may seem to be unconquerable obstacles, having the intestinal fortitude to hang in there is an asset. It is easy to say, "I can't succeed because I'm a female," "I can't succeed because of racism," "People show me disfavor because I'm short," "I can't make it because I'm handicapped," etc. All of these excuses are legitimate if what one wants is an excuse for failure. What one should look for is an opportunity for success. The people who offer up excuses still want the same necessities of life and the extras that hard work brings.

Despite the controversy caused by his views on politicians and a host of issues, Rush Limbaugh is a man whom I greatly admire. Not so much for his political satire, but for his attitude towards success. He has 'Stick-To-It' plastered all over him. He stated that it was always his dream to be a radio disc jockey. Coming from a family that by any measure has to be considered successful, Rush Limbaugh was the outsider. He was the guy who didn't fit into the mold that his father had cast for him. I vividly recall his stories about being so broke that he frequently ate peanut butter sandwiches and potato chips. He has divorced twice, not because of any abuse on his part, but because of complications brought about by the pursuit of his dream. Now he is enjoying the fruits of his labor and life-long passion. No one should be envious or jealous of this man. He has paid his dues and was relentless, steadfast in the belief that one day his break would come.

I have an acquaintance whom I come into frequent contact with now, who is on the verge of making his first million. We worked together for a company that is no longer in existence called Fisher Body. Freeman Webster was always a dreamer and was quick to tell all those who would listen what he had planned. He was fond of horses, so he bought a piece of property in the town of Milford, Michigan that would accommodate a small stable of horses. He bought the property for a reasonable amount and sold it after three years for four times what he paid for it. With the proceeds, he started a small engineering design firm. He had a building built very close to his primary customer.

Freeman opens and closes his firm daily and gives input into every job. He works six days a week and puts in 16 hours a day. Freeman worked this maddening schedule for seven years before things started going well for him. Right now he is reaping the rewards, but it was not always so. He will be the first to tell you that it was, and still is, hard work. That is why he is able to keep a level head on his shoulders while accumulating his toys. The enormous home, the stable of Arabian horses, two Jaguars, the trucks, the vacation home in Florida are all because of someone who believed in himself and his dream. He knows the price that was paid to get them and it keeps him humble. Freeman told me that he could lose it all at any time but he wouldn't be discouraged. "I've had nothing before and survived. If I lose it all, I'll start all over again."

There is no such thing as equal opportunity. There will never be. You don't get in life what you deserve. There are a lot of people who are glad of that including me. In life, you get what comes and you try to direct your path in front of the good stuff that's coming and not the bad. All you can hope for is an opportunity at the plate and try to maneuver to make it happen. I use this metaphor because sports is analogous to real life. What better way to make the starting line-up of a baseball team than to hit a pinch hit home run? When the opportunity presents itself, make good use of it. How many people do you know who squander their opportunities? Some of them get more than one chance at the plate and blow it every time. We don't get what we want because we're not ready when the time comes. One of my favorite movies is one that stars Bette Davis entitled "All About Eve." The theme of the movie was, dream dreams and when the time comes, take full advantage of the opportunity placed before you.

It takes hard work, focus, persistence and dedication to get you what you want and there is no substitute for it. People try to bypass the tried and true method by buying lottery tickets, gambling and committing crimes. A very few make out. Most of them don't. We can get what we want through working hard at some type of employment. The good news is, **"you can get a better job."** Dreams are of no use alone, they must be acted upon. To quote Mohandas

Gandhi, the former leader of India, "I am indeed a practical dreamer. My dreams are not airy nothings. I want to convert my dreams into realities as far as possible."

Some Good Advice

Do not become envious of the rich nor resent them for their wealth. Your ill feelings towards them will not help you, and it could hinder your progress. Envy, jealousy, and resentment are powerful and destructive emotions. It matters not whether the wealthy have earned their money or inherited it. There are lessons that can be learned from them. What can you learn from the wealthy? One of two things can be learned. You can learn how to act when you become wealthy through hard work or you can learn how not to act. You want to emulate the good behavior and avoid the bad. The rich and well-to-do provide economies around the world with the ability to earn a living. They make purchases out of their excesses, not their needs. What is meant by this? The wealthy buy bigger homes, purchase multiple vehicles, buy more clothes and spend more money on these items than do most of us. These things, plus countless others, provide jobs for all who manufacture and fabricate the articles previously mentioned.

Those who depend upon their weekly paychecks to survive cannot spend money excessively. They will tend to make fewer purchases and spend less money on each purchase. What is needed is more wealthy people spending out of their excess. With hard work and diligence, you can become one of them. Anything is possible in this great country. When you observe the wealthy living lavishly, it is easy to develop a vision of your own. A vision of what you would do if you were in their place. What has been popular is the thinking that the rich have gained at the expense of everyone else. If you can picture a pie having a definite size and being sliced, bigger pieces for some would mean smaller pieces for others. Some may only be left with the crumbs. This type of thinking leaves you with no hope of rectifying your situation.

We believe that there is no limit to the size of the pie that makes up our economy. The pie just gets bigger as the need grows. That leaves room for everyone willing to pay the price to get a bigger piece of the pie. For example, Microsoft's head, Bill Gates, has made more of his employees millionaires than any other person in history. He is second only to Sam Walton, the founder of Walmart, in making individuals wealthy. Those who bought stock in Walmart in its infancy know this to be true. However, they were not necessarily employees of the Walmart stores. Bill Gates increased the size of the pie as Microsoft grew. Some employees of Microsoft were rewarded for their ingenuity and hard work. If they came up with a good idea, they were allowed to develop it and reap some of the reward. These new millionaires did not gain their wealth at the expense of someone else. There was no one else!

Negative speech is contagious whether it originates from you or is directed at you. If the latter is the case, do not embrace this type of language. If you engage in self debasing thoughts and speech, stop it. Positive thinking and speech is all that should be entering your mind and coming from your lips. There are a million books written on the power of positive thinking. A man or women saying, "I can" releases their energy to make it happen.

The origin of positive thinking can be found in the Bible, The book of Genesis, chapter 11, verse six states, "Nothing will be restrained from them which they have imagined to do." This was reiterated later in the book of Proverbs, chapter 23, verse seven, "For as a man thinketh in his heart, so is he." What you say or how you feel about yourself will come to pass. If you utter the words, "I can't," or make a habit of offering excuses why it can't be done, you won't do it. This will not prevent someone else from doing that very thing. Why shouldn't it be you? Believe that you can achieve your goal. Spend time visualizing yourself in a successful environment. This will help to keep you encouraged, thus providing you with the strength to attain your goals.

Avoid negative speech from all sources, even from those who are close to you. Shun the abuse of others. Stay in the company of those who will edify you. When a person is instructing, promoting you intellectually, and praising you, you are being edified. These are the kinds of people to seek out, people who will build you up, not tear you down. I have listened to individuals explain why they, or members of their family, would never amount to anything. They felt as though their futures were cast in stone. This is because of the words that were repeatedly spoken to them. For example: "You will never amount to anything because you're a Harvey. The Harveys have never been anything and never will be anything." We say, use their condemnation as inspiration to prove them wrong. The more they insist that you can't, the more intense your efforts should be towards succeeding. There could be some substantial reasons why the Harveys have never been anything. Perhaps the heads of the households were alcoholics or drug abusers.

We know that children learn from the examples set before them. If all they see is a lifestyle of alcohol and substance abuse, what vision will they have of their future? That cycle must and can be broken. You could be the one to do it. Others have succeeded in climbing out of the pit of despair. I have always believed that anything can be done as long as there is a will to do it. Difficult tasks are not completed overnight. They take time. If you focus on the enormity of the task, you can be overwhelmed by its size.

Yes You Can

Listing the job descriptions for a position is a very common practice. It is also common for would-be applicants to become intimidated by the tasks listed as job duties. Consider the following. Did the president of this great country know how to perform the duties of the oval office before he became President? Did the governor of the state in which you reside know how to perform as governor before taking office? Did the COO of the Disney Corporation, Michael Eisner, know how to perform his duties before taking office? The answer to all of these questions is resoundingly, "no." As a matter of fact, Michael Eisner's degree is not in business.

Take the case of the ex-professional wrestler who became governor of the great state of Minnesota, Jesse Ventura. Where did he learn to become governor after being elected in 1998? Did he go to governor school where they teach you how? Of course not. Did not having any prior political experience deter him from his mission? No it didn't. He persevered and won the election based upon his offerings to the public. Running a state is more difficult and has more responsibilities attached to it than most jobs. He has to balance his actions between the state legislator, the judiciary and the citizens of Minnesota.

What is the point? You can learn the job! Do not become intimidated by the listing of the job duties. It is a rare person who knows how to perform every task listed on a job description. Jobs are seldom as difficult as they are described. Sometimes excess verbiage is added to the job description to make the job seem more important than it really is. What is vital is that you show the aptitude to accomplish the tasks at hand. Convince yourself that you can perform at the job in a manner that is fitting. Convincing yourself of this will go a long way towards convincing the person who is interested in hiring you or conducting the interview.

Attaining your goals will not always be easy. If it were easy, everyone would make it. The only true difference between those who win and those who do not is that the winners are willing to pay the price for success. What all successful people have in common is their desire to win. You will only fight for success if you feel you deserve it. Tell yourself, "I deserve it!" You must see yourself as a winner and fight with all the might that is within you. When you reach a point where you feel your strength is failing, fight on. As the motivational speaker, Les Brown, says, "It's not over until I win." You must stay inspired at all costs. When you lose your inspiration, you also lose your desire to press your way forward. When you no longer desire to move forward, you will be standing still. When you are standing still, you are done.

DISCOVERY

There are practical aspects to winning that job of your dreams. You may not get every job you go after. That is akin to losing a battle. Losing a battle is not a sufficient reason to stop trying. In any case, expect to win. Bear this in mind at all times. You will never possess that which you are not willing to pursue. As discussed in the chapter, **"A Job Well Done,"** you will reach your goal incrementally. Each job that you take should be used as a stepping stone for the next. Each step you take will be "up" if your **"performance"** is up to par. With each job, the lessons learned, and analytical skills used, prepare you for the next level. Thus, your discovery is a culmination of many tasks performed and lessons learned.

What I hear very often is one of two, or sometimes both, statements, "I don't know what I'm good at," or "I don't know what I want to do." So, what if you do not know what you're good at? How do you discover where your talents lie? This is vital because the natural tendency is for people to perform well doing the things they like to do, instead of things they have to do. I often tell individuals, "Do what you have to do until you can do what you really want to do." You will not discover what you would like to do remaining idle, wasting time watching television. You would be doing yourself a tremendous favor by declaring a moratorium on watching television. It is the contention of the authors that discovering where your talents lie is easy. Making money using your talents isn't so easy. That takes time and development to make it a reality; time to discover who has the need for what you know how to do. But first, more on the discovery process.

Discovering where your talents lie can arise out of the need to survive. When you have a good job and are being fed, you feel secure. You are not hungry. There are no pressing needs. Why should you begin an exercise in discovery? You wouldn't. I recount the story of Wally Amos, who founded Famous Amos cookies. Destitute and short on possibilities, he baked cookies and sold them to those visiting the beaches. Perhaps his real talents did not lie in baking, but he did what he had to do until..... What he did have was the "I can do that" attitude. You are more likely to be successful doing something that you love doing. When you find it, you won't be motivated, you'll be driven. Motivation doesn't last, passion does.

I've come across a number of people who work well with their hands but have no aptitude whatsoever for schooling in the traditional sense. They feel that it is a waste of their time to be in school and in some cases, it is. Their grades and attendance reflect those feelings. Their efforts would best be spent developing their skills into something that can sustain them. Some of these individuals are painters, sculptors, woodsmiths, glassmakers, and other artisans.

The persons who choose these routes are secure in their ability to take care of themselves. This is not a tacit endorsement of truancy from school. All people can benefit from having a formal education through high school. Though rare, there are exceptions. There are very few of us who possess the intellect of that great inventor, Thomas Alva Edison. Thomas Edison was an American inventor with more than 1,000 patents to his credit. The most famous of them is the electric light bulb. In books that tell of his early upbringing in Milan, Ohio, it is reported that his teachers felt he was retarded. At eight years old, young Thomas Edison had lost all interest in school. He was bored with the traditional activities of the classroom. His was to be a life of tinkering and inventing.

Michael Dell is the founder of Dell Computers, one of the largest computer manufacturers in the country. He was able to zero in on what it was he wanted to do while in college. He loved tinkering with circuit boards and computers. It was his father's dream for his son to become a doctor. On one occasion, Papa Dell made a visit to his son in college. It is reported that upon finding his son tinkering with computer circuitry, his father became enraged and threw the components out of the dorm window. The lack of Papa Dell's approval did not deter his son, Michael, from discovering where his talents lay or from pursuing his dream. Stories abound of individuals who forsake traditional schooling in order to pursue their dreams. They were fully persuaded that their outcomes should be in their own hands.

Some people are molded into place by their parents or others who act as their guardians. Such is the case many times with those aspiring to become professional athletes. They cast their lot in that direction early on in their lives. We all know who Michael Jordan is. If you don't, where have you been hiding? But before Mr. Jordan came on the scene, there was a round ball prodigy by the name of George Gervin. It was said of George, while playing in the public school basketball leagues, "He is a man playing with boys." It was as if he were one with the ball while playing. Even with all of the awards and records achieved by Mr. Jordan, he still does not possess the pure artistry with a ball as George did. He was poetry in motion.

Many tales have been told of George's dedication to basketball. Some say that he was given the keys to the gym because he stayed long hours after school to practice his shooting and dribbling skills. George was not a party-goer. He thought it was a waste of his time. If it didn't involve basketball, he wanted no part of it. George Gervin did go on to play professional basketball in the American Basketball Association and later in the National Basketball Association. He attended Eastern Michigan University for a very short period of time. It was there that I had the privilege of seeing him play basketball.

Continuing on the theme of sports, Wayne Gretzky, perhaps the greatest hockey player ever to lace a pair of skates, was groomed for hockey at an early age. On a special segment hosted by the Canadian Broadcasting Company, Wayne's dad told of how he placed a pair of skates on his son while Wayne was a toddler. "There was no question what Wayne was going to be. He was going to play hockey," stated the elder Gretzky. The family even moved, to place Wayne in a better youth hockey league district. That is taking things to the maximum, allowing the avocation of the child to dictate where the family will live. Did all of the time and energy invested in Wayne's career pay off ? Yes, it paid off big time.

What is the point? If you have discovered what you are good at and it is your intention to devote yourself to its maturation, you had better become great at it. Life is littered with people who left themselves no option. They put all of their energies into one crop. When the crop did not provide a good harvest, they lost out. The process of discovery need not be clouded with mystery. There are aptitude tests that can be taken at many local community colleges and adult education facilities. These tests are designed to identify your strengths, weaknesses and emotional state. If you are unsure about where your best abilities lie, tests such as these will help to pinpoint them. Too late in life you say? Nonsense. It is never too late. There are numerous individuals who are late bloomers in life, not finding their place until their forty's or fifty's. So do not become discouraged.

If you have a special talent, there is someone somewhere willing to pay you to exercise it on their behalf. In cases such as these, it is not always necessary for you to find them, they'll discover you. The chapters **"A Job Well Done"** and **"Getting Along With Others"** will expound on how this will come about.

MOTIVATIONAL REFERENCE

Ten Days To Self Esteem

by

David D. Burns, M.D.

A Quill Publication

You Can Make It Happen

by

Stedman Graham

A Simon & Schuster Publication

Concrete Confidence

by

Sam Horn

A St. Martin Press Publication

Feel The Fear And Do It Anyway

by

Susan Jeffers, Ph.D.

A Fawcett Columbine Book

Stairway To Success

by

Nido R. Qubein

A John Wiley & Sons Publication

A JOB WELL DONE

"Those who have missed the joy of work, of a job well done, have missed something very important."
William J. Bennett

We have all heard the saying "If a job is worth doing, it is worth doing well." This cry is universal, "It is hard to find good people." If I have heard this said once, I have heard it said one hundred times. The shortage of good employees is becoming more acute as the years pass. This is due partly to the times in which we now live, where immediate success and gratification is lauded. The definition of what constituted a good job used to come from our parents. I began to reminisce on "How it used to be." Those were the days when we were not so consumed with television talk shows and tabloid newspapers. The focus was not on rock concerts, what was playing at the movies, and other things that absolutely have no added value to our well being. If you were a person willing to do odd jobs for pocket change, your work performance was spread by word of mouth, albeit good or bad.

When you were given a task, it was in your best interest to do the job right the first time. There was a penalty for not conforming, the least of which was a loss in credibility. There would surely be an occasion when you desired some extra consideration from your parents. In those days, your credibility was everything. You wanted to be able to say, "I did a good job." If the job was not done properly, you were made to do it again. It could have been something as simple as cutting grass that was wet or too long. When it reached that stage, the clippings clumped together and made for an untidy appearance. You saw the clippings and you knew what was required. A decision had to be made. Do you go back and expend the energy to make it right, or do you try and get by with not doing a good job? No excuse would be good enough when you were asked, "Why did you leave the lawn like that?"

I have long been an advocate of the saying "You'll be good at what you practice." When you practice doing things the right way, you will become good at it and the tendency will be towards doing everything the right way. It will not be a burden, but a constraint. Conversely, when you practice being sloppy, careless, and lackadaisical, performing in a substandard manner, you will become good at that also. That will now be the normal mode of operating for you. To perform in any other fashion would be difficult at best. As a matter of fact, you will not be able to distinguish between performing poorly and a **"Job Well Done."** You cannot become a conscientious, detail oriented, trustworthy worker just by wishing it to be so.

We are becoming a socially-interdependent, "cyber society" where it is thought that our federal government, with the aid of computers, has the solutions to all of our ills. As we have moved towards making less use of manual labor, the skills that enabled us at one time to be the premier producers of finished goods have rapidly diminished. The new direction is towards an economy based on services instead of one based upon manufacturing. The backbone of manufacturing was, and still is, the "skilled trades," the die setters, tool makers, electricians, machinists and so on. The skilled trades are some of the last vocations where the apprenticeship programs that are in place assure that the end product, the skilled worker, meets all the criteria set forth. There are rigid rules and regulations in place that protect the credibility of each skilled trade. All of this is a sort of guarantee that the person will be able to perform as expected. That is fine for the few thousand of skilled trades persons employed in our nation. What about the rest of the country? How are they going to get the message of doing a job and doing it well?

What are the attributes of **"A Job Well Done?"** Too many to describe, but you know them when you see them displayed in various individuals. They consist of performing tasks beyond what is necessary and also describes tasks that are performed without the worker being asked to do so. **"A Job Well Done"** describes the performance of the U.S. Postal Service worker who received the coinage for a first class letter taped to the letter because the mailer didn't have a stamp on hand. When the postal worker is asked by a patron, "Will that work?" the postal worker replied, "I'll make it work." Then, there is the postal clerk who received letters that have no zip code placed on them. Instead of rejecting the letters, which in turn would anger the patron, the worker looked up the correct zip codes and applied them to the letters. That deed may have gone unnoticed by many, however, the postal worker had become good at what was practiced, doing above and beyond what was required. This attention to detail and customer assistance will pay off sooner or later.

"A Job Well Done" describes the performance of the bank teller who went above and beyond the call of duty. You desired 200 brand new single Treasury Notes to use for tips while on vacation. The teller was gracious and polite in manner, even though it meant extra work for her. She ordered the notes for you and had them ready, prior to your departure. She understood your explanation that brand new bills took up less space than used, tattered ones.

"A Job Well Done" describes the efforts of an employee of a garbage disposal firm. Each truck has a single driver who is also the disposal mechanism operator. While heading away from his prescribed route, the driver noticed a plastic garbage bag off to the side of the road. The bag is on the opposite side of the wide thoroughfare. Its contents have spilled and is in jeopardy of dispersing. There was no apparent explanation for the garbage in the street. Neither the driver nor anyone else from his company had anything to do with this mishap. A private contractor performed the garbage collection in this community. The contractor won the bid by a strategy of competitive pricing and a good "Quality Statement."

The garbage would have been assumed to be the responsibility of his company. All complaints about the service rendered to the community would be investigated. If found to have merit, the company would be issued demerits that would count against it. This would give its competitors an advantage. Too many demerits and the company would be disqualified from future bidding. The driver stopped the truck, turned on the emergency flashers and proceeded to gather the garbage strewn in the street. The driver did not report this event. Nothing extra would be done for him, not even a thank you. It was his belief that anything done to help the company he worked for, helped him.

"A Job Well Done" describes the behavior of a particular sales associate at one of the local home improvement stores. When asked if an item was in stock because it didn't appear on the shelves, the sales associate said, "Just a minute, Sir, I'll look and see." Moving over to the counter where the stock sheets are kept, the sales associate went through the stock listings until he discovered that the item in question is indeed in the store. However, it was on the very top shelf and hidden behind several boxes. The sales associate left, and returned with a forklift to retrieve the item from the top shelf. Happily, he opened the shrink-wrapped box and gave the item to the customer. All of this is even a more astounding effort because the item only priced out at $1.50. The sales associate could have very easily stated, "It's out of stock," after discovering that the inexpensive item would take considerable effort to retrieve. The customer would never have known.

"A Job Well Done" is performed by the brick mason who was hired to repair the cracks in the mortar on a previous home that I owned. He came highly recommended and his services were difficult to acquire. This was a person you did not ask, "How much do you charge?" The question you ask him is, "When can you come and do the job?" Upon visiting the area that was in need of repair, I could not believe how fabulous the job was. Then it occurred to me, "This is why Mr. Hill is so much in demand. He is indeed a craftsman." Being so thoroughly satisfied with his work, I instructed him to go around the entire house and do what needed to be done. With a person whose services were in as much demand as his, it would be a long time before he would be available again. After completing the job, he cleaned up. There was no trace of debris. He was paid far above the fee he asked.

"A Job Well Done" is performed by the mechanic working on your car at a garage. Your disk brake wear indicator tabs were squealing up a storm. You were certain that you needed new front disk brake pads. You were not certain about the condition of the brakes at the rear of the vehicle. The rear brakes are drum. Without asking him to do so, the mechanic took the initiative and inspected the rear brakes. It was a good thing he did. There was very little lining left on the rear brake pads. Continued travel on them would have resulted in excessive costs, due to the rear drums being damaged. There were instances where this same mechanic found the rear brakes on other vehicles to be in good working order. He truthfully revealed the condition of the rear brakes when asked.

"A Job Well Done" is performed by the employee at a fast food eatery. Despite the pressures of serving a lunchtime crowd, the employee maintains a patient, courteous attitude while awaiting the customer's order. Several minutes pass by before the customer decides on his food order. After the food order has been taken and the money exchanged, the customer changes his mind. A different entree number was requested, requiring a void of the first order.

The initial order could only be voided by the manager on duty. As fate would have it, she was occupied with other tasks. Customers continued to enter this popular eatery. As the order line lengthened, some patrons became boisterous. The attendant maintained her composure. Before this customer departed, he said, "Give me lots of sauce." His request was noticeably absent of a "please." The attendant reached under the counter and placed a fist full of sauce in his bag. He said, "Wow, you gave me a lot."

"You asked for a lot and it's my job to please my customers." She said that with a smile.

"A Job Well Done" is performed by the person double-bagging your groceries at the supermarket when he notices you have items that are heavy. The last thing he wants to have happen is breakage due to a lack of concern. You walk away thinking, "What a thoughtful person." Anyone can do a job well that they like. What about the job that no one likes or wants to do? Perhaps you worked in the accounts receivable department of your company, a department where there was no pressure. Your work was outstanding. The senior accountant never had to correct any mistakes made by you. There is a vacancy created in accounts payable because the person who had the job previously couldn't withstand the constant pressure that the job entailed. You are asked to fill in temporarily, knowing full well that management desires you to take the position permanently. You take the new position as a challenge and perform more perfectly in it than in the prior position that you liked so well.

"A Job Well Done" describes the performance of an employee of a company that specializes in the packaging and transporting of goods. You have been asked by your boss to oversee the transporting of special prototype parts to a specific engineering facility. It is the intent of management to display this prototype to a prospective customer, hoping to garner new business. The prototype parts have to be there the day of the meeting. The company best capable of performing the task has been contacted and is eager to begin. There is one problem. The person who could assure the on-time delivery of the prototypes is scheduled for a vacation. His family has planned this vacation for months. However, he has enough foresight to determine that aiding your company in its time of need will give his company a favorable status when it comes to obtaining future business. He postpones the vacation for a couple of days. The delivery is made on time. The prototype was impressive. So much so that the company interested in it provided funds to develop a production model. The delivery company was given a contract to deliver all production parts leaving the assembly line.

All jobs that are well done require attention to detail and a respect for one's own output. How do you describe the performance of a roofer who applies an intricate pattern of expensive fiberglass shingles in order to simulate a cedar shake roof? In an obscure corner at the rear of the home, he notices that he has a portion of the pattern wrong. No one will ever see it, or if they see it, will not recognize that the pattern is wrong. However, the roofer knows. He tears off the shingles and starts all over. The pride that he has in his work will prevail and his self-esteem will not allow him the luxury of trying to get by with his mistake.

What about the school janitor who is charged with keeping the school clean and free of debris? The janitor not only cleans where it will be observed, but also cleans where no one will ever look, in the nooks and crannies of booths that may be in the back areas, in the corners, in the dark. To top it off, the janitor places a white glove on his hand and wipes the window sills of the school to detect items that have not been cleaned.

How about the mechanic who is charged with changing the spark plugs of a motorized vehicle? Knowing that the area around the spark plug collects crud, like a magnet collects iron filings, he wipes the area clean with a rag so that the gunk will not fall into the cylinder vacated by the spark plug. All of these are real life examples of **"Jobs Well Done."**

One of the keys to securing a better job is performing well on your present job. This ties in well with the segment on **"Attitude and Performance."** I make reference to the segment on **"Attitude and Performance,"** specifically because of my old roommate, Ron Holbrook. I revealed how Ron was employed by the management of Howard Cooper Audi-Porsche-Volkswagen to wash and porter the vehicles. The job also required that Ron wash the car of the dealership owner, Howard Cooper. Mr. Cooper's radio was never tuned to another station when Ron was in the vehicle. Ron never tampered with the glove box or removed items from the vehicle unless asked to do so. These are antics that infuriate many when they go to car washes that require the drivers to exit their vehicles.

Why these dryers assume we all have the same taste in music is beyond me. Is it not their job to just dry the vehicles? The radio station should remain tuned into the frequency of the owner's choosing. Some drivers stated that they made sure the radio was turned off when entering the car wash. To add insult to injury, the small change that is left in their ashtrays usually disappears. They discover this a few days later when the change is needed. If the vehicle dryers do this throughout the day, that small change adds up to be some pretty heavy coin. To avoid this, some vehicle owners no longer patronize car washes that require them to exit their vehicles. Those car wash owners lost my business. I imagine that there are vehicle owners that have similar experiences and sentiments.

Performing well can also aid you in obtaining more money in your present position. This is especially true in jobs that are truly service oriented. For instance, if you work in a car wash, it should be your goal to become a crew leader or some other position of authority, working your way up through the ranks, thus securing your job as best as possible. When there are slow periods, the persons who are told not to report are those who are not interested in performing well. You will begin to establish yourself as someone who is dependable and a person who can be trusted with responsibility. Who can say where that will lead? A lot of big things emerge from small beginnings.

TRUE STORY

My youngest son, Devvan, has proof that these principles work. Like any young man his age, 15 years old, he can't wait until he gets his first job. For some kids, their first job is a paper route. For Devvan, it was the opportunity to work at the neighborhood grocery store, which happened to be in walking distance from our home. His motivation was to acquire enough funds to purchase a bass guitar and amplifier. There was tremendous competition for only a few positions as grocery baggers and shopping cart retrievers. Devvan secured one of the positions early by having his work permit in order and his application and recommendations neatly typed. The pristine preparation of the documentation I attribute to his mother, the consummate educator. Being his first job, he was excited about having an opportunity to earn some money instead of having to receive an allowance from his parents. You can't brag to your friends about getting an allowance but you can boast in receiving a paycheck.

The excitement gradually wore off after a few months of working. The work was hard, tiring and compounded by the fact that it was winter. A caravan of shopping carts was difficult to maneuver and made more difficult when the carts had to be pushed through the snow. Nonetheless, Devvan persevered and was determined to be a good employee. He waited for his turn to rotate back to bagging groceries inside. On the next occasion of cart retrieval duty, Devvan began gathering the carts to place them back at the entrance. However, he noticed that the carts were filled with sales papers. Without being told to do so, Devvan returned inside and got several plastic grocery bags in which to place the discarded paper. Unknown to him, the manager was watching this event and took note of it. Later on, at the end of his shift, the manager commended Devvan on **"a job well done."** The manager remarked that none of the other boys took notice of the debris left in the carts. "The customers will appreciate a clean shopping cart, Devvan." That one action, along with his excellent work habits, caused Devvan to be moved permanently inside to the produce area. He was now a very happy young man. There would be no more shopping cart caravans in the winter. I believe the manager thought as I would have. "If he will take care of a little thing like that, he is likely to take care of other things without having to be told, making my job as manager a little easier." It was good to see that all of my cajoling was not in vain.

****

Just as there are examples of jobs that are well done, the inverse applies, too. There are many jobs that are not well executed. We all have experienced them. A gratuity (tip) is defined as "A favor or gift, usually in the form of money, given in return for service." The key word here is service. What is meant by the word "service?" A former colleague of mine was of the opinion that tips should not be given in restaurants. The price of the meal should include the serving. "How else would the meal get to the table? Are the patrons expected to go into the kitchen and bring the meal out themselves." He felt that it was not the fault of the patrons of the restaurant that the management was underpaying their employees. To him, tips were a subsidy, a hidden cost that should be properly reflected in the cost of the meal by being placed on the menu. Does the offering of a tip or, in some cases, a mandatory tip equate to a job well done? Not in all cases. If that is the situation, a tip should not be taken for granted, and truly earned by the receivers.

Those who travel by air and park their vehicles at long-term lots can identify with this. There are two, huge, privately-owned parking lots in two different cities. They both are in the immediate vicinity of a major airport. Both of these lots have shuttles that ferry people to and from the airport. The shuttle driver in city "A" is very unpleasant and does not assist the passengers with their luggage. The shuttle driver from city "B" not only greets the patrons with a smile and a cheerful hello but exits the vehicle and assists every rider with their luggage. Upon arrival at the airport, shuttle driver "A" is courteous enough to let the riders off at each respective airline. Shuttle driver "B" not only lets each rider off at their respective airline but assists them with their luggage again. What's the point? Shuttle driver "A" has a box for tips located at the front of the vehicle. There are a few dollars stuffed in it. Sometimes, individuals place money in their own tip box to persuade others to follow suit. Shuttle driver "B" has no tip box but is relying upon the riders to recognize **"a job well done."** I left a tip with one of these persons in accordance with their **"performance"** and **"attitude."** Which driver received it?

Another humorous event happened while attending an exterior car wash. Car wash attendants have become accustomed to receiving tips when they have completely dried your vehicle. There are those individuals, of which I am one, who make a judgment on whether they have performed services that merit a tip. On this occasion, when my vehicle reached the end of the line, I was approached by the dryer. He beckoned me to roll down my window. I obliged him. "Sir, I'm gonna to do a real good job drying off your car. I just wanted you to know this beforehand. I want you to feel free to tip me if you feel like it. I know that you're gonna do the right thing." Was that a solicitation or what? I did do the right thing and rewarded him accordingly.

TRUE STORY

I am reminded of the embarrassment I endured while dining out with some friends from Florida. Everyone likes to have the area in which they live portrayed in a good manner. For that reason, the decision was made to visit one of the finer restaurants in the Detroit metropolitan area. The wait staff was inattentive. After requesting coffee for the third time, and constantly being told "just a minute," I went over to the coffee station and retrieved a pot of coffee myself. I then poured coffee for my guests and for a group of people at a neighboring table. Our request for coffee was not an unreasonable demand placed upon an overburdened staff. These people just didn't care. When the bill was presented, I accepted it with a smile, the same manner in which it was presented. The bill was paid by credit card, all except the tip. That portion of the statement was crossed out, so as to not be added in later. Instead, I left the tip on a napkin next to the statement. On the napkin, I left a nickel and scribed these words, "This is what I think of your service." It would seem to me that the wait staff took the gratuity for granted. My party and I departed. I have never been back to that restaurant and would never recommend it to anyone.

I would imagine that members of this wait staff will, at some time, seek out employment elsewhere. How can they expect to receive a good appraisal to use as a reference? If I were a maitre d' or waiter at an upscale eating establishment, my pockets would be full of money at the end of every day. Taking nothing for granted, I would perform to the best of my abilities at every turn. Servicing the public can be difficult. It is easy for me to emphatically declare what I would do in a given situation. One thing that I would do for sure is stay focused by keeping my eyes on the prize. In this case, the prize may not be relegated to just another job, but more money. If by a good performance (attending to the needs of the public is like performing) I can increase my monetary status, the attitude to adopt is clear. It becomes a matter of how much I can take and for how much money.

Just to set the record straight, I am not cheap. I salute people who work hard for their money. There was a restaurant in the city of Troy, Michigan that I would visit every Wednesday for lunch. It had a reputation for good food at a reasonable price. At the writing of this book, Sophia's is still in business. Upon first attending the restaurant, I was not sure about the reception that I would receive. There have been occasions when I have not been waited on promptly, although that has not happened in recent years. The waitress was polite and attentive beyond belief. She was everything a patron could want. After the meal, I left a tip that was more than the cost of the meal. I wrote a message to the waitress and left it on a paper napkin, thanking her for the courtesy and care she displayed. Upon departing, I turned to see the reaction of the waitress. It was just as I would have suspected. She was a very happy woman. Performing a job and performing it well over a period of time pays off in the long term. The next Wednesday when I appeared at the door, there was a stampede of waitresses, each vying for my attention.

****

From time-to-time, a short stay in a hotel is required of me. A short stay being defined as a week or less. Forever cognizant of the fact that there is no place like home, I try to make the hotel stay as pleasant as possible. I attempt to accomplish this by bringing my own pillow, the same one that I have had since I was 10 years old. In addition, I bring my own mattress pad so that I can have a comfortable night's sleep. I hate those inferior imitations of mattress pads that are nothing more than thick blankets. As you toss and turn at night, it becomes easily removed from its initial placing.

I am not an early riser. I stay in bed until it is absolutely imperative that I arise, foregoing the traditional breakfast settings. Needing some type of nourishment in the morning, I usually have some fruit on hand in the room. That includes various melons. Knowing that they can be messy, I prepare for any mishaps by having adequate paper towels and garbage bags on hand. When finished, I bag everything up and leave it in plain view of the person assigned to clean the room. It has always been a habit of mine to leave a generous tip for the person cleaning the room. This accomplishes two things. It acts as a safeguard against having my personal possessions rifled through and, in some cases, items taken (that does happen). Secondly, it acknowledges to the person doing the housekeeping that I know I have added extra work to their work load and says that I am appreciative of their service.

If I am visiting a city where I have been previously, I will stay in the same hotel if it was a pleasant experience. Doing that often enough, the personnel of the hotel become familiar with me and have any special room requests taken care of before my arrival. One stay in a hotel started out as routine as ever. I did my shopping for the usual items and prepared for the next business day. I have this funny little quirk about business travel. If at all possible, I arrive at my destination the night before, ensuring a prompt and punctual meeting with my party the next day. It also gives me extra time to prepare notes, documents, and gain my composure.

I left the room the next morning with the obligatory tip laying next to the small garbage bag hosting the breakfast refuse. Returning to the room in the evening, to my surprise, the garbage bag was still there. However, the tip was taken. This prompted me to do a thorough inspection of the room to ascertain what else had not been done. The bathroom hadn't been cleaned to my satisfaction. I didn't place a call to housekeeping, I went down to the front desk to lodge my complaint. I was informed that the woman who usually cleaned my room was out, sick. The replacement was a young lady whom they had just hired. What impression had she made upon me and her supervisor? This was indeed a person who had practiced doing the wrong things and had become good at it.

****

It is difficult to get this message of **"a job well done"** across to this younger generation. Those who seize the message will be head and shoulders above their peers. I have found that this is more difficult than it should be, to draw a correlation between where they want to be and what it takes to get there. It is an age of instant gratification, where the young have seen that you do not have to work hard. You have to be lucky, which is the message that can be gleaned from the many legal lotteries across our country. I have never bought a lottery ticket in my life and I am most proud of this record. I believe and counsel that it is through the application of proven principles and attention to the details, that success is achieved.

In the building that houses one of my clients, there is an area where standard business forms are placed. The forms are placed in a tower that can be purchased at any office supply store. There were approximately nine shelves in the tower, making it convenient to place the forms in it and retrieve them when needed. I was asked to oversee the caretaking of this document tower until some formal procedures could be put in place. When the tower was low on some of the forms, I asked the person responsible for replenishing it to make additional copies. He just happened to be a new hire in his early twenties. The next day, I visited the document tower again and was somewhat upset at what I thought was inaction with respect to my request. After querying him, he informed me that he had indeed made additional copies. The problem was that the amount of copies that were made was so minuscule, it was easy to assume that the count hadn't changed. I picked up one of the copies and noticed that is was crooked. That is a common problem when making a reproduction on a copy machine.

Because he was young and willing to learn, I felt that I could make an impression upon him. No one wants to feel as though his message is falling upon deaf ears. I explained to him the necessity of inspecting his work to make sure that it was presentable. In addition, never leave a question in the mind of supervision as to whether a request was executed. I further explained that the machine doesn't care how many copies it makes, his boss does. If you're asked to make copies and no certain number is requested, make plenty. He was new to that environment and the only place there was for him to go was up or out the door. The lack of adhering to the principles of **"a job well done"** will pave the way for him to be out! The young man was appreciative of my heartfelt concern and continued to excel in his job performance.

****

One owner of a very small business relayed to me his experience with some students seeking employment for the summer. The young men were not complete strangers, having grown up in the vicinity of the owner's home. Rather than do a mass mailing, this small business owner had predetermined to saturate a particular neighborhood with handbills. Using this method, he could control where he was advertising his business and thus be more cost effective. Two students were to be paid a straight hourly rate, and were told beforehand where to begin, and end, with the distribution. It occurred to these young men that they could feign a complete distribution of handbills after meeting only half of the stipulated requirement. Having disposed of the remaining handbills, these guys showed up after what they thought would have been an appropriate amount of time. They then made their way back to the office of the company owner for their wages.

Being a streetwise and crafty person, the owner had enough foresight to follow the young men. He observed them actually dumping the handbills in a dumpster in the rear of a restaurant. When confronted with the fraud that they had committed, the two young men confessed. What was the point in denying that which was obvious? They were paid and were not used again. When young people are attempting to put a resume together, it is imperative that they make full use of every employment experience. That is the method by which prospective employers will be able to determine if you are worthy to be hired. These two young men only cheated themselves out of a good recommendation, they burned a bridge behind them. Small business owners operate on a very tight budget and do not have funds to waste. That business owner will never forget that experience and the young men failed a test of **"a job well done."**

I am often asked the same question of a great number of people: "Who do you know who is good?" It gives me great pleasure to recommend individuals for various jobs. It matters not whether they are domestic jobs or jobs related to business, the principles remain the same. Practicing good working habits has thc grcatcst influence on your continued employment and the advancement to something better.

****

Working for a very demanding boss can be some of the best training that you can get as an employee. The difficult boss or leader can be comparable to a tough drill sergeant in the military. He is not much fun when the training is going on, but the training will prepare you for the tough road ahead. The chances are that in your workplace experience, you'll only have one "Captain Bligh" type boss. The bosses that are meticulous provide the best training. He or she may be of the mindset that no one can do the job as well as they themselves can. They make sure you cross your t's and dot your i's, even when you think that it doesn't matter. It does matter. Retype it, redo it as many times as you are asked to do so. Your gut instincts would be to tell your boss, "I've had it with this job," or some other exclamation of complete frustration. Resist the temptations to give the boss a piece of your mind. You will have just burned a bridge and there will be no recommendation for the next employment **"opportunity."**

Be mindful of this. You are indeed in training when you are working for a difficult boss. If you can work for him or her and make sure the jobs are done well, you will surely be able to withstand the challenges of the next boss. You are always looking towards that next job. Each experience is an opportunity to gain knowledge which can be parlayed into a better position. Knowledge is power!

TRUE STORY

Anyone who runs a business can attest to the fact that good help is difficult to find. In fact, those employees who are in the classification of "one of the good one's," can usually receive preferred treatment from management. There are instances when a manager may find themselves in a bind, manpower-wise. Such was the case with this particular client. They were in need of a person to fill a spot in their Computer Aided Design department. I was charged with filling this spot on a temporary basis. The project was estimated to take three weeks for completion. Trying to find someone to fill a spot for three weeks was a formidable task. No one wants to be looking for another job after three weeks of employment.

A project that lasted longer would have been easier to man. In addition, designers are in great demand and can command working conditions that are favorable to them. The chapter entitled **"Opportunity"** explains this further. Nonetheless, it was my responsibility for finding, interviewing, and hiring this person. I received a call from an agency that had a person who was willing to fill the spot for the time allotted. The resume was faxed to me and the credentials were verified by the agency that made the initial contact. Time was being lost and I had to get someone.

Left without much choice, I consented to hire this person. When he arrived, I had a private meeting with him and explained the urgency of the project. I was assured by him that there would not be a problem. That gave me a warm and fuzzy feeling, the kind you like to get. That feeling soon began to disappear as it became apparent that this person had misrepresented himself. He was not as adept in the particular design package as was needed. Moreover, he failed to sense the urgency of the job and demonstrated this by talking excessively on the phone. My clients became quite upset at having to pay the wages of a person who was not performing as expected or required.

To top it all, he left the job without giving notice. This person forgot what was revealed to him in our first conversation. Although the duration of the project was for three weeks, the chances were very good that he would be retained, depending on his **"performance."** I received a call from a recruiting agency asking me to give an assessment of this person. What was I to say about him? His **"performance"** was not an example of **"a job well done."**

Some Good Advice

Guard your employment with a passion. "To Thine Own Self Be True." There is no neutrality when it comes to job performance. You are either influencing someone in a positive manner or they are influencing you in a negative manner. Job performance is something that is easily observed. Do not allow someone else to cause your performance to decline. Chances are, he will not allow you to influence his in a negative manner. What happens when you are being visited by a co-worker who has nothing to do? He begins to bother you and disrupt your activities on the job. He is bored and wants someone to talk to.

There are two administrative assistants, Sally and Jean. Sally works on the third floor. Jean works on the fifth floor in the same building. Sally is swamped with work, while Jean has barely enough to keep her busy. Sally and Jean are good friends on the job and enjoy each other's company. The problem is that Sally's boss observes that Jean is spending a lot of time at Sally's workstation. If she complains about having too much to do with insufficient time, her boss will render a remark that signals why she can't get her work done, too much fraternization. Sally is mindful of the looks she is getting from her boss and tries to do something about it. "Come on, Sally, you can take a break."

> "No, I can't. Really I can't. This report has to get out and be distributed by the end of the day, Jean, or I'll be in real hot water with my boss."
>
> "Oh, your boss is such a jerk. Besides, he's always giving you things to do at the last minute. You can take a break. You don't smoke. Look at how much time the smokers get for breaks."

Because Sally values the friendship and is not true to herself, she relents. Now Sally becomes seriously behind. The five-minute break stretches into 45 minutes.

The roles become reversed in a very short time. Because of a recent merger, Jean's department is now the hot bed of activity. Jean comes in early, works through lunch, and stays late. She now has the **"opportunity"** to improve her standing with management by showing them how dedicated she can be. Sally notices that Jean hasn't been over to see her in quite a while. Sally's workload has now lessened. She goes to visit her friend. "Hi, Jean. Let's go for a break and sit down in the cafeteria. Boy, have I got some news to tell you."

"I can't get away right now, Sally. I've got too much to do. This is the first of the month and the Cost Allocation Account information has to be completed and faxed to all of the manufacturing locations by the end of the day. Sorry, some other time." Sally goes away, somewhat dejected. She remembered how busy she was and allowed Jean to not only interrupt her, but place her in precarious situations on numerous occasions. In addition, Sally appeared to be slothful in the eyes of her boss. When it came time for her annual review, she would not be bargaining for a raise from a position of strength.

THE COMFORT ZONE

"If you want something you've never had you must try something you've never done."
M. Murdock

We have comfort zones. It matters not whether you are familiar with the term, you'll recognize the description. The comfort zone means different things to us as individuals. Humans are creatures of habit and order. We have a tendency to do the same things repeatedly. If you shop often at a mall, perhaps you park in a place that is conveniently located by a particular entrance, affording you ease of entering the mall and exiting. You have parked in the same location so long that it takes no effort whatsoever to remember where your vehicle is. Perhaps you attend church on a regular basis. Without thinking about it, you move to a certain section of the church to listen to the sermon. If you cannot reach the exact place you usually take, you get as close to it as possible. Sitting in another section of the church just isn't the same. You have to turn your head in a different direction to observe the members of the congregation.

The same can be said for your favorite restaurant. If you happen to be a regular patron, it is possible that the wait staff remembers your preferred seating arrangement. In my case, I'll take a table anywhere as long as I am not sitting with my back to the aisles. That is very unsettling to me and I must be in a position to observe who is coming in and going out of the restaurant. I confess, that is a bit of paranoia on my part. It stems from the story of Wild Bill Hickcock being shot, with his back turned to the door. You have just entered the cafeteria at your place of work. There are two tables in the immediate vicinity of each other. One of the tables is unoccupied and there is one with a person sitting at it whom you do not know. Where do you choose to sit? No doubt, you would choose the table that is vacant. It is a process of natural selection. We subconsciously choose those things that bring us comfort. To put it more succinctly, our comfort zones make us feel at ease. We're able to relax.

Grown children living at home know all about the comfort zone. They don't have to worry about such things as where to get their laundry done, shopping for food, and for that matter, cooking food. All they have to do is go to the refrigerator or freezer and take out something that has already been prepared. That child, no matter what the age, does not want to leave the nest that his or her parents have created. Any number of excuses will be given as to why he does not leave and establish his own homestead. At the heart of the matter is the fact that going out on his own has some uncertainty to it. What if he fails and can't take care of himself? Will he be able to come back home? There is fear of the unknown and only the most hearty souls take it on with a "full steam ahead" attitude.

The neighborhood where you live brings on familiarity. You know where all the stores are that will provide you with the accessories necessary to run your household. More importantly, your neighbors provide you with a sense of well-being. There is comfort attached to seeing faces that are familiar to you. In older neighborhoods that have elderly residents, they depend upon the familiarity of their neighbors as sort of a unified protection. They learn each other's habits and can tell when something is not in order. There is predictability in the delivery of the mail, the route the UPS delivery person takes. If you moved to a new neighborhood you would have to deal with the arduous task of starting all of this over again.

There is the comfort that comes with human familiarity. When a man and woman first meet, they are at their very best, performing and attempting to impress one another. This is done regardless of any romantic inclinations. One or both may hope that this meeting leads to romance. There will be a point in the relationship when the couple will become "common." I use this to describe the condition of being comfortable with the presence of the person. The need to impress has long since passed and things will be done and said now that would not have been done or said in the early stages of the relationship. There are no surprises. You know what to expect of each other. When you are with this person, you are in your comfort zone.

All of the previous examples were given to expound on the fact that we all have our comfort zones. They may differ in their depiction, but the essence is the same. They cause us to relax and be at ease with ourselves and our surroundings. That is a good thing except when it comes to your working environment. Comfort zones are tantamount to dropping your guard, not paying attention to what is going on. When this happens, you will lose your competitive edge. That is what this is really all about, staying on top, being at your peak performance as much as possible. It is the competitive edge that distinguishes the average employee from the good, the outstanding employee from just the good one. The place to be is outstanding.

That is where the greater rewards are. In order for that to happen, a person must leave his comfort zone that has been established at his place of employment.

That is easier said than done. Who wants to start a new job with all the anxiety and stress that accompany it? One gets used to coming to the same place and doing the same thing, day after day. There are the days you plan to be off, sick. It is just a coincidence that these sick days happen to coincide with days of sunshine and 80-degree weather. You are at home at the job. Your colleagues are analogous to your neighbors. There is no need to perform at your peak, no one else is. Your compensation is set in place and most of the people around you are compensated in a similar fashion. Then there is all that vacation time you have got coming. Why would anyone in their right mind give that up?

When a person starts a new job, he knows that all eyes are upon him, the new person. He will come into work, go to lunch, return from lunch and finally, leave at the end of the day at the proper times. This is sometimes called the probationary period. When I was first employed by General Motors in 1983, the probationary period for new salaried employees was six months. It was the view of management that a person's true character would be revealed within that time frame. The severity in which one had to adhere to the rules depended on the department's management. The test of time revealed that as younger employees were hired, they could be on their best behavior for six months, standing on their head. If the truth is told, a person would have to do something terrible to be terminated. Your attendance was not one of those items that would get you fired. You would perhaps be reprimanded and made to sit in the corner (that's a joke) but there was really no penalty for performing poorly.

At the time of my departure, G.M. had revised its policy on probationary periods. It was a policy that was more subtle and was not written down in a manual. Instead of the new hire being placed directly on the G.M. payroll, the person would be contracted in through any one of the temporary employment agencies. Temporary was defined as being as long as G.M. stipulated. I have firsthand knowledge of engineers who were contracted into G.M. on a temporary basis for more than three years. That lengthy period was because the individuals were not dealing from a position of strength and because their skills were those that could be found elsewhere. Positions of strength and hiring policies are covered in the segment entitled **"Strategies."**

Complacency is a job "killer," because with it comes a lack of hunger. The hunger that I am speaking of is the hunger to enhance or sustain one's standard of living. The mistake most people make is thinking along the lines of, "It will always be this way because it always has been this way." If you are working for a company presently, there is no guarantee that that will always be the case. Continuing your education will surely bring a disruption to your life. There are so many other things that we would rather do with our time, things that bring us pleasure. In this day and age of constant change, a rationally thinking person must stay on the cutting edge to remain a valuable employee. You cannot count on the company for whom you work to make the decisions for you.

When you first begin to work for a company, the two parties have agreed to certain conditions. The stipulations need not be in written form. Your best interest and that of the company you work for coincide. Frequently, over a period of time, your best interest and that of the company you work for begin to diverge. When it becomes in the best interest of the company to sever your employment, that is what it will do. The goal must be to have your employer feel that it is in his best interest to retain your services as a laborer. This is accomplished by making an investment in yourself through continued education or acquiring a skill that is in constant demand. These topics are covered in detail in the segment on **"Education."**

TRUE STORY

Because I don't have permission to use her real name, "Karen" will do. At the time, Karen and I were employees of the same corporation. This corporation was comprised of several divisions. Karen worked for the division that was located in the city of Flint, Michigan, while I worked for the division that was located in the city of Detroit, Michigan. In a move to streamline the corporation, mergers were announced. That is always an unsettling event because more rumors abound than truth. Nonetheless, when the details were fully disclosed, the total number of people who were to be employed after the merger of these two divisions was approximately 1,200. The total before the merger was approximately 2,400 people. The only people who are safe are those who have skills that are in demand. Even at that, you may choose not to wait patiently for a new assignment. You begin to make phone calls to your old bosses and friends to see what they can do for you. The very first people to go scrambling for positions with other non-participating divisions were the executives. It made sense that there would be no room for all of these [shooters] in one combined division. They are the ones who have the most to lose, having worked so hard to attain those positions.

Appealing to the old bosses for cover was useless. They could not provide cover for themselves. Karen was one of those individuals who was left uncovered. Her services, after 25 years, were no longer required. Needless to say, she was devastated. A very proud woman she was, trying to hold back the tears from her eyes. She felt rejected by the same company that she had shown so much loyalty to. She said to me, "Al, what did I do that I shouldn't have done and what was it that I should have done that I didn't do? I thought that if I needed more education, the company would tell me." That was no time to be truthful with her. The corporation's interest and hers had diverged and she was not watching as it was occurring. How do you say that to a person after she has lost her job? The corporation was not to blame, she was. She had been in her **"comfort zone"** and wanted no disruptions.

ATTITUDE AND PERFORMANCE

"I'd rather change my mind and succeed than on my own way and fail"
Robert Schuler

Social psychologists define attitudes as beliefs that predispose us to act and feel in certain ways. What are the origins of our attitudes? We learn them from our experiences and from other people. What can affect the way you feel about yourself or the way your employer feels about you more than your attitude? Someone once said that "Your attitude will affect you altitude." Plainly stated, it is the attitude displayed concerning our job and those around us that will ultimately determine what plateau we reach in life. That is, unless you are independently wealthy and you do not have to work for a living. In a recent presentation that was made by a banking official, the following text was released: "Our attitude is not determined by our circumstances but how we respond to circumstances. Our minds determine our attitude. We can respond positively or negatively. It is how we react to events, not the events themselves, that determine our attitude."

In the daily pursuit of my activities, I meet individuals who display the types of attitude that are so outstanding and I am compelled to compliment them. There is always a smile on their faces. I am cognizant of the fact that there had to be some days when they were not at their mental or physical best. One could not tell this from outward appearances. Their attitude towards how they performed their jobs said a lot about them. That is why attitude and performance are linked together. Your attitude towards your job and how that job is performed is inseparable. A good attitude can be a difficult thing to maintain when dealing with the public. However, you never know who you may meet and where you will meet them. What does all of this have to do with getting a better job?

Because of my position as a consultant, I am asked occasionally to make recommendations for hiring people to perform specific tasks. I am also asked to review the performances of individuals and make recommendations for terminating the employment of individuals. My phone will ring and it will be a [headhunter] asking me, "Do you know someone whom you can recommend for......" When I meet people with outstanding attitudes, their demeanor is inviting enough that I make inquiries of their future aspirations. "Are you happy and satisfied with what you are doing?" That is a typical question that I would ask. If they are forward thinking, they will give the proper response, which will be, "I am always looking for a better job."

TRUE STORY

We have many job experiences in our lifetime. Some of them are good and some are not so good. One of the good experiences for me was when I worked for a small company in 1979, called Special Engineering. This engineering firm was located in a very old section of the city of Dearborn, Michigan. The building was a dump in every sense of the word. The cinder block walls had cracks in the mortar so large that we could see the sun rising in the morning. At one time, the room was heated by a gas stove-like appliance that vented through the wall. The cylindrical hole in the wall was never filled. It was merely covered with a piece of plastic. Although the place was unsightly, it provided me with some of the best work I ever had. No day or job was the same. When I first entered the building, I said to myself, "I am the best guy in here." I was not the most talented designer in the building nor was I the most experienced. What I did have was the best attitude. I had a very good understanding of the needs of that company. I was an employee who was on contract (temporary employment) to perform work for their customers. Their major customer happened to be Ford Motor Company Experimental Engineering. The engineers would come in with requests to do designs that were for a limited number of vehicles.

Because the work was experimental, it entailed making frequent changes to the designs. All of the work was performed on vellum paper. The drafting boards were 4x8 sheets of plywood on top of saw horses. Those were extremely crude furnishings, but it was functional. When times are good, automotive designers are in demand. The wages paid reflected that demand. At that time, the going rate for a designer was $15.00 an hour and $22.50 for every hour over 40 worked during the week. Those numbers did, and still do, give a great number of designers attitudes of haughtiness. Making that kind of money would require individuals of exceptional character to maintain any semblance of humility. Thus, when the engineers required a change to a drawing, there was huffing and puffing, complaining, and a general display of impatience. I would see the designers feed off each other and almost compete to see who could be more obnoxious with their responses. This behavior was not in the best interest of Special Engineering, nor was it in the best interest of the designers.

The Experimental Engineering building was in close proximity to Special Engineering. That was their trump card. The engineers did not like to travel far. The majority of the engineering firms were located in the suburbs northeast of Detroit and catered to General Motors. G.M. was by far the largest user of [outsourced] engineering expertise. When changes had to be made, it usually meant that the designer had to do some erasing of what he had already labored over. Some of the work took considerable effort. The designers could not be blamed altogether for their lack of enthusiasm in having to do some erasing. A lot of rubbing with an eraser could be involved. On the other hand, when I discovered that the engineers had a tendency to change the direction of the designs, I bought an electric eraser. That would make any changes to the designs more tolerable and less time consuming.

All one had to do was think about the situation to come to a sensible conclusion. I was paid by the hour. It did not matter whether I was placing lines on paper or taking the lines out. In addition, if changes were being made, that prolonged my attention to that particular project. That meant my temporary employment status was extended. I was quite amazed at how the engineers approached me. They were almost apologetic. I assured them that their request for changes would not be met with hostility. "After all, you guys are the customer," would be my reply. "What a refreshing attitude you have, Al." It didn't take long before I was swamped with work. I noticed that certain engineers were requesting me to work on their projects. That was good for Special Engineering and myself. The engineers would continue to bring their projects to Special Engineering and I would continue to make a pretty decent wage.

The programs that were allotted to Special Engineering began to dwindle and that meant that some people had to be laid off. The more significant problem was that the entire auto industry was in a downsizing mode. Cuts were being made in every area, which included giving overflow work to engineering firms. The pendulum was now swinging in the opposite direction. There were more people desiring work than there was work available. Being laid-off meant that there was a good chance that a person might not find an equivalent job making the same amount of money. The programs at Special required 50 people. After 18 months, the programs only required 11 people. I was one of the 11 who remained employed at Special Engineering.

The owner, a gentleman by the name of Mike Vargo, called me into his office because he heard that I was contemplating leaving. He wanted to assure me that they had no intentions of any further reductions. If it became necessary for them to reduce the staffing levels, I would not be one of those they let go. Then he said something very interesting. "Just as you guys get together and talk about what shops are good and which ones not to go to, we owners do the same thing. We talk about you guys and inform one another on which of you to avoid hiring. If it came to a point where I had to let you go, I would call one of the other shop owners and ask him to give you a job. You set a good example for the shop. The Ford people really like you." Thus I proved my premise that having the right attitude can assist you with future employment.

****

That was something that had never occurred to me, the fact that the owners would get together over lunch or dinner and discuss the contract employees. What had I done to merit such praise? I had done nothing spectacular. Was I worthy of it? I think not. It was the little details that made the difference. I came to work everyday on time. I went to lunch on time. I came back from lunch on time and then I punched out at the end of the day. Yes, we had time clocks. I was careful of who I associated with when the shop was at full staff. I stood out because

I stayed focused on my goal. I wanted to learn as much as possible in as short a period of time as was allotted.

Staying employed there gave me time to learn what I didn't know by taking design classes after work. In the meantime, I kept my eyes on the prize. There were those who were hiding in our number. The ones who tried to do as little work as possible. There was always an excuse why they couldn't complete a task. They didn't last long. They never do. After a while, they are relegated to the lowest paying jobs around because their reputations have preceded them, as Mr. Vargo had stated.

****

The right attitude can cover a multitude of deficiencies. The skills necessary to perform a job can be learned. Unlearning a bad attitude is more difficult. No one comes into this world having knowledge. We learn the things we need to know over time. Employers, for the most part, have great patience for those who show a willingness to learn, even though their performance may not be up to par in the beginning. They are given time to bring themselves up to speed because they display the kind of demeanor employers are looking for.

"If they paid me more money, I would do better."It's a troubling declaration that I have heard from employees many times. Did it ever occur to these individuals that if they performed better they might be paid more? They have it all wrong. More money will not translate into an employee who displays the proper attitude. There are better methods that can be used to achieve the goal of better compensation. A bad attitude is something that emanates from within the mind of the individual and money will not change that. Being a disgruntled employee and having an unpleasant disposition will not get you more money. It may, in fact, get you fired. How many times have you been to a grocery store, a fast food restaurant, or a discount department store and witnessed rude behavior by the check-out clerk? This is all too common. Perhaps there was a scowl on the face of the person so fierce that the customers dared not to ask him for assistance. These displays of repugnant attitudes are visible for all to see.

Let's acknowledge the fact that dealing with the public is a difficult undertaking. Some patrons can be impossible to please. It is as if their mission is to be as obnoxious as possible. When the employees are a part of a large company, they can get away with performing in a manner that is not favorable to the company. Acting inappropriately can be interpreted as speaking harshly towards the store patrons. Careless actions can also describe the treatment my wife received while at a drive-through window at a burger joint. I'll ignore the fact that the order was incorrect. That can happen. It was the throwing of the change back to her that was objectionable. It was in the evening and she could not retrieve the money until arriving home.

People will not stop shopping at a discount department store or a fast food restaurant because they were treated poorly by one individual. They may complain to the management or shop at another location. These individuals are motivated to shop because of the low price of what they are shopping for. The same cannot be said for upscale department stores and finer restaurants. Their employment requirements are much more stringent. They scrutinize each employment candidate and screen out those who will not project mannerisms that are favorable to the company. They are usually better educated and more articulate than their counterparts at the low-scale stores. The patrons of the upscale establishments will shop at another similar store when treated poorly. Money is not an issue with them, service is. The employees who work at these high profile stores are paid accordingly.

If you are a patron of a finer eating establishment, you have an expectation of good, if not exceptional, food and service. I personally will provide a restaurant with a second opportunity to disappoint me. There are many who share my sentiments on this issue. What are those people with poor attitudes overlooking? The fact is that you never know who is observing you and your behavior, good or bad. I am not the only person who admires and acknowledges those who display outstanding attitudes. Business owners occasionally shop at some of the discount department stores. They also notice the good and bad behavior and attitudes of employees.

The same can be said for restaurateurs. Restaurants compete against one another for patrons. This competition can also involve persuading wait staff and other workers to leave their present employers to come work for them. It stands to reason that only those displaying the proper attitudes will be courted.

Those who have "bad tudes" have no hope of bettering themselves if they continue in the mode that they are in. They become locked into a downward spiral without a clue as to how to get out. Hopefully, reading this book will provide some remedy for their situation.

DON'T EXPECT ACCOLADES

Don't expect your boss to pat you on the back every time you perform a job well. It does feel good to receive praise for our efforts and performance. We call those, "at-a-boys." Doing a job well should be praise in itself. You should not feel slighted if you condition yourself to perform at your peak, regardless of attention being paid to you. Your performance and attitude can diminish if, for some reason, you did not get the credit or praise you felt you deserved.

RESPECT FOR AUTHORITY

What can be identified as one of the major hindrances to progress is not having the proper respect for authority. As stated elsewhere in this book, "If you take the king's ransom, you must do the king's bidding." This is translated into modern-day English as, "Do as your boss asks you or find another job." The lack of respect for authority is a phenomenon that is becoming more prevalent in our society. It starts with a lack of the proper nurturing of young people at home and escalates throughout their lives. It is learned behavior. When children feel it no longer necessary to obey their parents, it signals the beginning of disrespect. If there is no penalty for disobedience or disrespect, the behavior worsens.

This behavior is something that is foreign to most immigrants who come to this country. In some of these cultures or ethnic groups, disrespect or disobedience of parents is not tolerated nor is it imaginable. Studies have shown that there is a direct correlation between the relationship of parents and their children to the child's scholastic performance. When the child no longer deems it necessary or prudent to obey his parents, there will be no restrictions to his behavior. He will have no fear of punishment because his parent's dominion is minimal at best. The classroom teacher now becomes the recipient of the child's lack of respect. It then proceeds to the lack of respect for the law and law enforcement officials.

This is not to say that all of these individuals will be disposed to a life of crime. What is clear is that there will be a propensity for disrespectful behavior. That does not play well in the work place. At General Motors, Ford, Chrysler, IBM, EDS and other large Fortune 500 companies, there are three grounds for immediate firing. The first is fighting. The second is stealing. The third is insubordination. Insubordination is a fancy way of saying, "disrespectful."

This could be as simple as your boss asking or telling you to do something that lies within your classification and your refusal to do so. Whether the task is one that should be obeyed is what arbitration boards and union officials determine. One of the reasons why some ex-military personnel are sought after is their ability to follow directions (orders) and their respect for authority. It has also been found that these ex-military types often make good leaders because of their training. Redundancy is built into military procedures to ensure a successful outcome.

Many great books have been written on the subject of leadership and management. Leadership is a skill that is learned and developed. This is contrary to some who believe that leaders are born. In my opinion, the theory of "born leadership" is erroneous. A person can become a good leader by reading about and practicing leadership skills. But a person cannot become a good leader without first learning to become a good follower. Becoming a good follower is difficult. It takes humility of spirit and confidence in one's own abilities to take orders from someone else.

At the heart of taking orders is recognizing who is the boss. There is an old saying that says, "I am paying the cost to be the boss." This is usually true, the person in charge being the one responsible when things go wrong. That is why it should be done his way. His way may not be the best way, but there are ways to exert your influence over decisions that are made. Develop a reputation for cooperating with your boss. Not only will he appreciate it, he will speak of your cooperation to others. You could receive a glowing recommendation when you are searching for another job. Remember, you are always looking for another job. Everyone should be the recipient of respect. Whether they are deserving of respect is a separate issue. The "Golden Rule," "Do unto others as you would have them do unto you," is always applicable. When displaying a disrespectful attitude, it is certain that you will become unemployable at some point.

TRUE STORY

In 1974, I witnessed an example of how having the proper **"Attitude"** and adhering to the principals of **"A Job Well Done"** can pave the way for a better job. Ron Holbrook was the person with whom I shared an apartment in Ypsilanti, Michigan. Ron was also a full-time student at Eastern Michigan University. Coming from a home where the merits of work were stressed, it was no surprise that he would take on a part-time job to earn extra money. What was surprising was that he took on two part time jobs. Both were at the Briarwood Mall in Ann Arbor, Michigan. Ron, an impeccable dresser, had the gift to sell. His personality was conducive to the vocation of sales. He was articulate and very well-mannered. Skalaar's International and J. Riggins, both men's clothing stores, were the places of his employment.

When school recessed for the summer, Ron took on a third job because he was already working the maximum number of hours available at both clothing stores. In the immediate vicinity of the mall was an automobile dealership by the name of Howard Cooper, Audi, Porches, Volkswagen. There, Ron was employed as car washer and porter. The job of porter was to ferry the vehicles to and from different locations. Occasionally, I aided Ron in performing vehicle swaps with other out-of-state dealerships. To some, this might have seemed beneath their abilities. Who would want to wash cars and perform the role of go-for? Ron looked at it as an **"opportunity."** The location of the dealership afforded Ron the convenience of attending to all three jobs without losing time. Ron's duties included the daily washing of Mr. Howard Cooper's personal vehicle. Being a car lover also, Ron was attentive to the details of cleaning Mr. Cooper's car, employing the principles of **"A Job Well Done."**

At the end of the day, Howard Cooper would exchange pleasantries with Ron and be on his way. After several weeks, Mr. Cooper began to engage Ron in more substantive conversation. Mr. Cooper took notice of Ron's ability to express himself, his attention to detail and his mannerism. Ron's goal was to become a new car salesman. He would get his chance. The sales manager was the person given the task of tutoring Ron on the particulars of car sales. Ron was an instant hit. The exact number of his monthly sales escapes me. He did well enough to quit the two part-time jobs and school also. You have heard it said that luck happens when opportunity meets preparation. Here was a prime example of someone who was prepared when the opportunity arose. The work was honorable and his attitude towards the work was the key to his success. His positive attitude had a positive effect on his performance. His performance placed him in a position of opportunity.

It has been several years since the last communication between Ron and I. After learning the intricacies of selling cars, Ron moved to Azusa, California. He informed me that he was selling ultra-expensive luxury cars at a dealership where they do not ask how much. They ask, "When can I get it?"

****

You cannot make people like one another. People choose their friends based on a lot of different factors. Any means used to force them together does the opposite of what was intended. Just as water seeks its own level, people will generally destroy their own stereotypical attitudes. It happens when they meet and get to know someone of the nationality or race which they have defamed. Usually they find out for themselves that he or she isn't so bad after all. It is up to you, the individual, to maintain the proper attitude towards people. In 1984, I was hired into a department in General Motors where one of the employees of 40 years standing was retiring. The entire complex was under a hiring freeze and you could not add to your personnel head count. You could only replace those who retired or quit. The department was comprised of 14 people. The two guys with the most knowledge were very agitated at my admission to their group. They said nothing to me, but I knew my presence was not appreciated.

Raymond Edwards and Lowell Johnson (not their real names) had been in the department the longest period of time and knew its operation inside and out. The manager was new to the department, having been promoted and placed there two years prior to my arrival. All was swell with the rest of the members of the group but I knew Raymond and Lowell were two nuts that I was going to have to crack. The two of them had their desks at the front of the room and right behind one another. Everyone had to walk by them to get to their own desks. These two guys made it a point to greet everyone in the morning as they passed by except for me. They made sure that I got the message that they weren't going to welcome me. I guess what angered them more was that I often got a laugh out of their behavior. The two of them never spoke a word to me in six months. Yes, it was six months. We're talking about General Motors in 1981.

Now you may wonder how this could go on, but our functions were so dissimilar in the department that verbal communication between us wasn't necessary. It was obvious to the manager that something was wrong. We had a group meeting every month and their demeanor was something other than cordial if I had to sit next to one of them. The manager asked me into his office and began apologizing for the behavior of Raymond and Lowell. He asked if there was anything he could do. I assured him that everything was just fine and I insisted that he not intervene. The three of us had to work to together I told him. There was no law that said we had to like one another. I told the manager that I would handle the situation my way. In reality, there was no situation. Those guys didn't know me. That was the problem. I made sure I spoke to them every morning, a simple and unpretentious "good morning, gentlemen" as I passed their desks. Just because they were acting foolishly, it didn't mean that I had to. There was never a response from them.

In order to make a short story even shorter, I'll get to the point. Our paychecks were handed to us twice a month and I always made sure that I picked up their paychecks and handed them to them. I heaped kindness on those guys and displayed my competencies. I was fighting fire with water. Water takes the heat out of the combustion process. It took a while, but I took the heat out of those guys. It was directly beneficial to me because Robert gave me an outstanding endorsement to Simon Marshall, a Director of Engineering. Robert was someone whom Marshall respected for his engineering skills and gave credence to his recommendations. Marshall had me promoted. I would not have gotten the promotion when I did without Robert's intervention. Yes, I deserved it, but you do not always get what you deserve in life. Having the right attitude will help get you what you want, a better job.

Some Good Advice

Just as you would protect your body from physical harm, you must protect your spirit from contamination. You say you don't have an inner spirit? Of course you do. When someone whom you love says something terse or cutting to you, are you not wounded? But the wounding was not of a physical nature. Why then do you feel hurt?

Because your inner spirit was damaged. The "contamination factor" attacks your human spirit and adversely affects your attitude. Without getting into the proofs of the existence of man's human spirit, there are those who knowingly or unknowingly can bring you down from the heights of exuberance. You have experienced that before. All is going well at that particular moment in your life. As a greeting, you asked someone "How are you doing today?" You really didn't mean for him to give you a detailed description of what was wrong in his life. Nonetheless, he continues on. The high that you were on is now gone. You have been robbed of your inner joy. He has imparted upon you his misery, and misery loves company. The next time, you will be sure to avoid him. The same can be said for disgruntled employees. They are to be avoided at all cost. The reasons for their degrading attitudes are too numerous to list.

The disgruntled are individuals that who no sweetness in their lives. Something unfortunate happened to them and rather than getting over it, they make it their goal to contaminate the minds of other people. Bosses see this happen quite frequently when there is a new hire on the property. The disgruntled employee begins to fill the mind of this person with all of his workplace prejudices. These people poison the environment in which we must work. They are a boss's worst enemy. They do their jobs well enough so that there are no grounds for their dismissal. However, what they do is far more destructive than not performing their jobs. You say that you do not have a bad attitude? If you continue to fellowship with a disgruntled person, you soon will. He does not have the ability to enhance his position by complaining nor can he enhance yours. The fruits of your association with him will be misery and cynicism.

The disgruntled are easy to pick out. There will always be something wrong with someone else's work except theirs. They'll seek to gather a supportive group around them to help insulate them from being singled out by management. These are powerful individuals and have the ability to influence others in the wrong manner. What you will begin to notice about yourself is that you will take on their characteristics of criticism. The things that never bothered you before now seem to irritate you. An unbiased examination of the topic, item, or work procedure would reveal that the issue is altogether different than how it is being portrayed. All humans are susceptible to making mistakes. Humans are, by nature, filled with faults. We make mistakes. What should be one's goal is to seek to be as mistake free as possible. The disgruntled are this way. When they like you, they can overlook any of your faults. When they don't like you, you can't do anything right. Everything you do will be criticized.

In the work place, everyone has an agenda. Some agendas are openly voiced by the management. Some are overt and some are covert. The disgruntled employees have agendas too. Theirs is to subvert the activities of the workplace. They proceed in covert activities and are individuals in need of psychological help. They stir up the waters that would otherwise not be muddy. When the waters become muddy, they are not pleasurable to drink from. When that person(s) is removed from the scene, the waters settle once again. There is peace and harmony.

Any manager who is in tune to his environment knows who the disgruntled are among him. They are the last to get promoted and get the lowest amount of money in the form of merit increases. If the employee happens to belong to a bargaining unit, all a boss can do is hinder favorable actions towards him. This could be in the form of not looking the other way when there are discrepancies in starting and quitting times. The disgruntled employees' bad reputations go before them just as do good reputations. You want to continually be in search for better employment. Obtaining a bad reputation by way of association is not conducive to this goal. Surround yourself with people who are edifying and full of cheer and praise. What you will be taking on is part of their uplifting spirit.

PERFORMANCE

Your attitude about the job you perform and your job performance are directly related. If you feel good about your work, the natural tendency is to do a better job. When you practice doing a good job, the act of performing that job well becomes ingrained in you. A **"job well done"** becomes second nature. Your job performance may be noticed by someone in a position to advance your career. Not only is your job performance known among your present colleagues, but those with whom you used to work remember you. When they are asked, "Do you know anybody who's good?" your name will come up. It should be apparent that what is being described is a cycle of interdependency.

The opposite could also be true. When you do not have good feelings about the work you perform, just getting the job done is paramount. Perfection or anything close to it is out of the question. Furthermore, just getting to the job is a chore in itself. As Dr. Edward Deming, the author of the *Deming Principals of Quality*, stated, "Work should be fun." Anyone reading this book can identify with this. You are either loving what you're doing or wishing you could do something else. If the question you are asking is, "What if I don't know what I want to do?" or "What am I good at?" That scenario is covered in the chapter entitled **"Dreaming And Discovery."** I have had jobs that I loved and many more that I couldn't stand. Deep within, I envisioned a day when I would no longer have to endure the misery of those jobs. That was my motivation. For the ones that I loved, the work was hard at times but it fit into my job skills. I was well suited for it. Even if long hours were required to complete a task, it wasn't as if I dreaded every minute of it. In fact, the hardest thing I had to do was get up out of bed in the morning. Once I got to the job, it was "show time." (I borrowed that from Earvin Magic Johnson).

Employees have expectations of their employers. The order in which they are listed may not have a bearing on their importance to employees:

- They want to be paid promptly and without complications.
- They want a clean and safe place to work.
- They want their task to be clearly defined.
- They want regular increases in their compensation.
- They want to be able to take scheduled time off work.
- They want room for advancement, someplace to go besides where they started.

Employers have expectations, too. It is meeting and exceeding the expectations of your employer that sets you apart from everyone else, performance wise. Another key to securing a better job is being able to measure how you are performing in the job you have. If there is nothing special about what you are doing, how will you stand out from your colleagues? Employers expect that their staff will report to work every day. Employee absenteeism is still, and always has been, a problem with the larger and mid-sized companies that manufacture products. Usually, the staffs responsible for the manufacture or the assembly of the products are comprised of individuals with little or no post-high school experience. How that figures into the equation, I am not quite sure.

I have worked in several factories in my lifetime and the rule of thumb was that Monday would be the day of greatest employee absenteeism. Friday was the day in which the hourly employees were paid. The wages that were being paid made it less costly to miss a day of work. These were all union jobs, so there was very little that management could do to curb this trend. It is my understanding that today, as an inducement to come to work on a regular basis, some companies offer money for each day's attendance. In addition, some of these same companies pay a cost-of-living allowance. The cost-of-living allowance is based upon the amount of hours a person works. Therefore, the windfall can be great when you consider what these individuals are being paid. Not bad work if you can get it, even if they are bargaining unit jobs. One should consider why all of these offerings are necessary. Because the work isn't any fun.

In addition, on the subject of the expectations of management, having an understanding of your employer's needs will, in itself, help to secure your job. Bosses want employees who can anticipate what to do and not stand around waiting to be instructed. This is especially true in cases where routines are repetitive. If it is abundantly clear what must be done, don't wait to be told to do it. Take the initiative and perform the task. If you are the type who has to be instructed in every detail, there is nothing special about you. The unemployment lines are filled with people like that. A versatile employee is invaluable, one who is willing to do what has to be done, and a person who doesn't complain about how hard every task is. Employers want to hear, "Yes, it can be done," even if the task is difficult. These are the types of people who try to see how much they can get done in an eight-hour day, not how little they can do.

I have known individuals such as this. To say that they were outstanding does not do them justice. When a task had to be completed within a certain time frame, they came in early and stayed late, assuring that the task would be completed on time. This was done without any indication that they would be paid. If you are surmising that these were salaried employees, they were not. They were contract employees who were paid by the hour. However, they did not allow the term "hourly employee" to preclude them from doing what had to be done.

In terms of productivity, being a smoker is a liability. Although it is not at that point yet, soon you can expect job discrimination issues to arise. That is because employers can make the case that smokers are less productive during the day than non-smokers. In theory, that sounds plausible. There are several smokers in the building of my major clients. The same faces can be seen every hour, taking a 10-minute or more break for a smoke. If one were to multiply that 10 minutes by eight hours, 80 minutes of productivity is lost per smoker. If I am an employer, it is much more beneficial for me to employ those who do not smoke. I have not considered the health concerns involving smoking in this scenario. It is a fact that smokers have more time off work due to illness than do non-smokers.

The flaw in this scenario is the inference that a non-smoker is more productive because they do not leave to smoke for 10 minutes every hour. The non-smoker might talk excessively on the phone or visit colleagues for the same amount of time required to smoke a cigarette. It is plausible that a smoker can get as much or more done than the same non-smoker. The individual persons have a great deal to do with whether this argument has validity. However, all things being equal, when I am interviewing two candidates for a position, if one smokes and the other does not, the non-smoker has the advantage.

If you work for a business that deals directly with the public, you must also consider their expectations. If the business is scheduled to open its doors at 9:00 A.M., it is not a good practice for you to stroll in two minutes before the doors open. The customers have very little patience for that sort of thing. Most likely, there is set-up involved with every task. Getting the set-up in order takes time. Arriving at your job early gives you time to get things in order without rushing. Your boss takes notice of who comes in at what times. You may not even be late. What you will become good at is showing up promptly. That is because you have practiced it.

Bosses also want employees who are not "mice." This refers to that saying "When the cat is away, the mice are at play." Every street-wise boss knows that people, in general, do not like to follow the rules that have been established. The more rules there are, the more rebellious the attitudes toward them. A smart boss also knows that every one of his employees wants to get away with something. What he or she must do is narrow the avenue of what they can get away with. In addition, it is beneficial to direct the focus of the lax behavior. As an employee, this lax behavior should never take place while your boss is absent from the scene. That is the time when you want to be on your very best behavior. The last thing your boss wants to hear are tales of how the people under his supervision went berserk. A feeling of betrayal and mistrust becomes planted in him. You want to be the one that he knows will do the right thing, in his presence or out of his sight.

One of the local television stations in the Detroit Metropolitan area did an exposé on county workers. The object of the exposé was to show how little was being done, at the taxpayers expense. A television crew followed a group of workers with hidden cameras. Specifically, these workers were given the assignment of cutting the grass on selected highways. Without going into all of the details, it was quite evident that these men worked only four hours out of an eight-hour day. One of the gentlemen was actually asleep on his mower. The mower was in the middle of a median that divided the highway. The foreman, director, manager, or boss of that crew was not a very happy person. Is it possible that any of the men on that crew would receive a favorable recommendation for a promotion or another job? I don't think so.

Having worked as a contract employee for many years, my senses were sharpened on the needs of my employer. Anyone that has worked in [job shops] can attest to the fact that it is not here today and gone tomorrow. If one does not perform up to expectations, it can be here today and gone the same day. I have seen this happen. The gentleman misrepresented his abilities and it did not take long for it to be discovered. He happened to have his first day of work coincide with a weekly project review. The project manager peered keenly at the work he had performed in those few hours, asked him a couple of questions, then told him to pack his tools. Being told to, “Pack your tools” was the same as saying, “Get out of here, you are fired.” What this did was keep you focused on your mission. You came in and did your job. The reward was a paycheck and a healthy check it was. The details of job shops are covered in the chapter entitled **“Opportunities And Possibilities.”**

Working in the job shops was some of the best training a person could receive. It helped to establish a form of discipline. One could get by with a mediocre performance when times were good and the jobs plentiful. The true test would be when the jobs were not plentiful, as happens in the cyclical world of the auto industry. There are other industries that are cyclical in nature. When the downturn occurs, they must reduce the size of their staff. The attraction of job shops is that its premise is truly “Pay-For-Performance.” You are a free agent who negotiates the hourly rate you will work for. Your reputation and skill level as a designer is a very important factor in establishing your free agent hourly rate. As a contract employee for a company called Stellar Engineering, I was placed within the confines of the General Motors Technical Center in Warren, Michigan, specifically, Fisher Body.

I was one among many contract designers who was on site at Fisher Body. My attitude was the same as it had always been. I was going to focus on the needs of the customer. Continuing on as I had always done, I came to work every day on time. I went to lunch and came back on time. At the end of the day, I left on time. After several weeks had passed, the design room supervisor began to pay closer attention to my work. I was being queried on the methods used to perform specific procedures. These were tests to determine my competencies but this would not be revealed until sometime later.

After three weeks, I was summoned into the office of the Engineer-In-Charge (EIC). The EIC's position is that of a high level executive. I was being offered a direct job working for General Motors. I hadn't asked to work for General Motors nor was it a part of my overall employment strategy. I was not even required to fill out an application. The EIC said to me, "We're going to give you an increase over what you are making now plus we'll be paying your health insurance premiums. You'll also be getting cost of living allowances and several paid holidays." What was I going to say, no? This was indeed a better job than the one I held. My reply was, "The offer is completely acceptable to me."

I was placcd in a group that had several senior designers in it. The person most responsible for me was a gentleman by the name of Jordan Divitto. It was Jordan who gave me day-to-day instructions. After I returned from a physical, Jordan came over to me and said, "I told the supervisor to take a closer look at your work. There was going to be an opening in the group because of a retirement. We could not increase our head count but we could replace people that retired or quit. I liked your **"attitude"** towards your work. You came to work everyday, put your head down and stroked lines (a slang term that means to draw lines on paper). You weren't goofing around like those other guys, shooting rubber bands and talking on the phone all day. You stood out like a sore thumb." Automotive designers are notorious for coming up with ways to reduce the monotony of drawing lines all day.

I made some instant enemies within the department. Some of the remaining contractors felt that I took a job that one of them should have had. With their lack of understanding the principles of **"Attitude and Performance,"** there existed only a small chance that one of them would have been hired. After all, some of them had been on location there for several months before I came along. Bear in mind that I was not the best designer. I had the best attitude and performance. When those two exist, you are given time to come up to speed. I knew the fundamentals of design, but the department in which I was to work had a specialty. Only time could bring on the experience needed to gain proficiency in that discipline. Having the right attitude and high level of performance will not guarantee that you will get a better job. It will place you in the arena where the better jobs are. Let it not be forgotten that you will be good at what you practice. When you practice being a sluggard, you become good at being a sluggard. The same can be said for **"Attitude and Performance."** At times it will be hard to sustain both of these at high levels.

My experiences are not unusual nor are they unique. At the heart of the matter is the theme **"performance."** General Motors had an expectation of performance for the price they were paying for contract services. What they were asking from the temporary staffing was not unreasonable. It would be the same for any employer. Come to work everyday and work a reasonable amount of time for the money being paid. As your level of responsibility increases, your job performance expectations increase also. On every job there are times of panic, emergencies, or hot projects. These are times when your employer is looking for commitment.

Most people plan their vacations and recreational activities well in advance. They do not foresee any emergencies or hot projects. So what do you do when they arise and you have planned your leave months ago? There is no set answer to this. It depends on the severity of the emergency and how much time and money is invested in the leave. If family members are involved, how will they take any postponement? I can attest to the fact that those individuals who make the sacrifice, and it is a sacrifice, rise to the top of every field they are in. It matters not whether they are wait staff, file clerks, carpenters, janitors or engineers, the sacrifice is not forgotten by management. It does not have to be something as grandiose as a vacation. It could be that you have planned to go to a sporting event or concert after work. What should you do? Weigh the benefits of staying versus the costs of leaving them in a jam. Consider this, being flexible, even when it hurts, is a strategy that can be used for getting a better job.

If you are in a job that prohibits you from performing at a level at which you are confident, your choice is simple. Be diligent in seeking something else. Performing poorly at your present job will not get you a better one. I often hear the incurably ignorant make a statement along the lines of, "What do you expect for that kind of money?" Being underpaid is not an excuse for performing poorly. It will be used as a reason to terminate your employment or lay you off. An employer has an expectation of a job well done. A job is only worth what an employer is willing to pay. The level of performance and how much a job pays are totally separate issues. One only has to look at how hard some immigrants and migrant workers toil, compared to what they are paid, to come to the conclusion that these two are independent entities. The assumption is made that these individuals have only minimal education as compared to U.S. standards. Though the tasks they perform are relegated to mostly manual labor jobs, who can argue that these individuals do excellent work and are dependable? However, the market place is determining what they are to be paid. If the owners of businesses have difficulty finding workers at an established wage, the wage will increase until people are willing to work for that rate. Their performance level remains unaffected by the wage being paid.

THE MYTH OF EQUALITY

Your attitude and performance on the job must be separate and independent of what others are doing or not doing. There is no such thing as equality in the work place. As a matter of fact, there is no such thing as equality on the face of the earth. There are different rules for different people. Even in a political system that had its origins based upon the premise of equality, we find that there exists levels of privilege. For the most part, the politics of the work place determine what privileges are awarded. Even in work environments that are governed by organized labor in the form of unions, the politics exist. Union activity is politics in the purest form.

If you are a woman, you are not awarded the same privileges as men in certain fields. When men are standing around talking, it is assumed that they are discussing the job. They may or may not be. When women are gathered in one place, it is not assumed that they are discussing issues involving the work place but that they are gossiping. They may or may not be. No one said that this is fair. Fairness has nothing to do with it. As Bruce Hornsby's song says, "That's The Way It Is." Now that you know this, be prepared to deal with it and make it work to your advantage. This can be done by developing a strategy for advancement. There are exceptions to this unwritten rule. The higher the educational level required to secure the job, the less the differential of gender is apparent. This holds true because competency is the governing factor and not output. Female doctors, scientists, engineers, etc. are not evaluated by their output but by their competency in performing their trade. However, a female assembly line worker, Post Office clerk, or secretary have their performances measured by their output. In these cases, unions do tend to equalize the output required to satisfy the employer. The flip side of that coin is that the union guarantees that there is no reward for superior performances.

There is something about having a tougher way to go, and adversity, that makes one better. The United States Marine Corps boasts of this and has made it part of their allure in their advertisement, "Be the best that you can be." You are guaranteed to get the most stringent training available in the Marine Corps but you will be the best at what you do. When there are skirmishes that involve U.S. military services, which group goes into action first? The U.S. Marine Corp goes in first. What does that mean for you as a female in the work place? Knowing that the scale is tilted in favor of men, you have to work harder to achieve the same level of compensation and status. That will serve many purposes, the most important of which is, you'll be the best that you can be.

I am not able to explain why adversity brings out the best in people. All sorts of sayings revolve around the same issue, adversity bringing on improvement, such as, "When the going gets tough, the tough get going." The one that I have used on occasion is, "The same sun that melts the wax, hardens the clay." What are you made of? If it is wax, you will melt under the load. If it is clay, you will become hardened by the experiences and become impervious to the distractions. The result will be a person who has the ability to remain focused on his goal, increasingly better employment.

If you happen to be a member of an ethnic or gender minority, you are not afforded the luxury of complacency. That is, if you want to get ahead of the crowd. It becomes an exercise in futility to complain about how there is unequal treatment among ethnic groups. Nowhere in the world does real equality exist. Renowned economist, Thomas Sowell, visited this issue of equality and many others in his book, *Preferential Policies, An International Perspective*. This work was a global view of the theme of equality and preferential treatment of individuals according to race, nationality and gender. His conclusion: Nowhere in the world does this idea of equality truly exist. The United States, with all of its imperfections, is the country that is closest to enforcing equal treatment for everyone, thus allowing some individuals to fulfill their dreams.

What is the bottom line? If you are a minority, you're in the spotlight. There is no getting around it. It is a mistake to focus on getting away with the same things and wanting to do what other people do. Stories abound of members of ethnic minorities who achieved greatness through adversity. No doubt, many of these experiences were uncomfortable and some, unbearable. Yet, they persevered and allowed their performance to speak for them. After the lengthy review of the life and times of Jackie Robinson, I am even more convinced of my premise that adversity can bring on great performances. There is no ethnic minority member living in this country who will ever have to endure the shameful treatment or anything similar to that given to Mr. Robinson. He paved the way for all minorities to follow. What shall become of that great personal sacrifice made by him? Are you wax or clay?

Your performance has a great deal to do with the kind of preferential treatment that you receive. If I am a boss, I am going to be more tolerant and a giver of breaks to those who have cooperated with me. These are individuals who have made it clear that their mission was to make me look good as a boss. In fact, I have told my previous bosses that very thing. I accomplished this by paying attention to the details and performing above and beyond the call of duty. I didn't have to be watched to see if I was performing as expected nor did I want to be. I used every assignment as an opportunity to display my abilities. As I recall, many of the assignments were not glamorous. What I thought about was how would

I want an employee of mine to perform in the same situation. I would have an expectation of cooperation from them. In exchange for that cooperation, I would make allowances for variations of established policies. Cooperation and consideration is a two-way street. Those who do not cooperate should not have an expectation of consideration.

This one thing I know to be true beyond a shadow of a doubt. There is tremendous competition for qualified, exceptional employees. They are qualified because they have attained the necessary skills. They are exceptional because they consistently go above and beyond the call of duty. They are the ones who set the bar higher for everyone else, performance wise. They place tremendous pressure on the mediocre and those who think good enough is good enough. These individuals are in short supply in every occupation, in every city and in every state of this great union. Your goal should be to become one of them.

One final word concerning performance, there is no neutrality when it comes to one's performance. Someone is either affecting you for the worse or you are affecting them for the better. More clearly stated, keeping company with the wrong people will cause your performance to suffer, depending on who has the stronger character traits. If you keep company with serious-minded, sober people, you will find yourself acting more soberly. If you begin to keep company with those who act foolishly, you know what the results will be. "How can two walk together except they agree?"

PREPARATION

"For all your days prepare, and meet them ever alike."
Edwin Markham

This may be one of the most important chapters in this book. It deals with the **"preparation"** for a better job. This **"preparation"** covers the basics of what is needed to prepare oneself for the job that will ultimately bring the satisfaction and personal fulfillment that is sought after. What can be more important than being prepared? The answer is, nothing! How does one prepare for a better job? The preparation takes three forms. There is the **mental preparation,** the **spiritual preparation** and the **physical preparation.** You are not going to have time to get ready for the job when the opportunity presents itself. You have to be ready ahead of time. Not believing in luck in the mystical sense of the word, I will support the saying that "Good luck happens when opportunity meets preparation." A person becomes mentally prepared through education and the development of vocational skills; both require a commitment. To stay committed, you must practice being committed. Without practice, dedi-cation, and a commitment to be your best, you'll always be living beneath your privilege. That is because you will not be accruing wages that allow you to live better.

MENTAL PREPARATION

A person becomes mentally prepared by taking care of the personal matters in his life and by the acquisition of knowledge through education. It has been said to me a countless number of times, "But you don't know what I have been going through." They are absolutely correct, I don't know what they have been going through. What I do know are the steps that must be taken to leave the place of stagnation and get to where you want to go. Things that involve your children (if you have any) or matters of the heart cannot be brought into the workplace. Each case is independent of the other and there are no quick or easy solutions. They all require you to deliberate on the problem and perhaps get some help in the form of family counseling. Interruptions in your daily workplace activities because of problems with your extra-income projects outside of work will not be looked upon with understanding.

Employers are becoming increasingly more sensitive to the needs of their employees. What we see are companies answering the call for assistance by providing on-site services such as day care for the children of their workers. In addition, to aid in solving some financial problems, some employers provide space in their buildings for credit unions. Some problems are more deeply rooted and require legal assistance. As part of the compensation package, some employers are including legal assistance. However, unless you target working for a company because of these benefits, you should not count on them being made available.

SPIRITUAL PREPARATION

A person becomes spiritually prepared by adhering to a set of rules and principals that have been proven to be reliable over time. They are biblically based and begin with, "Thou Shalt Not…" These are also the rules that cause us to obey the common laws of man even when they may be unwritten. They are the rules that are inbred, unspoken, and handed down from generation to generation. No one has to tell you that stealing and lying is wrong. There is that still, small voice that speaks to us all to let us know when we have done wrong. Man, being a free moral agent, has the ability to ignore his conscience. A commitment must be made by the individual to establish a set of personal laws that will not be violated. These laws should govern what you will and will not do to your employer. I place such things under the general heading of, "Doing the right things."

PHYSICAL PREPARATION

A person becomes physically prepared by taking care of his personal affairs before seeking employment. They are the affairs of everyday life that we all experience. When you are seeking a new employer, you must have your affairs in order. One problem that comes to mind is transportation. If one does not own a motor vehicle, getting to work can be a chore. I am not capable of covering every transportation problem. The fact remains, you must get to work on a regular, timely basis. If all that you have available to you is public transportation, you have my encouragement, not sympathy. I have first-hand knowledge of how undependable public transportation can be. It will, however, not be an adequate excuse for less than prompt arrivals on the job. Whatever means of public transportation is being used, depart from your residence in sufficient time for something to go wrong. Get schedules for the transportation so that you can leisurely plan your arrival at work.

If you have a vehicle whose performance is less than stellar, you have two choices. Apply enough resources to bring it up to a state of dependability or get rid of it. I know for certain that this is one of the last things a person wants to do, get rid of his car. A car represents personal freedom, thus, explaining the love affair Americans have with their automobiles. If you cannot depend upon your car to get you to your destination, it is a hindrance. Employers have very little tolerance for the call-in excuse, "I'm having car trouble." What must be faced is the hard reality of the situation. The last thing you want to have happen on a new job is to be terminated because you cannot get there on time. When you are making attempts to move forward, you cannot allow these types of things to hold you back.

****

It takes time to prepare for most things in life that have worth. For the individuals who say they do not have time, my reply is direct and to the point. "You have time. What you do not have is time to waste, not if you want to get ahead in life." A sacrifice of time must be made. What is the sacrifice of time? It is the determination of what is important to expend time on and what is not important. In fact, several things can be important enough to demand some of your time, but only a few of them can be chosen. While working on my undergraduate degree, I learned to make the sacrifice of time. That was the only way I could complete the task set before me. There were many things that had to be done and they were all my responsibility. The tasks were prioritized as far as importance to my family. There are very few sports that I love. I happen to love football, collegiate as well as at the professional level. One of the things I had to sacrifice was Monday Night Football and some collegiate games being played on Saturdays. It was heartbreaking to say the least. However, I was maintaining a full time job, taking care of an ill parent and an in-law, while taking a full load of classes in the evenings. I did not have the luxury of time to waste on entertainment.

A great deal of time can be wasted on the quest to be entertained. That is the biggest complaint I have about television. It stifles productivity. It is all too easy to become engrossed and mesmerized by the daily offerings of talk shows, soap operas, and situation comedies (sit-coms). One thing you should consider while sitting idle in front of the television set, is that the individuals that you are watching have achieved success. As the saying goes, "They have gotten theirs." You should be trying to "get yours." You may have to forego going to the movies, musicals, sporting events, and other activities that rob you of what limited time you have to accomplish your goals.

You must make the sacrifice of time to prepare for success. That can only be accomplished by partitioning your time so that each of the really important items can be attended to. Time is so important that whole industries have been started espousing the conservation of and the better use of our time. Donald Trump, the flamboyant New York real estate developer, owes some of his success to the prudent use of time. In his book entitled, *The Art of the Deal,* Mr. Trump said that he takes advantage of the time when his competitors are sleeping. He reportedly only sleeps four hours a day. That means that if his competitors are sleeping eight or more hours a day, there are deals being made while they are asleep. There is no one that has achieved success without toil. Those that were born into wealth had a head start on the rest of us and did not have to work as hard. However, just because you have wealth now, that does not always mean it will continue to be that way. As a wealthy gentleman said to me, "You have to stay wealthy to be wealthy." Staying wealthy takes **"preparation"** also.

KNOWLEDGE

While making a visit to the main branch of the Detroit Public Library with my family many years ago, I happened to look up and observe the words inscribed in marble over the entrance. The words were "Knowledge Is Power." Truer words have never been spoken to mankind. Just saying the word knowledge is incomprehensible. It encompasses a great many subjects, subjects that are as expansive as the universe. One thing for certain, there is always someone willing to pay you for what you know or know how to do. What one must focus on is increasing one's knowledge base on as many subjects as possible. One must guide oneself into the path of the people that want to exploit one's knowledge or skills. Exploitation is not being used disparagingly in this case. The meaning here is plain and simple. Make full use of your abilities.

Above the importance of acquiring knowledge, is gaining wisdom and an understanding of how to use the knowledge. Wisdom is the ability to apply the knowledge gained in the proper manner. An understanding is the full comprehension of why things work the way they do. Knowledge can be acquired in a relatively short period of time. Wisdom is quite different. One may never become wise. That is something that must be sought after by means other than conventional study. I have found that many people have knowledge, but very few have wisdom and an understanding.

EDUCATION

Education plays a very important role in anyone's quest to obtain a better job. There is hope for a brighter tomorrow in practical ways through education. Economic oppression and captivity come from a lack of education. Those who are undereducated suffer all sorts of indignities and afflictions. They do not possess the fundamentals of education. What are the fundamentals of education? The ability to read at the proper level, the ability to construct and write a proper sentence, and perform simple math problems, something as easy as figuring out a 10 or 15% gratuity. In our society, no one is locked out from a better education. There are many educational resources available no matter what station in life you may find yourself. With education comes greater **"opportunity."** Almost all employment doors are closed to you when you have not acquired knowledge or a skill through education. There are some uniquely gifted individuals who are so talented that they would not directly benefit from having a formal education. They are the songwriters, painters, sculptors that we hear about who rocket to stardom. Ask yourself this question, "What are my chances of becoming one of them?"

America is a very affluent nation overall. Despite this fact, there are a great number of our citizens who live in poverty. It is a fact that hundreds of millions of dollars have been spent on the so-called "War On Poverty," that was first initiated by former President Lyndon B. Johnson. This failure to progress these families boils down to one thing, the lack of education. Most of the children living in poverty today are the offspring of the generational poor. Poverty and illiteracy have a tendency to run in families. People who do not learn enough in school to become employable have little or no chance of escaping the grip of poverty. The amount of education required to become gainfully employed keeps changing as employers continue their search for qualified people. Therefore a high school drop-out or undereducated person cannot possibly obtain a good-paying job without acquiring a skill. The importance of education cannot be stressed enough. Education translates into marketability and marketability translates into employability. It is through the continuance of education that a person remains on the cutting edge of performance.

You are never too old to continue your education. Education has an intrinsic value in itself. It brings on a higher sense of self-worth and is a confidence builder. While working on my undergraduate degree, I became accustomed to participating in study groups. This particular day we met in the main cafeteria of the university. An elderly man walked in with his arms filled with newly purchased textbooks. I would estimate that his age had to be in the mid 70's. One of the members of the group remarked, "He's a little old to be going to school, don't you think?" That statement brought on some mild laughter from the other members. What I saw was a person who was not going to allow age to become an impediment to continuing to learn. We have to grow old. We have no choice in the matter. We do not have to become ignorant as time passes by. What better place for an elderly person to become more enlightened than a university of higher learning.

One of my clients offered to a select group of individuals a chance to learn a different computer-aided design software package. The company contracted with an outside training firm to administer the training. The training would require 60 hours to complete. The schedule was set at Monday through Wednesday, four hours per day, over a five week period. The individuals who were offered the training were considered to be the best in their field. The training would take place after normal working hours. There was a major sacrifice that these individuals had to make. They were working on projects that required them to work a significant amount of overtime. That overtime would have to be sacrificed in order to partake of the training.

I thought on the mindset of each individual. I wondered if they would sacrifice a short-term gain for long-term marketability. Although they would lose the overtime, they were going to learn another computer language that they would otherwise have to pay for. Knowing this new computer software package would make them more marketable in the long-term. Greater marketability directly translates into more money. Each of the individuals who were offered the training, took it. I know of several individuals who would not have done so. They would have insisted on being paid for the overtime, thus losing out on a golden **"opportunity."**

****

There is a great deal of clamor made over the need for a college education. Indeed, much can be said in favor of a post high school experience. It is common to see individuals with degrees working in fields other than what is specified on their diploma. For example, a person may have a degree in library science and be managing a restaurant or fast food eatery. Having a college degree does several things for you and all of them are good.

- A degree is used to screen out individuals whom an employer does not wish to consider employing. It is a minimum qualifier that discourages those who do not meet the standard from applying. Employers often impart more responsibilities to those employees with degrees because they associate the college degree with trust-worthiness, reliability and stability.
- Obtaining a college degree takes several years of hard work, no matter what field of study. It displays to an employer that you have stick-to-itiveness. If given a task, you will see it through to its completion. After all, you stayed focused on the goal of obtaining a degree and stuck with it until graduation. The individuals who attended school had a myriad of things that they would rather have been doing instead of busting books. They sacrificed enjoyment for education.
- A degree shows that you have discipline. It takes discipline to arise every morning, head to a specified destination, and arrive on time. Even more discipline is required when the student attends school in the evening. People who attend school at night usually do so because of being employed during normal business hours. In most

cases they are part time students. If a choice has to be made between two perspective candidates for employment and all other things being equivalent, the person who went to school in the evening gets the job. In my mind, those who work during the day and go to school in the evening have a more difficult task than those who just attend school.

- A degree shows that you can work with individuals in a group setting. That is one of the many practical benefits of the collegiate setting. In the workplace, you cannot pick the group members to handle a project, your boss does that. What you must now learn is how to cooperate with one another despite the difficulties that will arise. It is inevitable that conflicts will arise. The most common one being, a neutral place and convenient time for the group members. Then there is the matter of a participant not doing his fair share of the work, but benefiting from the results. Group projects in college provide that learning experience.
- A degree gives you confidence and a feeling of security. You become more marketable. It gives the bearer some possible choices of where to work and live. There is a sense of accomplishment that accompanies the degree. A person has that inward feeling of satisfaction, as perhaps a marathon runner receives at the end of the race.
- A degree broadens your horizons in a intellectual and humanistic sense. In a collegiate setting, there are all kinds of people from all corners of the globe. Myths and stereotypical ideas evaporate as you discover on your own that those who do not look like you are not necessarily bad people. It can be a cultural smorgasbord and that is a good thing. This explanation has validity in almost every discipline except for those of the sciences. Those are specialized areas of expertise and the degree acts as a pseudo guar-

antee that the person holding it is qualified in that area. For example, a pharmacist no doubt has a degree in pharmacy or chemistry. An electrical engineer may have a degree in electrical engineering or physics. It is not an absolute but it is a reliable statement.

****

College is not for everyone. For those who would rather work with their hands, perhaps following the avenue of a skilled trade is the answer. I am a fan of the way Germany promotes education. There are two paths that students can take as a post high school learning experience. Those with the inclination and appropriate academic foundation, can pursue the collegiate settings after graduation from high school. Germany also has an excellent program for students to enter into the skilled trades. The training is intense and is as demanding as the courses in the collegiate setting. The results in either case are well-trained people who can participate in German industries. This same model should be adopted in this country, giving as much emphasis to the area of the skilled trades as given to a college education. One thing for certain, we all can benefit from the exercise of education. The quest for knowledge should be never ending.

TRUESTORY

In 1986, General Motors began the production of its new line of vehicles that were of the 'E' car model in the Detroit-Hamtramck assembly plant. Specifically, these models were the Cadillac Eldorado, the Oldsmobile Toronado and the Buick Riviera. The Riviera had a central controlling unit for its radio, tape player, and heating and air conditioning. The unit was a monotone CRT (cathode ray tube) that operated by a static touch of one's finger. Instead of the usual dials, knobs and levers found in most cars, the driver or passenger would touch the display with a finger to activate these features. The unit resembled a small television screen. Prior to being installed in the vehicles, each CRT unit was tested by an electronic diagnostic machine that had the capability of pinpointing malfunctions. When there was a defect in the CRT unit, the color display of the diagnostic unit would inform the operator exactly what the defect consisted of. The color display was the size of a 19-inch television set. The size of the screen was a visual aid for the operator.

All automotive assembly jobs in G.M.'s manufacturing facilities are bargaining unit jobs. That is to say, that one has to be a member of the United Automobile Workers (UAW) union to retain a job. This particular union handles all in-plant assignments by use of the seniority rule. The individuals who have the highest seniority within a manufacturing facility have the first choice of which job assignments and job shifts they will work. Because the CRT diagnostic area had this 19-inch color screen as a tool, it appeared to be a cushy job, and it was. What was a key element of the job and considered fundamental to its execution, was that the diagnostic operator be able to read. At the end of the assembly lines is where all the excitement is in an automotive assembly plant. That is where the vehicle is started up and driven off the line. If the vehicle functions properly, it is placed in the lot to be shipped. If the vehicle does not function properly, it is moved over to a repair area for servicing.

On this particular shift, several vehicles were sent to the repair area. The problem was the same on all of them, non-functioning CRT units. The decision was made by the production supervisors to visit the CRT diagnostic area to determine how all of the non-functioning CRT units escaped detection. Arriving at that station, they found an elderly gentleman who had just "bumped" into that job. "Bumping" is the term used to describe the removal of and replacement of a worker by use of seniority. When questioned as to how the non-functioning units escaped detection, it was discovered that the person could not read. He wanted the job because he liked looking at the colors on the display. The UAW was cooperative in having this person placed in another job.

****

No matter what station in life you may find yourself at this point, there is always hope for you to become better than what you are. If you have not finished high school, you can study to obtain a General Educational Development (GED) certificate. A GED can be obtained by continuing educational study in daytime or evening hours. For information on where to find institutions that support GED study, consult your local high school or community college. It is never too late to further one's education. Whatever excuse you may have for not doing so, that excuse is not good enough. If you are the parent or legal guardian of small children, your day does revolve around the care and nurturing of the child. However, when they are in school all day, you are presented with an **"opportunity"** to go back or start school yourself. This one singular action sets things in motion for you to obtain better or first-time employment.

There is a direct correlation between those individuals who have good English diction and their social, economic status. That is one of the common elements of poverty, poor English-speaking skills. English is our national language. Those who fare the best are people who learn to speak the language well and develop excellent vocabularies. The people you interact with make an association between the way you speak and your level of intelligence. Whether or not that association has validity is irrelevant. In cases such as this, perception is reality. Those who promote alternative forms of English by giving it a therapeutic name are doing great harm. There is no other form of English. What they are espousing is English that is spoken very poorly.

Language matters. It is the means by which we, as humans, communicate with each other. Having poor English-speaking skills may not necessarily emanate from the lack of education. In some cases, poor English-speaking skills could be the result of having a national origin other than the United States. Many intelligent people who have migrated to the U.S., have been, or could be, discriminated against because of their poor English-speaking skills. This discrimination is not the kind that is normally thought of. When seminars or presentations are to be conducted, management must discriminate in their choice of which person shall present the material.

I have been in the audience when important information was being presented by individuals with poor English-speaking skills. At the request of my clients, I attended this meeting, hosted by foreign businessmen. We, in the listening audience, were wasting our time. Heads turned several times as the question was mouthed, "What are they saying?" We understood not a word. I made the trip back from Chicago but not without noting how vital it is to speak English well when conducting business in this country. The U.S. dollar is the preferred currency of the world. The dollar is considered the international currency. In the same respect, English is considered to be the international language.

When a person is in the midst of a job interview, his or her communication skills will be observed. The first inferences will be drawn from the way the person speaks. The person being interviewed will never have a second chance to make a first impression. This is the time when it will be determined if you match the information placed on your resume. Being able to communicate properly is an essential element in obtaining better employment. If your communication skills are not what they should be, invest some time and money to improve in these areas. For those who feel they need to start afresh, check to see if there are remedial reading and speech classes provided by your local board of education or community college. Continued education in proper English grammar, composition, and public speaking can only help you in your quest for better employment.

HIGH-TECH STUFF

Let's face it, if you are not computer literate in this day and age, you are not going to be left behind one day, you are behind. People make jokes about not knowing how to program their video tape recorders, as if it is virtuous to be technologically ignorant. Not being computer literate seriously limits your employment prospects. In your prospective job, it doesn't matter if you will be interfacing directly with a personal computer, you have to know how they operate. A computer is a tool that allows you to do almost everything easier. It provides you with access to information that you would otherwise not have access to. Being an informed person is one of the keys to success. What you don't know can be detrimental to your livelihood.

Having a working knowledge of computers will provide you with the opportunity to perform tasks at home that previously required a personal visit. Just think, from your home computer, you can:

- Pay your bills
- Make transactions at your bank
- Check the latest news stories
- Review old news articles
- Check the availability of a library book
- Renew the library book
- Make travel arrangements
- Check the price of a new or used car

The list goes on and on. What is most important about the use of a computer is its ability to aid you with staying on the cutting edge of education. Staying on the cutting edge of education will make you more marketable. Becoming more marketable directly translates into a better job. Why spend time, energy and money on a tool to play a game? That is what you do when you buy a computer and place games on it. Although the computer can enhance the enjoyment of any game that can be played manually, how will that help you in the job market? I counsel all who will listen, "Get rid of the card games, the golf games, and the war games that are placed on your computer. Maximize the tool. Use it to increase your knowledge in something that is more tangible."

With the computer, you can not only construct an award-winning resume, you can post the resume on a bulletin board and it will be seen by a host of prospective employers. If you have been successful in getting an interview with a company, you should find out all the pertinent information about the company. Having knowledge of the company, the products offered or the services rendered can only help during the interviewing process. Having a working knowledge of computers will assist you in getting on the information super highway called the Internet. The Internet is the greatest thing to happen to personal computing since cheaper memory.

The Internet can be described as a collection of computer networks that are linked together and communicating by a common language. The Internet is more than a network of computers. It is a means by which a person can make use of **electronic mail** (e-mail), **network news, file transfers,** and **information browsing.**

- **Electronic Mail:** A method by which messages can be sent over the phone lines anywhere in the world. All that is required is that the recipient have an e-mail address. You and another person or group of people may correspond over long or short distances.
- **Network News:** A means by which you can participate in a wide variety of electronic discussion groups. There are literally tens of thousands of discussion groups on all types of subjects.
- **File Transfers:** A method of moving computer files from a personal computer to another personal computer on the Internet.
- **Information Browsing:** A means of obtaining an infinite variety of data from informational resources. The most popular informa-

tional resource is called the **"world wide web,"** thus the acronym, **www.**

If you do not own a personal computer, make use of one at your local library or community college. If you do not know how to use one, take an "Introduction to Computers" class at a local high school or community college. There is fear of things that are new. That is why some individuals boast in their lack of knowledge about their VCR's. It is not that they weren't capable of learning, they did not want to learn something new. The "fear factor" engulfs them. The "fear factor" can be described as a deeply rooted psychological barrier that is in place to protect one's psyche. Sometimes these fears are called phobias. Whatever it may be called, it results in the same thing, a person who thinks less of himself than he ought. Technology is not to be feared. It is to be used for our betterment. A computer should be considered an appliance just as one would consider a dishwasher or microwave oven. Computers may appear menacing and intimidating, but they are harmless. By having a working knowledge of computers, a person can gain access to a wealth of information. As previously stated, knowledge is power. Without knowledge, you have no power. You will depend upon the mercy of others.

CONSTRUCT A PROFESSIONAL LOOKING RESUME

There are some who argue resumes are an obsolete tool that should not be used to acquire a job. My reply is, "A resume is the easiest way to introduce a perspective employer to a candidate for employment." A good resume is indeed a requirement for any individual seeking a new job or different position within the same organization. The time and money you spend in preparing a good resume will reap major dividends. A resume is intended to be an extension of you. It provides factual data and it gives the reader some impression of the caliber of person you are.

It is a sales tool that is meant to provide an introduction to your potential employer.

You have perhaps two minutes to make an impression upon the person doing the hiring. All he has is that piece of paper representing you. It has to be a good representation. For these and other reasons, the resume should be placed on as high a quality paper as possible. Preferably, your resume should be placed on paper that is 100% cotton with a laid finish. The color should be white, not one of the many pastels available today. A resume should give enough information about you and be constructed in a manner as to entice someone to call you. Because of the fonts and graphics that are available, copy centers, print shops, and some professionals, are more than qualified to construct a very nice looking resume.

There is such a thing as a resume not matching the person whose name appears on it. I have seen resumes from individuals who were outstanding, only to be disappointed at the interview. If your resume is being prepared by someone other than yourself, it would be beneficial for the two of you to talk and agree beforehand on the contents of the resume. I am very skeptical of employment candidates who have credentials that are remarkable. They have been Senior Vice Presidents, Chief Engineers, Plant Managers and designed everything except the Space Shuttle, and are 25 years old. Your resume should be realistic. The rule that I have abided by is, if someone's resume seems too good to be true, it usually is. The interview will reveal all that is false and overstated. No one gets a job because he had a fantastic resume alone. He had a good resume in conjunction with a positive interview. That is the sole function of the resume, to provide enough information as to say to the reader, "I'm the person you're looking for, let's talk."

A good resume should be one page in length if you do not want it to end up in the trash can. Employers are not impressed by the lengths of resumes. However, they are impressed by their brevity, conciseness, and neatness. Foremost on your resume is your objective. Do not play to vagueness as a symbol of humility. You will not take just any job (although you might). You want a specific job and that is the one to place as an "objective" on your resume. So if you are scouring the classified ads for a job, find something that you like or feel adept at. That is your objective. Avoid placing information on your resume that could be prejudicial, therefore detrimental. What kind of information could be construed as being prejudicial? Providing your age, your gender (you can't always tell gender from the name), your marital status, how many children you have, etc. Have some business cards made with your name, phone number and the title or position that you hope to attain. This makes for a very becoming presentation. Present your cover and resume enclosed in a folder that has slots for your business cards.

There are some don'ts concerning resumes that must be mentioned.

- Do not place your resume on paper with a conventional typewriter if you are preparing it yourself. The only thing that looks worse than a typewritten resume is a typewritten resume with stains on it. Be mindful that there is always the possibility of someone drawing the wrong conclusions from your address. While making a presentation to a prospective client, I was asked "And just where do you live?" How the question came to be asked is not important to this segment. Let's just say that there can be political or social significance placed upon your mailing address. In the same respect, I do not advocate placing a false address on these types of documents. Not being truthful can come back to haunt you.
- Do not get carried away with wildly colored stationary, no matter how expensive it may be. Fluorescent-colored papers are not impressive. They are a turn-off. Keep it simple. Place your resume on a very good grade of white or cream-colored bond paper. The

paper should have at least 25 percent cotton fiber, preferably a laid finish.

- Do not provide information about your personal status, such as how many children you have, if any. A future employer could equate children with time taken off work to care for sick children. You will not be told why you did not get the job, but if other job applicants do not have dependents, you are at a disadvantage.
- Do not provide personal information such as your hobbies or recreational activities on your resume. You do not have the luxury of space when the goal is to get everything on one page. Besides that, no one really cares what your hobbies and recreational activities are. It may seem like the thing to do, to show how well rounded you are, but it is quite unprofessional. When I see that kind of thing, it hits the trash. Bear in mind what the readers of the resumes are trying to do first, separate the good resumes from the bad ones. That is done by taking a quick glance at the key elements of each resume. They have now reduced the pile to a manageable number and will give each one a closer look for critical information. The critical information is that which qualifies you for the job. Perhaps you are thinking that the readers are being too harsh in their selective process. It acts as a separator that works well. A conscientious individual, a person who pays attention to the details, is not going to present a poorly done resume.

Chances are that a sluggard is not going to present a good resume. How else would they be able to weed through the pile except for critiquing each resume? You want to make sure that your resume does not end up in the trash.

A resume should also have references, a person(s) that can be contacted to verify the information provided on the resume. The person(s) that you are choosing as a reference should be someone who has stature and whose title is impressive, so the reader will infer credibility. Bear in mind that the purpose for listing them as a reference is so that they will say wonderful things about you. Before listing someone as a reference, get his permission. There is nothing worse than a manager receiving a "cold call" from a recruiter or HRM'er, asking about a former employee. You are startled and ill at ease at what to say. Individuals have been known to initiate lawsuits because unfavorable information was given. Asking permission places in the mind of the referenced person that they may be asked to provide such information. They have ample time to prepare an appropriate response.

A resume should also be accompanied by a cover letter. To use a fishing metaphor, the cover letter acts as the bait to get the reader hooked on your resume. An interesting and well constructed cover letter entices the reader by saying to them, "There's more good stuff to come." Conversely, a bad cover letter indicates that there is more bad stuff to come. Another thing to consider is the fact that you are not the only person applying for the position. What you want is that competitive edge that a good cover letter can give you. A cover letter should be short and concise but constructed in a manner as to mention the position you are applying for and your strong points. The cover letter should be written on the same type of paper as the resume.

Under no circumstances should there be typographical errors or mistakes in the resume or cover letter you are preparing to send. This is the one document that represents you before an interview takes place. One bad resume or cover letter translates into no interview. It is absolutely imperative that both the resume and cover letter be flawless. Take as much time as needed to get it correct. You will not get a second chance to make this first and very important impression. What is the message given to a perspective employer about you when care is not given to these documents? Have the documents proofread several times before sending or taking them anywhere. A good resume and cover letter will not guarantee that you get the job you're after but a bad resume will guarantee that you do not get the job.

For those individuals who are computer literate, you can have your resume posted [online] on a [bulletin board] or a [web site] that will host your [home page]. There are also companies that will act as host to your resume. One company that provides this service is "Intellimatch." An item to consider is that when you post your resume electronically, you are making certain information about yourself available to anyone to see and perhaps make use of. Examples of reasonably well constructed resumes and information on electronic job postings are contained in the **Preparational Reference** section at the end of this segment.

After the interview has taken place, it is always fitting to send a follow-up letter. This is most commonly referred to as a "Thank You" letter. As stated by Harold E. Meyer, author of *The Book of Letters:*

"A follow-up letter after a job interview can often be the extra push that gets you the job. A letter received two or three days after the interview will keep your name in front of the employer."

REVERENCING PUNCTUALITY

This is a fancy way of saying, "Learn to be on time." When I first started out in the field of design, an elderly and experienced checker said to me, "It is sometimes better not to show for work than to show up late." Although his statement is not entirely true, there is validity in its premise. To be habitually late displays an **"attitude"** of "I don't care." In not showing up for work, the assumption is made that something unforeseeable happened, such as an illness or accident. While working in the Test and Development department for General Motors, I acquired a new respect for timeliness. The job required that I arrive at certain destinations to conduct testing. I was given a window of time to use the vehicles that were shared among many engineers. Any late arrival on my part not only delayed my testing, it hampered the activities of those who followed after me.

The rule of thumb has always been to arrive at the airport one hour before the scheduled flight departure. My rule is, arrive at the airport two hours before the scheduled departure. In this manner, if there are any obstructions in the flow of traffic, such as accidents, construction, or a flat tire, you have ample time to recover. After being entrusted with the awesome responsibility of certifying vehicles for domestic and foreign sales, I could not render a feeble excuse of, “I missed my plane.” My management would have been sorely disappointed.

Some engineers routinely missed their main flight due to delays caused by commuter flights. The Detroit Metropolitan Airport was approximately 75 miles from their location. It was not mandatory, nor necessary for them to take the commuter flight. They could have driven the distance. Having their flight originating from the local airport did offer them 750 more frequent flyer miles, at the risk of arriving late. How does this relate to you as the perspective job seeker? Your arrival to the interview, your first day at work, your departure for and arrival from lunch, should all be examples of someone who reverences time.

Some Good Advice

If you already have a job and are soliciting another one, it may not be permissible for you to receive phone calls at work. If you must make contact with other job prospects during normal working hours, use a pay phone. You will attain a greater degree of privacy and will not have to worry about being overheard. Some employers look unfavorably towards their employees who solicit jobs while in their employ. You risk revealing your hand if your attempts are discovered and you may be terminated before you are ready to leave. This termination of employment can greatly affect your employment strategy. It is a fact that if you already have a job, it is always easier to get another one. The reverse is also true. If you do not have a job, getting one is made more difficult. That is because of the psychological effect of association.

If you are not employed, the questions from a perspective employer are, "Why doesn't he have a job? Is there something wrong with him? Surely if he were any good, someone would have hired him." If you are already employed during normal business hours and have no one at your residence to take phone messages for you, the appropriate thing to do is to get an answering machine. Refrain from placing exotic introductions or wild music on your answering machine. It allows people to pre-judge you. You want the judgment of your prospective employer to be based upon substantive things such as your resume and interview. A simple greeting is sufficient.

****

In your quest for education, be careful of the institution or organization that is offering you "pain free" knowledge. If there is no pain, there is no gain. What is meant by pain is the traditional exercises in the quest for retained knowledge. They involve study, memorization and recitation. Be leery of the offerings of "Earn your degree at home through correspondence." There are some legitimate "study at home courses" that are accredited and can provide you with proof of it. There are also many scam artists who eagerly await the opportunity to separate you from your money. Read the declaration of the training course carefully. Are they offering free job placement or job placement assistance? If what they are offering sounds too good to be true, it probably is. Many of these so called "training institutes" make their money off the sales of books and tapes that you are required to purchase. There is no substitute for a practical learning environment that is presented in a classroom-like setting. Do your own research to determine if there is a market for the skill or degree you are interested in.

PREPARATIONAL REFERENCE

Resume

Cynthia Adams

OBJECTIVE: PHARMACEUTICAL SALES

EXPERIENCE: 1990–1994 Pickway Shoes Detroit, MI

Area Sales Manager

- Increased average area sales from $5 thousand to $10 thousand per week.
- Doubled sales per employee.
- Suggested new shoe styles that increased earnings by 26%.

1985–1990 Gantos Women's Apparrel Southfield, MI

Senior Sales Representative

- Increased sales revenues for each sales associate.
- Implemented sales to include mass market accounts.

EDUCATION:

1971–1985 Wayne State University Detroit, MI

B.A., Business Administration and Computer Science.

ADDITIONAL SKILLS:

PC Literate, including Word Processing, Spreadsheeets, & Presentation Graphics.

12345 MAIN STREET • ROYAL OAK, MICHIGAN 12345-6789
PHONE (123) 456-7890
FAX (810) 098-7654 • E-MAIL ME@MYCOMPANY.COM

PREPARATIONAL REFERENCE

Resume

Karla Marshall **14927 Lucas St. Akira City, CA 90236**

OBJECTIVE Technician, Data Processing Operations

EXPERIENCE

1995–1997 Globe Data Services Southridge, SC
Executive Assistant
- Managed the distribution of incoming data requests.
- Organized clients' conference times.
- Prioritized CEO's daily schedule.

1993–1995 Greene Family Dentistry Southridge, SC
Receptionist
- Distributed incoming calls.
- Delivered executive memos.
- Implemented training course for new receptionists.

1991–1993 Clintwood Drug Store Tempe, AZ
Stock Clerk
- Maintained appropriate product levels throughout the store.
- Received and inventoried all incoming shipments.
- Oversaw store cleanliness.

EDUCATION

1995 to Present Fisk Community College Southridge, SC
Computer Science Major, Sophomore

1989–1992 Groves High School Groves, AZ
- Salutatorian
- National Honor Society Vice President.

PREPARATIONAL REFERENCE

Resume

Carol Wright
1005 Kitchener St.
Detroit, Michigan 48215
(313) 331-9172

Objective A challenging position that will both utilize and strengthen the organizational and motivational skills acquired in over 11 years of diverse, demanding responsibilities.

Experience Recently completed over 11 years as an urban homemaker and mother of three children, with success and skill in the following areas:

Budgeting - Accountable for the control and disbursement of an annual budget of $49,200.

Prioritize - Established schedules, met deadlines, and coordinated diverse tasks.

Training and supervision - trained, instructed, and directed three junior associates, whose development was under my jurisdiction, in a wide variety of skills.

Interviewed, selected, and hired a wide variety of professionals, including handymen, physicians, and baby-sitters.

Purchasing - Analyzed and initiated purchase of low-budget to high ticket items, such as automobiles, an 18 cubic foot freezer, living room and bedroom furniture.

Education Graduate, 1973 Southeastern High School
Voted "Most Likely to Succeed"

References available upon request

PREPARATIONAL REFERENCE

Cover Letter

Addressee Name
Addressee Address

Date

Dear Sir/Madam,

With the hope that there is a position available within your company, I am submitting my resume for consideration. As my resume reflects, my experience has been primarily automotive related. However, I have demonstrated competencies in many areas and disciplines. I can and have performed as a company liaison, group supervisor, and a host of other functions.

I have a valid U.S. Passport and am familiar with the protocols of work-related travel, both domestic and foreign. Upon contacting me via any of the methods indicated, an interview can be scheduled. In this manner, you may further evaluate the potential of any contributions I may add to the further success of your company.

Respectfully,

Job Seeker

PREPARATIONAL REFERENCE

Cover Letter

Addressee Name
Addressee Address

Date

Dear Ms. Jones,

Your company is well-known throughout the employment industry. I've also seen your advertisements in various publications. As the enclosed resume indicates, my background includes management of several insurance divisions. Some of my more noteworthy contributions include:

- Reviewing entire division's operations and reducing annual expenses by $300,000.
- Improving processing time in three areas by 20-30% without increasing operating costs.
- Developing and presenting several different training courses, with $100,000 in related savings.

I am also thoroughly knowledgeable in cost control, accounting systems, and administration.

My company's recent reorganization and staff reduction have encouraged me to seek a new position. Rather than accept a transfer that would not take full advantage of my abilities, I've decided that this would be an excellent time to look for a more appropriate and challenging opportunity. The company has agreed to assist me in this process.

I would appreciate the chance to discuss personally any position that appears to be a good match with my qualifications. I'll call you next week to arrange a time for us to meet.

Sincerely,

Job Seeker

* Cover letter taken from *'The Resume Handbook'*

PREPARATIONAL REFERENCE

Reading Material

The Resume Handbook

by

Arthur D. Rosenburg & David Hizer

An Adams Media Publication

A clear and easy-to-follow handbook that shows you how to create an outstanding resume and cover letter that will best showcase your abilities and experience.

Winning Cover Letters

by

Robin Ryan

A John Wiley & Sons, Inc. Publication

This book contains tips from hiring managers and human resource personnel to common mistakes to avoid in constructing cover letters. It points out how to target letters to get the interest of employers you want to work for. It also contains successful cover letter samples that landed interviews.

Cover Letter Almanac

An Adams Media Corporation Publication

This book contains 600 professionally written cover samples that have actually landed jobs. Advice is given on how to structure cover letters to respond to classified and blind advertisements. Also included in this book is advice on how to write a "cold letter" to a potential employer.

PREPARATIONAL REFERENCE

Reading Material

Gallery Of Best Resumes
by
David F. Noble, Ph.D.
A Jist Works Inc. Publication

This offering is a collection of more than 200 quality resumes written by professional resume writers. The book is geared towards those seeking a job or changing careers in the 1990's.

Resumes In Cyber Space
by
Pat Cristo
A Barron's Educational Series, Inc. Publication

This a comprchensive, user-friendly guide to job hunting in what is called "Cyber Space." It offers the learning of basic skills of the Internet and electronic mail (e-mail). You will learn how to search the most current job banks and tap into thousands of job openings around the world.

Encyclopedia Of Job Winning Resumes
by
Myra Fournier & Jeffrey Spin
A Round Lake Publication

This book contains 400 success-proven resumes that are ready to customize. Every major industry is covered, from entry level to Chief Executive Officer. It offers advice on what to include in your resume and what to leave out. There are resumes for students and new college graduates.

PREPARATIONAL REFERENCE
Reading Material

The Windows Internet Tour Guide

by

Michael Fraase

For anyone wanting to learn about the Internet the easy way, this book is an excellent choice. It is easy to read because the technical jargon is kept to a minimum. The book comes with everything you need to navigate the Internet with convenience.

PREPARATIONAL REFERENCE

Technical Training
Computer Graphics

The following is a brief description of the computer graphics systems that will be mentioned.

AutoCad
Owned by AutoDesk Systems and used by a host of tooling shops, suppliers, and original equipment manufacturers.

Computer Aided Three-Dimensional Interactive Applications (Catia)
Owned by Dassault Systems and used by Chrysler Corporation and a host of original equipment manufacturers and suppliers.

Unigraphics (UG)
Owned by Electronic Data Systems (EDS) and used by General Motors and a host of original equipment manufacturers and suppliers.

Computer Graphics System (CGS)
Owned by General Motors and used by the parent company and its suppliers.

Prime Development Graphics System (PDGS)
Owned by Ford Motor Company and used by the parent company and its suppliers.

PREPARATIONAL REFERENCE

Technical Training
Computer Graphics

BADENCORP
Offering classes in Computer Aided Three Dimension Interactive Applications (CATIA). The training includes literature and the classes are taught on state-of-the art IBM and Hewlett Packard workstations. Certificates are awarded upon completion of classes.

101 Sunnytown Road, Ste. 208
Casselberry, Fl 32707
Phone 407.260.2777
Fax 407.260.0584
e-mail: baden@iag.net

COMPUTER ENGINEERING TECHNOLOGIES (CET)
Offering classes in Computer Aided Three Dimension Interactive Applications (CATIA), and Unigraphics. The training includes literature and the classes are taught on state-of-the art IBM and Hewlett Packard workstations.

18025 Fifteen Mile Road
Clinton Twp., MI 48035
Phone 810.790.2700
Fax 810.790.2703

PREPARATIONAL REFERENCE

Technical Training
Computer Graphics

DESIGN ENGINEERING CONSULTANCY SERVICES (DECS)
Offering classes in Computer Aided Three Dimension Interactive Applications (CATIA). The training includes literature and the classes are taught on state-of-the art IBM workstations.

Wilshire Plaza North
Ste. 214
900 Wilshire Drive
Troy, MI 4808
Phone 248.362.2604
Fax 248.362.2841

ADVANCED DESIGN TECHNOLOGY
Offering classes in Computer Aided Three Dimension Interactive Applications (CATIA), AutoCad, Computer Graphics system (CGS), Unigraphics, and Prime Development Graphics System (PDGS).

32500 Concord Drive
Ste. 306
Madison Heights, MI 48071
Phone 810.588.9398
Fax 810.588.9313

PREPARATIONAL REFERENCE

Technical Training
Computer Graphics

EDS UNIGRAPHICS EDUCATIONAL SERVICES

Offering classes in Unigraphics at the five locations listed below. The training includes literature and the classes are taught on state-of-the art Hewlett Packard workstations.

Boston Center
Reservoir Place
1601 Trapelo Road
Waltham, MA 02154

Cypress Center
10824 Hope Street
Cypress, CA 90630

Detroit Center
38701 Seven Mile Road, Suite 335
Livonia, MI 48152

Niagara Falls Center
570 Glendale Avenue
St. Catherines, Ontario Canada L2R 7B3

St. Louis Center
13736 Riverport Drive
Maryland Heights, MO 63043

PREPARATIONAL REFERENCE

Technical Training
Electronics

INSTITUTE OF ELECTRONIC TECHNOLOGY

The courses enable the students to not only understand theory, but allow a hands-on experience in analyzing and troubleshooting on many types of electronic equipment. There is instruction in Communications, Computer Electronics & Sales, System Analysis, and Data Transmission.

Institute of Electronic Technology
509 South 30th Street
Paducah, KY 42001
Phone 502.444.9676 800.995.4438

ITT TECHNICAL INSTITUTE

ITT provides post secondary education and training for its students in many fields of study. They offer instruction that leads to a degree in Electronics Technology or Computer Aided Design. They have schools in the states of Alabama, Arizona, Arkansas, California, Colorado, Florida, Idaho, Illinois, Indiana, Kentucky, Massachusetts, Michigan, Missouri, Nebraska, New Mexico, New York, Ohio, Oregon, Pennsylvania, South Carolina, Tennessee, Texas, Utah, Virginia, Washington, and Wisconsin.

ITT Technical Institute
1522 East Big Beaver
Troy, Michigan 48083
Phone 248.524.1800 800.832.681

PREPARATIONAL REFERENCE

Technical Training
Skilled Trades

Pattern Maker

These are the individuals who form, shape and mold objects so that their original images can be rapidly reproduced. These are the organizations to contact for training:

American Foundrymen's Society
505 State Street
Des Plaines, IL 60016-8399
Phone 800.537.4237

Glassmolders, Pottery, Plastics and
Allied Workers International Union
PO Box 607, East Baltimore Pike
Media, PA 19063-0607
Phone 619.565.5051

Plumbers and Pipe Fitters

These are the individuals who design, install, and maintain water piping systems, heating and cooling systems. These are the organizations to contact for training:

National Association of Plumbing,
Heating and Cooling Contractors
P. O. Box 6808
180 South Washington Street
Falls Church, VA 22040
Phone 703.237.8100

PREPARATIONAL REFERENCE

Technical Training
Skilled Trades

Plumbers and Pipe Fitters (continued)

United Association of Journeymen
and Apprentices of the Plumbing and
Pipe Fitting Industry of the
United States and Canada
P. O. Box 37800
Washington, D.C. 20013
Phone 202.628.5823

Mechanical Contractors Association
of America
1385 Piccard Drive, East Baltimore Pike
RockVille, MD 20850
Phone 301.869.5800

Robotics Technician

These individuals are responsible for the maintenance and repair of automated robots that are used in industry. This is the organization to contact for training:

Robotics Industries Association
P. O. Box 3724
900 Victory Way
Ann Arbor, MI 48106
Phone 313.994.6088

PREPARATIONAL REFERENCE

Technical Training
Skilled Trades

Roofers

As the title implies, these individuals place various form of compositions on structures to seal out weather. These are the organizations to contact for training:

The United Union of Roofers,
Waterproofers and Allied Workers
1660 L. Street
Washington D.C. 20036

Roofing Industry Educational Institute
14 Inverness Drive East
Building H, Suite 110
Englewood, CO 80112-5608

National Roofing Contractors Association
10255 West Higgins Road Suite 600
Rosemont, IL 60018-5607
Phone 847.299.9070

PREPARATIONAL REFERENCE

Technical Training
Skilled Trades

Sheet Metal Workers

These are the individuals who form and shape sheet metal for a host of industries. They range from ductwork for the heating and cooling of buildings and homes to stamped and roll formed sheet metal for consumer products. These are the organizations to contact for training:

National Training Fund for the
Sheet Metal & Air Conditioning Industry
Edward F. Carlough Plaza
601 North Fairfax Street Suite 240
Alexandria, VA 22314
Phone 703.739.7200

Sheet Metal Worker's International Association
1750 New York Avenue, NW
Washington, D.C. 20006
Phone 202.783.5880

Tool and Die Makers

These are the individuals who make devices that hold, form, shape, and cut materials that are used to produce products for OEM's (Original Equipment Manufacturers). Tools and dies are also used to make products for companies that produce consumer goods. These are the organizations to contact for training:

PREPARATIONAL REFERENCE

Technical Training
Skilled Trades

Tool and Die Makers (continued)

National Tooling and Machining
Association
9300 Livingston Road
Fort Washington, MD 20744
Phone 301.248.6200

United Aerospace & Agricultural
Implement Workers of America
Skilled Trades Department
800 East Jefferson
Detroit, MI 48214
Phone 313.926.5000

Construction Worker
These individuals are the talented people who build our homes. They are the brick layers (masons), the rough and finish carpenters, the cement masons, and the heavy and light equipment operators. This is the organization to contact for training:

National Association of Home Builders
15th and M Streets, NW
Washington, D.C. 20005
Phone 202.822.0200

PREPARATIONAL REFERENCE

Technical Training
Skilled Trades

Welder

Many industries use and have need of welders. They are too numerous to name. The major industries are those involved in construction and manufacturing, and those companies that have need of piping to move their products. This is the organization to contact for training:

American Welding Society
550 NW Le Jeune Road
Miami, FL 33126
Phone 345.443.9353

Iron Worker

Iron Workers are primarily individuals who participate in the erection of structural steel. The builders of large office buildings are the main users of structural steel. These are the organizations to contact for training:

National Erectors Association
1501 Lee Highway, # 202
Arlington, VA 22209
Phone 703.524.3336

National Association of Reinforcing
Steel Contractors
10382 Main Street, Suite 300
Fairfax, VA 22030
Phone 703.591.1870

PREPARATIONAL REFERENCE

Technical Training
Skilled Trades

Job and Die Setters

These are the individuals who prepare machine and production tools for use in manufacturing or the fabrication of finished or semi-finished products. These are the organizations to contact for training:

National Tooling & Steel Contractors
10382 Main Street, Suite 300
Fairfax, VA 22030
Phone 703.591.1870

Tooling and Manufacturing Association
1177 South Dee Road
Park Ridge, IL 60068
Phone 847.825.1120

Machinist

These are the individuals who shape and form metal products with the use of industrial machinery such as lathes, shapers, milling machines, drill presses, and grinders. These are the organizations to contact for training:

Tooling & Manufacturing Association
1177 South Dee Road
Park Ridge, IL 60068
Phone 847.825.1120

PREPARATIONAL REFERENCE

Technical Training
Skilled Trades

Machinist (continued)

National Tooling & Machining Association
9300 Livingston Road
Fort Washington, MD 20744
Phone 301.248.6200

Millwright
These are the individuals who are responsible for the construction and assembly of light and heavy duty industrial machinery. Machines such as presses, stamping machines, roll forming machines, boilers, and a host of other machines are used in this industry. These are the organizations to contact for training:

United Aerospace & Agricultural Implement
Workers of America
Skilled Trades Department
800 East Jefferson
Detroit, MI 48214
Phone 313.926.5000

United Brotherhood of Carpenters & Joiners
101 Construction Avenue, NW
Washington, D.C. 2000
Phone 202.546.6206

PREPARATIONAL REFERENCE

For additional institutions that offer career training, the **"Career Information Center"** is a valuable resource. This reference material offers information on literally hundreds of occupations. It provides the salary range, educational training needed for each job and the employment outlook. For the convenience of the searcher, the training available for each profession is categorized for every state. For instance, if you are interested in becoming a carpenter, the training institutions for carpentry will be listed from Alabama to Wyoming. There are 12 volumes of this publication. The **"Career Information Center"** may be found at your local public library.

General Training

The Ford Motor Company has a unique general training center located in Dearborn Michigan. It is called, "Fairlane Training And Development Center." The classes range from the technical to the humanities. For some classes, college credits can be awarded. For more information:

Fairlane Training & Development Center
P. O. Box 6055
19000 Hubbard Drive
Dearborn, Michigan 48121-6055
Phone 313.845.7301

PRESENTATION

"Image is everything."
Andre Aggasi

As unfair as it may seem, people make judgments about you from the way you look and speak. You and I cannot change this fact and we shouldn't waste time trying to do so. What the focus should be is doing what you have to do to get to where you want to be. This is not a "Truth," but it is a fairly accurate statement. "Wearing the right clothes will not guarantee that you get the job, but wearing the wrong clothes will guarantee that you do not get the job." The originator of that statement is unknown. What you wear as clothing says a lot about you. How do you know that a person is in the Army, Navy, or member of any military service? Their uniform tells you so. How do you know that a person is a member of a gang? Their colors are displayed. The group they are among reveals this to you. All you have to be is observant. How can you tell if a person is married? The wedding band will, in most cases, be displayed on the ring finger. The process of making judgments like this is called profiling. It is making use of all the stored knowledge gained through many years of experience and applying it. That is why it usually works.

What you wear is thought to be an expression of your demeanor and character. Placing confidence in a judgment based upon the way a person looks is a very weighty matter. It is not 100 percent accurate, but it is good enough for most people. When I interview candidates for a job opening and I am confronted with an individual with purple hair, I am liable to be apprehensive about employing him. My apprehension is increased if there is a chain connecting his or her nose ring to an earring.

In my opinion, those are symbols displaying rebellion against some of the established norms of our society. It is logical for me to conclude that that person would likely place himself in opposition to some other established work rules and regulations, rules that have been put in place to contribute to a cohesive, congenial working environment. What those who see you may not know about you, they surmise. It is done by way of perception and perception is reality. If you can give yourself an advantage by dressing in a manner that is in the affirmative, take it. I experienced infinitely better treatment by having on a shirt and tie than not. Because this works, I have a special tie that I wear to the hardware store. It is appropriately called, "the hardware tie."

Women are in the workplace in every field today. There are very few occupations that have not been visited by them. Despite what feminist organizations would have you believe, women are not free to wear whatever strikes their fancy. Women are judged much more harshly than men. The right or wrong of this is not being expounded upon here. It happens to be a statement of fact. For those women who want to be taken seriously and see their vocations as more than just a job, it is imperative that they look the part. There is attire that can oppose this goal:

- The wearing of high-heeled shoes.
- Skirts with lengthy splits up the sides and back.
- Dresses and skirts that are too short.

- Attire that is too revealing or too clingy.
- Ankle bracelets and excessively long nails that are painted every color in the rainbow.

These are just a few of the things that can signal something other than what may be intended. If I were allowed to do so, I would point every woman who needed instruction to a female engineer that I had the pleasure of working with. Liz McDonald epitomized the perfectly dressed woman in an office setting. Her attire was right out of Jos. A. Bank or a similar conservative woman's clothier. She was treated the way she dressed, respectfully. She got things done without having to jump through hoops as did some of her female colleagues.

Large corporations have a culture and structure all of their own. "Corporate culture is a corporation's set of values, beliefs, and symbols that help guide their behavior." Corporate structure is defined as "The basic framework of positions, groups of positions, reporting relationships, and interaction patterns that a corporation adopts to carry out its strategy." A company's culture can be retrieved from its mission statement, if one exists. The structure of a company can be determined from an organizational chart. When a candidate is applying for employment within a large corporation, it is assumed by management, that the person will cooperate in terms of norms for that company. **"Presentation"** plays a major role in this adaptation.

There are positions within companies that require a specified uniform. Commercial airline pilots, flight attendants, nurses, and law enforcement personnel come to mind. It does not sit well with management to have someone rebel against established norms. Yet it is done, day in and day out. Only the courts are brought into the picture because the company is being sued over the matter. I am reminded of the court case in Canada that involved a man of Eastern Indian heritage who wanted to become a member of the Royal Mounted Canadian Police (RCMP). The major problem was that this man practiced the Sikh religion.

As part of his religious beliefs, he was required to wear a turban and refrain from cutting his hair. This was in direct opposition to what was traditionally required by the RCMP authorities. The RCMP hat was to be worn and an occasional hair cut was in order. You guessed it. The matter wound up in the Canadian courts. The Sikh community backed their man and a larger segment of the Canadian population was in support of the RCMP hierarchy. It is the opinion of this author that the Sikh candidate had no Canadian constitutional right to be allowed to become a [Mounty]. This is at the heart of the idea of corporate culture. If you want to be a part of an organization, be willing to adapt to its requirements and fulfill them.

****

A business owner whose employees have direct dealings with the public has every right to dictate how the company is to be perceived. That representation is made by his employees. They are acting as agents of the company when they are on the job. Persons who consider themselves to be free spirits, in some cases, can be a liability. I would not want to place a person of that mindset in a conspicuous place where his appearance could affect the performance of my company or business. Take for instance the position of the receptionist/clerk who greets you when you enter the lobby of a business. To give the best image of the business, people are chosen according to their appearance, appearance in the form of personal grooming and aesthetics, not ethnicity or gender. If you are applying for the job of receptionist, you should consider what that job entails. It is an image that the company or business is trying to display.

Large corporations know this quite well. They place articulate, cordial, and aesthetically pleasing persons in those positions. As a receptionist or greeter, the individual receives a great deal of exposure. That exposure can translate into a better job if the individual focuses on having an admirable attitude and good job performance, while providing an excellent presentation. That is why companies have dress codes as part of their of rules. These dress codes are usually contained within the pages of a manual that is given to new hires. Dress codes provide uniformity and help establish what the norms are for that company. In corporate America's attempt to relax a bit, many companies have adopted casual work days. This has presented some companies with more problems than they envisioned.

The articles of clothing that comprise business dress is well established, while everyone's idea of casual attire is different. For example, in a school where uniforms are required, there may be few variations allowed. If a school has a policy of no jeans, it will be assumed to mean blue jeans. But does that include all articles made of denim? What about the brand of denim that is called Dockers? They come in colors other than blue. Are they considered jeans? It is not possible for the management of a company to review every iteration of what their employees consider casual dress. Some people will always stretch the limits to see what they can get away with. Women have worn halter tops, miniskirts and spandex on the job. As unsightly as it may have been, some men have worn spandex. Both genders thought sweat pants to be appropriate. If you think "hot pants" have passed off the scene, think again. I personally saw a woman wearing a pair in an office setting. If we were to talk about shoes, that would open up a whole new can of worms.

What you wear says a lot about you, even if it is unintended. You not only dress the way you feel, you dress the way you think. This allows others to easily cast a lot in a direction that may or may not be correct.

Why give an impression in the wrong direction? It has never been popular to wear ties in design shops. There were no dress codes to speak of. All varieties of opinions were represented by the clothing people wore. Despite that, I wore a tie everyday to work. I became known as Mister tie instead of Al. That was fine. I had a strategy. I wanted to look the part of a conscientious, meticulous employee, representing the engineering firm to the Ford Motor Company engineers. I know for certain that the management of the design shops appreciated my attire. I was treated accordingly. It is amazing how much respect a shirt and tie will garner. I have never been in favor of casual days. My retort to people who question my attire is, "I have to always be ready to conduct business, and there is nothing casual about business."

Large organizations sometimes have what is known as a culture. A culture can be described as a set of norms or rules that regulate conduct. For instance, at one time, the corporate culture for the Chevrolet Division of General Motors dictated that all salaried males wear white shirts, with their ties, in the design rooms. Any engineer or designer wearing a shirt with stripes or colors was sent home to change it. The dress code there is no longer as stringent. A person can make himself a spectacle by wearing outlandish hair styles and clothing in an office setting. While making my rounds in the accounting department of one my clients, I spotted a young man wearing a weird hair style. The best description I can offer is that it made him look like a rooster. It was raised quite high at his forehead and sloped downward towards the back of his head. He could not see how he was being mocked by the office staff.

His employment was only to be for a three-day period. He was filling in for someone on vacation. However, his appearance caused such a commotion that the manager asked his temporary employment agency to send someone else immediately. This person didn't have a clue. I wondered if I had given him the benefit of my counsel, would it have made a difference? Probably not. I have every reason to believe that he has been, or will be, rejected from other companies. When a person is employed through a contract agency and given a placement, the customer does not have to provide a reason for rejection. A person can only be rejected a set number of times before he becomes unemployable because of his presentation.

General Motors is one of many companies that provide college students with employment for the summer. On several occasions, I would have students assigned to me for use as I saw fit. Prior to the students returning to school, I also provided an evaluation on the summer student's performance. In addition, I made recommendations as to which students should be given employment the following summer or during semester breaks. Because of this, I took it upon myself to provide them with the sort of corporate doctrine that I was certain would benefit them. I spoke to them in a respectful manner, as adults and not as children. My point was easy to comprehend. The last thing you want people to be able to do is cast an unflattering opinion of you from your appearance. Gold chains, designs cut into the scalp, purple or blue hair, claw-like finger nails, grotesque tattoos, and wildly-colored clothing are all taboos in the corporate environment. The same can be said for the small business environment.

There are indeed jobs in which the employees attire has no effect upon the job function. A typical job might be working in the laundry room of a hotel or a mail sorter at a postal station. However, as a strategy for a better job, you should be a person who is always conservatively dressed. That means that you are ready to represent the company in a good light at all times. There have been many occasions when I was asked by my bosses to take their places in meetings. By being appropriately dressed, I was ready to represent my department. There were scheduling conflicts, but each meeting would present subject matter that was important to the department. When you attend those meetings, you are gaining exposure by being in the presence of people that you would ordinarily not come in contact with. You have now been presented with an **"opportunity."** You can ask for the business cards of the participants. This gives you a name and location of a person to whom you can possibly send a resume. All of this is made possible because of one's **"presentation."** Remember this, you never get a second chance to make a first impression.

****

Presentation involves a great deal more than what a person may or may not be wearing. A person's demeanor and personality also come into play. For these traits, let's call them "looks." In looking the best, I am not speaking of facial characteristics, although they may play a part. For any singular or multiple job opening(s), all skills being almost equal, the people that look the best will invariably get the job(s).

TRUE STORY

Because I don't have permission to use their real names, I will refer to them as Mary and Sue. Their names have no bearing on the validity of the story. There existed an opening for an executive secretary for one of the divisions of General Motors. This secretary would be in a highly visible position and made privy to some very important information. This person would be mainly servicing two executives. There were four executives in the office suite and one other executive secretary. Because of the fact that no new personnel could be added to the payroll, the solution was to move a qualified person from another area. All of the secretaries in the building were allowed to apply for the posted position. Someone coined a phrase that says, "Do you want to talk to the man in charge or do you want to talk to the woman who knows what is going on?" There is a great deal of truth in that statement.

I learned early in my career that the secretaries know what is going on. Because of this fact, I make it a habit to get to know the secretaries within a variety of departments. That is an employment strategy because information is key to any job opening. The top two candidates were individuals that I knew. In fact, they knew that they were the top candidates. I was made privy to their personal aspirations. They wanted that job. From the onset, I knew who was going to get the job. It all had to do with presentation. As far as skills, they were comparable.

Mary's attributes	**Sue's attributes**
Always impeccably dressed	Always impeccably dressed
Pleasant disposition	Cranky at times
Congenial	Bossy
Cheerful	Temperamental
Discrete in judgment	Bold in judgment
Modest	Forward

Is it any surprise that Mary got the job? It shouldn't be.

****

Despite laws against discrimination, we all discriminate in some way or another. Discriminating is the process of forming an opinion or making a judgment about a subject, person, object, etc. You cannot get away from making discriminating judgments. People who are considered obese have to fight more battles than that of their weight. When they appear for a job interview, judgments are already forming about them. These judgments in many cases are without merit and are baseless. The fact remains that if you are overweight, you may be considered a person who lacks self-control, a person who cannot moderate your eating habits. The state of being overweight could be caused by a medical condition.

Nonetheless, give yourself a fighting chance to acquire the job of your dreams. If you are a person who is overweight, lose it before going on your job search. It is not the intent of this author to insult or demean, just to tell things exactly as they are. Add to this, a lack of a good wardrobe and a loud or flamboyant hairstyle, mean decisions will have already been made about you. This may be unfortunate, but it is true.

****

Let's consider **"presentation"** in an entirely different format. As important and indispensable as computers are in the workplace, they can be a career stopper. I have never been one for computer games. In fact, I deleted them completely from my office computer (the ones that came with windows95). There is the tendency to become complacent and absorbed in the variety of games that can be played on the new generation of desktop computers. I am mindful of an incident involving several engineers at one of General Motors's engineering facilities. Because of the fact that there were not enough desktop computers for everyone to have their own, the three computers had to be shared. This was done via a walk-up station that was accessible to all in the department. One of these walk-ups was placed in front of the entrance to the department. Not a good place to be playing computer games.

As I strolled through one day, I saw four of G.M.'s brightest engineers playing the latest computer game on the machine. I thought to myself, "What a bad idea to be playing a computer game right in front of the entrance. Anyone could walk in and see them goofing around." How would they explain their behavior if a [shooter] walked in? They would not be able to. Not that I am adverse to having some fun, I would not be having fun in plain sight. A little discretion was in order. Just then, the department manager walked in. The look on his face said it all. He was totally disgusted. I can tell you what he was thinking, "This is what you guys do when I am not around? Don't you have anything else to do?" They were not scolded for their lack of good judgment. They were after all, well-paid professionals. They got the message without a word having been said. The impression they left would remain in the mind of that manager for who knows how long. These four made a very poor **"presentation"** of themselves.

One of my major clients had an administrative assistant who complained vehemently about being overworked. She told her boss, "I need help. I have more to do than anyone and do not have enough time to get all this work done." Her workstation was not in an office but in an open setting. Privacy was non-existent. Having a need for some documents to be signed by her boss, I approached her from behind to inquire of her boss's location. She was unaware of my presence. What was she doing? Playing solitaire on the computer in the middle of the day. "Not too bright," I'm thinking to myself.

She seriously damaged her argument of being overworked. If I could notice this, so could everyone else, including her boss. What was he to think of her request for help after seeing her poor **"presentation?"** "Let's see the situation here, you don't have enough time to get your work done but you have enough time to play solitaire on the computer. I know what I'll do, I'll get you some help so that you can have more time to play games." Does this seem plausible? Any rational thinking person would have to say emphatically no to this question.

Presentation Guidelines

- Your personal hygiene makes a profound statement about you. You can become known for the way you smell, albeit good or bad. How do you know if you smell badly? How could you not know? When people routinely avoid your presence for lengthy periods of time, you have to know that something is amiss. I recall interviewing several persons to fill a position in the Computer Aided Design department for a client. The resume of one of these individuals was impressive. I had received it a day or two prior to his arrival. When the gentleman arrived for the interview, he was dressed as I would have been in a similar situation. He wore a dark suit and was clean shaven. However, he reeked of body odor. So overpowering was the smell, that I made a reason for us to leave the closed setting of the conference room. As we entered the CAD area, I could tell that others caught a whiff of his "bouquet." He did not get the job. Not for that reason alone, but it was a factor. If a person was malodorous at a time when he should have been doing everything to make a good impression, what would his behavior be like once hired?
- Keep body piercings to a minimum. Multiple rings in the ears, nose, tongue, etc. signal rebellion to an employer. As previously stated, there are some occupations in which your attire has no bearing on your functioning in the job. It is no coincidence that the vast majority of these types of jobs are the ones that are high paying. I interpret 10 earrings as a person who is not able to restrain himself, having no concept of modesty. When the piercings become infected, as they sometimes do, it looks hideous. As a colleague and I were driving along a thoroughfare, I spotted a young man who had a ring

in his nose and one in his ear. There was a chain that ran down the side of his face that connected the two rings. What happens when the chain gets caught in something? Even more disastrous, what happens if the chain gets pulled by someone? It gives a whole new meaning to the term, "Someone yanking your chain." Anyone who has been around young children knows that they pull and grab things that we would rather they not pull and grab. When you come for an interview and you have multiple body piercings that are visible, you are at a disadvantage. Judgments have already been cast about you before you have spoken a word.

- Be businesslike in manner and speech. Don't be known as a jokester. You may think that people are laughing with you, but in reality, they are laughing at you. It becomes difficult for someone to take you seriously when they think of you as a joke. This does not mean that one has to be a prude. After all, work should be fun. But be about the business of business and save the levity for the proper time and place.
- There is a theme in advertising for automobiles that says, "You are what you drive." That is not altogether true. Sometimes you have to drive what you have because you have nothing better. As pretentious as it may sound, people make an association between the way your vehicle looks and you. I am not speaking of whether the vehicle you drive is dirty or clean. The issue here is the condition of your vehicle. Before I would drive a ragged vehicle to my place of employment, I would make use of public transportation. Doing this may inconvenience you greatly, but greater is the damage done to your **"presentation."** Remember, "Image is everything." If you are given the impression that I care about what people think, you

would be only partly correct. I care about what the right people think. Those who cannot bless me, I make sure that they are not in a position to harm me. Rusted clunkers are usually associated with vehicles that break down often. If there is one thing you need, it is dependable transportation. Bosses become intolerant quickly to absences or tardiness due to vehicles in poor condition.

- This may sound as if it is common sense, but common sense isn't so common anymore. Do not place your feet on top of your desk during working hours. Besides being a signal to your boss that you do not have enough to do, it is a sign of disrespect for the company you work for. The same goes for shining your shoes on company time. Once that is seen, you will not be able to take it back. When bosses see what you do when they are at work, their minds envision all sorts of things that you may or may not be doing when they are away from the job.
- Some office buildings have coffee stations where vending machines or other similar machines dispense food and beverages. It is a good idea to visit these areas alone, as to not give the impression that you are a goof-off. That can easily be done. There is something about a crowd that prevents it from being quiet. The more people there are, the more boisterous they will be. Your behavior is on open display for all to see. You cannot predict who will walk by and see you. It could be the very person that you want to interview next month for the job that was just posted. If you think that he or she will not remember your face, think again. If you must gather with a friend(s), do it in an out-of-the-way place. Discretion is the key thing here.
- Keep the use of business phones for personal use to a minimum. It would be unreasonable to ask that all calls be restricted to

business use. If a friend or relative knows your number, they are bound to make use of it. However, it becomes very evident that the conversation taking place is not related to business. The posture that is taken and the voice inflections are dead giveaways that the call is personal. This becomes more pronounced when the call has romantic overtones. Telephones are essential tools needed in any business. Even rudimentary communications demand telephones. Companies routinely publish documents, urging their employees to refrain from the use of company phones for personal use. This is something that is impossible to totally eliminate. What is hoped for is that the personal use of company phones be kept to a minimum. I have heard of companies that monitor the use of company phones by their employees. The employees were presented with bills for the long distance calls that were attributed to them. You can establish a bad reputation for always being on the telephone. That is not a good thing. One should always consider that his actions have consequences. Good actions bring on good consequences and bad actions bring on bad consequences.

- Always stay in control. Alcohol works against us in this area when it is consumed during working hours. You cannot be in control when a drug has infiltrated your body. Alcohol is a drug and this fact is generally known. What may not be so widely known is the fact that alcohol is a depressant. It is an enjoyable depressant because it reduces the inhibitions and alters the mood of those who partake of it. All sorts of hideous and shameful things have been done and blamed on alcohol. We all hear tales of the Christmas parties that have at least one character who gets out of hand after consuming alcohol. Having drinks at lunch time is a supreme “no no” when you are trying to climb the ladder of success. First of all, its odor will be detected on your breath or clothes. So much for your ability to be discrete. Your ability to work will be impaired. Even one drink alters the body chemistry. Because alcohol tends to remove the social inhibitions of people, there remains the possibility that you could do or say something that would be out of place. Once spoken, all of the apologies in the world will not erase the memory of what you said or did under the influence of alcohol.

TRUE STORY

My belief in this declaration was tested twice. I was on a very important trip with some lofty executives from General Motors. There were seven of us from G.M. in Cincinnati, Ohio on a mission to help the Norwood Assembly Plant. Along on this trip were two representatives from a supplier with whom we were doing business. When it came time for dinner, the supplier made reservations for the revolving dining room at the top of the Marriott Hotel. After dinner was completed, they ordered the booze. Several bottles of expensive wine were ordered by these executives. They were not paying for them, so they went all out. After all the wine was consumed, then came the cognacs. Two bottles of Chivas Regal cognac were downed. Now the execs are nice and loose. As happens when one consumes alcohol, one loses control. I was sitting at the far end of the table and somewhat obscured from the view of the main two executives who were acting in an unseemly manner.

They must have forgotten that I was there because the Engineer-In-Charge came out with an ethnic joke that was aimed at black people. It was funny and it took all that I could muster to keep from laughing. I was not offended because I have developed an usually thick skin. I acted as if I paid no attention to it while there was a deafening hush over the table. The EIC was told that I was sitting at the other end of the table and he turned as red as a beet. He had shown everyone at the table how not to act. Those comments, coming from the highest ranking person on board, set the tone for the rest of the trip. It would be all business after that. He apologized to me and I accepted it. What was I going to do, make a scene? I think not. Not if I wanted to continue working at G.M. That would have been acting contrary to my **"strategy."** The following morning, I was lauded for my restraint and poise by several people whom I respected. I had presented myself well. It also pays to develop a thick skin.

****

The theme of **"presentation"** is brought on because of what we see with our eyes. Once having seen, we deliberate on what it means. We then store that knowledge in our memory to be retrieved when later needed. The great tennis player, Andre Aggasi, said it well, "Image is everything." We would like for that image to be in our favor, not working against us. As will be repeated throughout this book, "You will be good at what you practice." When you practice making a good **"presentation"** of yourself, you will become good at it. Others who are in a position to make things happen for you will notice you. That is the point of this whole exercise, to get noticed.

OPPORTUNITIES AND POSSIBILITIES

"There is no such thing as security, there is only opportunity."
Charles Ricker

Time passes on and stands still for no one. While watching a Public Broadcasting System (PBS) offering one evening, I was captivated by the stories of how three areas of the country were severely affected by industrial changes. Specifically, the segment was on how the closing of steel mills in Pennsylvania, the coal mines in West Virginia, and the textile mills of the South changed the lives of the people who labored in them. Once the heart and soul of America's steel production, the city of Pittsburgh, known for its polluted air and high employment, was devastated by the influx of cheap foreign steel. Some of these steel mills failed to modernize and could not compete in the areas of price and quality. There was no market for what they were producing. They had to close and the jobs associated with these facilities were gone forever. One gentleman was interviewed at his home with his family surrounding him. It was a very moving scene as he revealed what his family was going through. "My dad was a steel worker, his father was a steelworker, and his father before him. I had hoped that my son would become a steelworker. I just want it to be like it was before." Although some can identify with this man's plight, reality has to come to bear. It is never going to be like it was. The same can be said for the textile industry and coal mining. As we have become a more homogenized world through rapid transit via air and sea, the efforts towards efficiencies in industrialization in one country has a global effect. My thoughts after viewing this were along the lines of, "What was binding these families to the areas where they were living? Why not go where the jobs are?"

With the advent of every new technology, there is an opportunity. I am mindful of the recent turmoil created by America On Line. With their haste to expand and capture a greater segment of the "on-line service" market, they suffered from a lack of qualified people to staff the new systems. What an opportunity for a new career. This scenario is repeated countless numbers of times as old methods pass away and new ones come into being. Why is there a reluctance to embrace these undiscovered territories? Because they require one to abandon his (or one's) **"comfort zone"** and accept the new technologies. The problem is compounded when a person is required to depart from an area where the surroundings are familiar and make a new location home. But one must go where the jobs are. Some persons who have found themselves out of work are not comfortable with the thought of relocating. If the mission involves some discomfort, that is not acceptable. However, we see immigrants not only relocate to a new area, but their relocation is on a much grander scale. It involves moving to a new country, a country where they may not be able to speak the language.

I cannot imagine a more difficult setting, trying to prosper in a new country where the customs differ, the people are strangers, and you cannot speak the language. Yet, the immigrants come to America and do well. To them, this is indeed the land of opportunity.

If it is a case of the newcomers starting up a business, the whole family becomes involved in the venture. One thing for certain, they all know the value of education. Do we not see the children of non-English speaking immigrants excelling in our school systems? There is nothing mystical about them. They do not hold a monopoly on intellectual capability. What they do have embedded deep within is the will to succeed. We have not resisted tyranny in this country to the point where our lives were at stake. Many of these people have, in their native countries. Having escaped the bonds of affliction and arriving in a country where they can live and prosper for their own sake, they wonder what is wrong with the people who are born here.

While awaiting my turn at a local cellular phone service center, I could not help but notice the deep accent of a women who was to assist me. After discussing issues relating to the phone service, I began to speak on personal items with Colette. "Where do you originate, if I may ask?"

> "I was born and raised in England. I came to this country in 1977, seeking employment. I have a brother and sister here with me also but the rest of my family is in England."
>
> "So America in now your home?"
>
> "America will never be my home, but it is where I choose to live. America is the place to be if you want to work."
>
> "Wasn't it the freedom, the flight from persecution, the ability to be free from government intrusions and all the things that are lauded as the greatness of this country? Aren't those the things that brought you here?"

She laughed as she replied, "Of course not. It was the prospect of employment that brought us here. You ask most people who come here. If they are truthful, they'll tell you that they came here to get a job. They would rather be gainfully employed in the land of their birth."

I have heard similar statements to this many times as my profession acquaints me with individuals from varying countries. America is the land of **"opportunity."**

LOSING YOUR JOB

Very few things can affect the lives of human beings more than the loss of a job. There is a great deal of pain and suffering that accompanies an event such as this. The death of a close friend or relative, in the mind of the authors, is the only thing that can surpass the grief associated with job loss. Working can be literally a life-saver to some individuals. It tends to give them a sense of worth. I have read that the average life span for a man after retirement is five years. The age of the person did not seem to be a factor. This statistic is open for debate. I believe that all of us have been surprised with the news of someone suddenly dying who recently retired. For some people, their vocation is not what they do, it is what they are. When that job is taken away from them or they are forced to leave it, the resulting grief, despondency, dejection and depression can be too much for them to bear. They either become sick and die or commit suicide. That is because attitudes and health are related. Even one's mental health.

The loss of a job can ignite turmoil within a family. When there are more bills left over than there is money to pay them, tempers can become short. Since there are distinct differences between men and women, the priorities set for household expenditures most likely will be different. There is not the same money available for entertainment and the token items that were purchased for one another prior to the job loss. The wife is trying to do the best with what she has been given. Let's consider that there are children in the mix. The constant attention and expenditures needed to clothe and feed them can be quite taxing. Eventually, extra items will come into play, like school supplies, money for the school trip, the yearly school pictures, etc. Everyone's needs cannot be satisfied and if there is no cohesive agreement, there are going to be arguments. Your automobile could be repossessed if not paid for. In addition, your home may be subjected to foreclosure.

Without gainful employment, you will be plunged into debt. Debt can kill a marriage like nothing else except the death of a child. Debt has a life of its own. It breeds and it grows and it draws one further into its clutches. Debt can string itself out for years, even decades, and can result in bankruptcy. Now that's total embarrassment. Your name is published as a debtor. Your friends and enemies know about it. What little unemployment compensation that is rendered is certain not to be enough. The truly sad part is, not only do you not have any money left for the essentials but you still have bills to pay. That can result in some serious and painful name-calling in the heat of the argument that is certain to ensue. Actions must be taken to head off these potential disasters. The only reasonable and sensible action to take is to immediately seek out another job.

The late 70's was a difficult period for the Chrysler Corporation. Their headquarters was located in Highland Park, Michigan. Lee Iacocca was lured over from the Ford Motor Company to become the head of the Chrysler Corporation. Decisions were made that adversely affected the lives of many of the individuals employed there, including this author. One of the first decisions made was an immediate reduction in staffing. There was to be a 15% cut across the board in salaried personnel and support staff. No levels or departments were to be spared. This was a very significant undertaking because it meant that 15% of the managing staff were going to lose their jobs along with engineers, designers, maintenance, administrative assistants, and so on.

Prior to the announcement of the reductions, it was business as usual. For the engineering community, it was full employment plus overtime. Fifty-eight hours had been the normal work week for years. People bought new homes, summer cottages, second, third and fourth cars along with an assortment of toys. There seemed to be no end to the gravy train. Power boating magazines were strewn all over the place. The individuals who purchased boats bought big ones. If the boat had sleeping accommodations for a certain number of people, the interest could be deducted from their federal income tax as a second home.

Then came the bad news. We were losing our jobs due to the downsizing. True tales spread around the building about men falling over dead from heart attacks. They realized that there was no way to continue their extravagant lifestyles. A few years prior to the downsizing, one of the senior design checkers, Stan Podzinski, took me aside and gave me words of advice. "If you were smart, (I inferred from this that I wasn't smart) you would leave this company and go work in the [job shops] so you can learn something. Don't become dependent upon this company for your livelihood. Big companies will let you down."

The thought of leaving Chrysler was out of the question. Why would I leave a company voluntarily that was providing me with a good wage and lavish benefits? After all, I would be departing from my **"comfort zone"** in a major way and heading for the great unknown. Stan's words proved to be prophetic. All of the designers employed at the Highland Park, Michigan location were members of the UAW. We had no choice in the matter. It was one of those rare occasions when a person can be a member of the UAW and a salaried employee also. My name was on a seniority list that had me near the bottom. The bottom was not a good place to be. Being a good and productive worker would have no bearing on my employment status.

There were people in the department going through the motions of working, without providing any tangible output. In addition, they gave the management a hard time. I was shocked beyond belief when the news came that my name was on the "good-bye" list. What was I going to do now?

My departure from Chrysler provided me with an **"opportunity"** to become better. I was forced out of my comfort zone and had to learn something new, even if it was learning how to get along with a different group of people. Learning new things brought on added value. Some may not view it this way because of their individual circumstances. I did have a skill that was in demand and I found work some months after the layoff. However, there are many hard- working Americans who have no special skills beyond that which are required for a specific job. These are the individuals who find themselves unemployable if they do not acquire additional training or skills.

Who is at fault when things like this happen? Certainly not the employer. They are making decisions that are in the best interest of the company. Each individual should be doing the same, making decisions that are in his own best interest. However, we become lulled into complacency. Because things have always been good, we think that they will continue to be that way. Such is not the case, as many too painfully discover.

Losing your job can be catastrophic. It would behoove those who become unemployed to consider this, it does not have to be the end of your usefulness. Those items lost, homes, cars, boats and a host of things, can all be replaced. How should those who become unemployed look at their situation? An **"opportunity"** to become better than they were. In the words of Mort Crim, renowned television news anchor and radio broadcaster, "There's only one thing to do when your world falls apart, put it back together."

TRUE STORY

The General Motors, Detroit-Hamtramck Assembly Plant is one of the most modern, efficient assembly facilities in the world. This facility is where the flagship of General Motors, the Cadillac is assembled. There is an area of the facility where the rear glass is placed in the body of the vehicle. Before being put into place, the glass receives a bead of polyurethane around the edge to seal out water and other forms of moisture. At one time, the operation required three men. One to apply the bead of polyurethane and two to lift the glass and place in into the opening at the rear of the vehicle. In order to apply the sealant, it had to be heated to a sufficient temperature to allow it to flow through the applicator tool. The proper amount of sealant had to be applied to prevent water leaks. Too much sealant, and it would protrude out onto the paint, right where you didn't want it. Either condition was undesirable. The assembly process was extremely [operator sensitive]. A quality seal was the most important thing. Even if a person were to be trained to perform this task to the optimum level and repeatedly for the entire eight-hour shift, what happens when he or she is not at work? The manufacturing engineers came up with the perfect solution, a robot.

As predicted, the union fought this change because, in their eyes, it was a job lost to a machine. When the robot was in place and functioning, it provided a consistent bead of polyurethane along a prescribed path. The robot even wiped its tip off after each application to prevent excess dripping. When I visited this operation, I happened to be there at the same time when an electrician was placing two of the same robots nearby. After making an inquiry, I discovered that the two extra robots were placed there to allow sufficient time for repairs and maintenance. It seems that there were not enough robotic technicians available to make timely repairs. Having an extra robot always on hand would provide the cushion needed until a technician could arrive on the scene. I immediately began to think, there is a new **"opportunity"** for someone. Any wage and availability curve will tell you that when the demand for a commodity is up and the supply of it is low, the price is high. Thus, anyone pursuing a career in robotics would be afforded an opportunity to have his wages rise with the demand for his services. I relayed this message to some of the assembly line workers. They were not interested, even after being told that they could receive the training at little or no cost to them. What was more important was their leisure time. They called it, "free time." Free time, I thought for a minute. What was free time? Time is not free. It is a case of time being used wisely or time being wasted.

****

One should not be beguiled by the momentary need for assembly workers advertised by industry, particularly, the industries that do not require their assembly personnel to have at least a high school education. Assembly jobs are referred to as monetary because they can be at, and are moved to, various locations. The pressures placed upon companies due to global competition require that these assembly jobs be moved to wherever the labor is cheaper. A careful examination of those items around us, the ones we use every day, will reveal this to be true. The labels read "Assembled in China, Taiwan, Indonesia," and other Asian belt countries that have inexpensive labor. The exceptions to this are, the aircraft industry and those industries responsible for the assembly of high tech military products. Those [vocations] require at least a post high school education. The manufacturing of the products is where many of the skilled workers are nestled.

Companies are reluctant to displace the manufacturing sector to foreign soil because, along with engineering, it is the life-blood of all industries. The requirements to fill those jobs are more stringent and demand more training. The [tool and die] makers, the electricians, carpenters, [jobsetters], and [model makers], are only a few of the occupations required for an industrial manufacturing entity. I do not advocate refusing to work as an assembler. As previously stated, the work is honorable. The focus of any person in this situation should be to take the assembly job while continuing on the journey for something more substantial for the future.

****

Where will the opportunities lie in the future? It is a safe bet that there will always be a shortage of personnel with technical skills and the skilled trades. That is the case worldwide. The principles of physics, mathematics and science are the same anywhere that one may travel. The language may be different, but the symbols are the same. The dedication and discipline needed to master these is what is really rare. Thus, the quantity of qualified people are scarce and the corresponding wages remain high. Try to get an electrician to come and service your home. His skills are in demand across the country. Everyone has need of one at some time or another.

Plumbers, heating and cooling persons, and a host of other home improvement specialists fall into the same category. A good friend of mine is a builder of custom homes. Being curious as to why it takes so long to build a home, his reply was, "Every builder is in need of those people with the skills necessary to build a house. Framing crews, drywall people, finish carpenters, and the rest, are in short supply. When hunting season comes, it gets worse. Hunting seems to be a tradition with these guys." This became even more apparent when he was constructing his new home, a modest abode of some 10,000 square feet. I was on hand when he was negotiating with plumbers to install the fixtures in his new home. They were going to be paid $65.00 an hour and they were still reluctant to show up when requested. The same held true for the electricians, only they were going to be paid a paltry sum of $55.00 an hour. They know that the demand for their skills is high and the supply of labor is low. Therein lies opportunities for those willing to invest the time and energy in learning these trade skills. Skills that can provide them with employment anywhere in the country and the world.

The job **"Opportunity Reference"** guide included in this chapter contains fields where the good jobs of the future are and where they may be located. It should be noted that your local newspaper can provide you with a barometer of where the demand is for employment. No doubt there will be little or no demand for common laborers or assemblers. The demand is, and shall be, for those who possess technical skills. Thousands upon thousands of these positions will go unfilled. There are just not enough people to meet the demand. As previously stated, with the demand being high for labor and the supply being low, the price paid for that labor will always remain high.

Living so close to Canada, we in the Detroit Metropolitan area are privileged to have access to the Canadian Broadcasting Company (CBC). After the North American Free Trade Agreement (NAFTA) was signed, the Canadian government proclaimed on national television that there was going to be an immediate increase in the demand for manufacturing being done in Canada. This demand could not be satisfied as is because there was already a shortage of manufacturing engineers in the country. To meet the demand of the private manufacturing sector, they estimated that upwards of 200,000 manufacturing engineers were needed, with no place to get them. They certainly could not siphon engineers from the United States. The manufacturers in this country needed every manufacturing engineer they could get their hands on.

As I listened to the Canadian Minister of Labor, I thought to myself, what an **"opportunity"** for those who are prepared. This is not a unique occurrence. In our own country, there is such a severe shortage of trained machinists, tool and die makers, and model makers, they are being imported from foreign countries. These individuals are the backbone of the manufacturing industry. One local news radio report concerning employment made the point very clear. The report stated that the need was so great for qualified tool and die makers in the Detroit Metropolitan area that a husband and wife tool and die team was brought over from Romania. When it comes to industry, it is manufacturing that is the lifeblood, not assembly. Manufacturing requires great skill and talent. Assembly can be done wherever labor is cheapest. As you begin to plot your course for the future, pay close attention to the demand side of the supply and demand curve. Focus your interest where there is a shortage of qualified people. When there are shortages it takes at least a decade for things to right themselves. How do you know where the shortages are?

I can speak with experience about the importation of foreign labor. The field of automotive design has suffered from a shortage of qualified individuals for decades. The shortage was so acute in the 80's that General Motors imported hundreds of contract designers from England and from other parts of the world. The contract that brought those men into this country was for a specified period of time. The U.S. Department of Labor was convinced by General Motors and other automakers that this was a field of specialization and that there were not enough qualified Americans available to satisfy the needs. Many of the people who were imported found the American lifestyle much to their liking. Rather than go back to uncertain employment futures in England and other homelands, they decided to stay. This was permitted by the Department of Labor because the shortage of designers was, and still is, very acute, despite all of the training that has taken place.

What does this mean to you as the reader? The message is clear and simple. There is tremendous employment opportunity for those willing to invest in themselves and learn how to become designers. Gone are the days when designs were done on drafting boards. The tool of choice is the computer. On it may be installed any variety of computer graphics programs. Almost everything that is made emanates from a design. Aircraft, oil refinery, building structures, automobiles, and many other disciplines have need of designers. Employment opportunities exists for designers all over the world. The Employment Reference Section at the end of the segment lists some of these job **"opportunities."**

For training and more information on becoming a designer, see the **"Preparational Reference,"** and **"Technical Training"** section at the end of the **"Preparation"** segment. The information on technical training is placed in that section because no college degrees are required as prerequisite. A person may acquire the knowledge of the field through study and practical application.

TEMPORARY EMPLOYMENT AGENCIES

Temporary employment agencies, also known as "contract employment firms," are not the newest thing on the employment scene, nor are they the oldest. These agencies have been around for many years. What is new are the numbers of individuals making use of these agencies as their source of employment. In addition, there is growing reliance on these agencies in all sectors of our economy. The term temporary employment can be deceptive and is ambiguous at best. At first glance, a person may have connotations of only working for a short period of time, thus the label "temporary." This is misleading. Temporary firms may give you a placement that is for a short duration, but they usually have another assignment for you, depending on your field of expertise.

Working for the same agency for many years is not uncommon. Companies are constantly looking for ways to increase profitability by cutting costs. The price they pay for labor is one of their major costs. Having a certain percentage of the staff employed as temporary workers gives the company the flexibility to bring on more people when the need is there and release people when the crisis ends. An example of this is all the merchants who employ people on a seasonal basis, particularly at the Christmas holiday season. These same companies reduce their staffs when they no longer have the sales to justify the number of workers on hand.

Companies need the ability to adjust the staffs in this manner or they will not remain in business. In times past, these merchants took on the added costs and burden of posting classified advertising, in addition to interviewing potential candidates. The objective of a company or business is not to employ people, but to earn money for the owners. In reality, a person may work for a temporary agency for a considerable amount of time while having varied assignments. This can be quite an outstanding opportunity for the individual who is looking to become anchored with one company.

Many companies use temporary employment as a screening mechanism for hiring permanent staff. A person can be on his best behavior for 30, 60 or 90 days. He may even be able to be on his best behavior for six months. However, no person is able to carry on a charade for a year or more. Your true work habits will eventually be revealed. Companies know this and make use of temporary firms as surrogates. After a sufficient amount of time has passed and your **"performance"** meets their standards, you may be offered a permanent job.

The gulf between the wages paid and the benefits offered by temporary agencies is narrowing every year. That is because the employment growth lies in the temporary employment sector. The temporary employment agencies are innumerable and varied in scope. Almost every field makes use of temporary employees. This places pressure on the firms to offer more money and benefits to stay competitive. As more and more companies are requesting these types of individuals to work in their venues, the temporary agencies compete for a limited, qualified employment pool. Therein lies the importance of **"preparation."** Some temporary employment agencies are so compliant, they will offer you more money in lieu of benefits. This could be to your advantage if you happen to have a spouse who has a good benefits package as part of his or her employment compensation.

What does this mean for you, the worker? It means that you will have tremendous flexibility in where you are able to work, and what you will be paid for your labor. There is no ideal employment situation when you work for someone else. However, working as a contract employee gives you the opportunity to have some control over your future. As previously mentioned, temporary employment agencies are all over the world. If your field of expertise is in a technical area, you can literally pick the country where you would like to work. The majority of the technical opportunities lie within the United States and Canada. I know of individuals who have taken working vacations in some very nice countries. They have worked as temporary employees in Australia, Germany, Italy, Great Britain, Japan, Korea, Saudi Arabia, China, and France.

Some contract employment firms are global. What is meant by global? A contract employment firm may be located in one state while employing people in an entirely different state. This is quite common. As a temporary employee, you are afforded the **"opportunity"** to work on different projects for various companies. As an added benefit, you'll gain some interpersonal skills. The chances are that there will be situations where the chapter on **"Getting Along With People"** will come in handy. These all become valuable workplace experiences that you can add to your resume. Your marketability is then increased, thus making it easier for you to get a better job. Some of the many temporary employment agencies are listed in the

"Opportunity Reference" section at the end of this segment. They are listed by their field of operation.

OPPORTUNITIES FOR THE HANDICAPPED

On one occasion, I had to make a trip to the bank where I do business. As I approached the teller window, I was greeted with a polite smile and a warm, "Hello, may I help you." There was something strange about her posture. She was sitting down and it appeared that the teller had her left arm behind her back. The dress she had on was of a dark print pattern, making it difficult to see. The background was also dimly lit which added to my curiosity. I was about to ask her why she was shielding her arm. "Are you cold," was to be the question put to her. Upon further discovery, I noticed that she did not have her left arm behind her back. Her arm was amputated at the elbow.

Along with feeling a bit stupid, I became intrigued at how she was performing her tasks. Handicap, what handicap? The young lady was performing the same tasks as any other teller, except it was being done with one hand. Upon further scrutiny, I understood why this person was hired. Her **"presentation"** was that which is to be expected of any employee of a bank, business dress. There were no series of holes along her ears with gaudy earrings hanging from them. Her hairstyle was not abnormal and she was extremely articulate. After my transaction was complete, she asked, "How may I be of further assistance to you today, sir?" If I were to give her a rating, her job performance was every bit a 10. This person could have been used as an example to all tellers, of how to treat the customers.

Moreover, she caused me to think of the plight of handicapped workers. Do they have the same opportunities as those without physical maladies? The answer to this question is both yes and no. There are jobs in which a physical malady could hinder or prevent a person from performing a specific job-related task. So, the answer to the first question is no. However, by making the proper career selection and with the right training, a person's handicap need not be a hindrance to her in applying for and getting a job.

The computer industry has a broad spectrum of applications that are perfect for persons confined to a wheelchair. The assumption being made here is that the handicap is not affecting the ability to think and make use of their hands. It is the law of the land that every public building provide handicap access ramps and be equipped with handicap access rest rooms. Many forward thinking companies are using barrier free furniture and their architecture is handicap friendly. The examples of jobs that handicapped individuals can perform are too numerous to list and expound upon. The answer to the second question is, yes. The point is, no excuse is good enough.

Where are those with handicaps to find the proper training and the resulting opportunities? That is the job of state and local social service agencies as well as vocational school guidance counselors. The focus of the handicapped should be on becoming productive citizens, not receiving a handout in the form of a government assistance check. The authors are not being callous nor are we without compassion for those less fortunate. It is our belief that all people should contribute to society if capable of doing so. If you happen to be a person with a physical disability, do not allow it to be a stumbling block to success. You have worth. Search for the **"opportunity"** and prepare yourself to display it.

OPPORTUNITIES FOR WOMEN

Millicent Hammond Fenwick from New Jersey served in Congress form 1975 to 1983. When asked a pointed question about the role of women in industry today, she gave one of the most intelligent and profound answers I have ever heard. The reporter was making an attempt to ensnare Congresswoman Fenwick by asking, "Do you think that women are qualified and able to do the same jobs as men?" Her reply was, "Nature should dictate what a woman should and should not do." It cannot be stated any simpler than that. It is a fact that women are assuming roles in the workplace that have traditionally belonged to men. The genders have gone through a melding, where the borders are no longer defined as to what role belongs to which gender. This is due partly to the increase in the number of single-parent homes headed by females. They are fully aware of the fact that the jobs men have traditionally held paid more money.

Jobs such as telephone repairman, truck driver, refuse collector, police patrolman, fireman, and a host of other occupations have all paid more than secretaries, clerks, receptionists, etc., and rightfully so. These professions demand more skill and learning and in some cases, more stamina. It would not be true to state that "Anything men can do women can do better." It would be accurate to state that "Most things that men can do, women can do also," provided that nature allows it. There are some positions, women are not capable of fulfilling because of strength limitations. That is not to say that they are inferior to men or that men are superior to women. It is an acknowledgment that the genders are different. In this light, men and women performing the same task should receive the same amount of compensation for those tasks. There should be no preferences for one gender over that of another nor should there be a different set of standards.

What does this have to do with opportunity for women? Plenty. Women are capable both physically and mentally to undergo the training to help fill some of the thousands of job vacancies. Women's groups should not waste time trying to get more money for doing jobs that do not command high wages in the free market. A person working a minimum wage job is paid the minimum wage because the free market has set it as such. Without external interference, that same job would require an increase or decrease in pay to fit what the demand is. When external forces come into play to set wages, there is less opportunity for all, not more. Women are fully capable of doing residential wiring to help builders complete their homes on time. The same can be said for plumbers. There are very few strength requirements for residential plumbers. Building framing crews do require considerable strength. Let's look at the industrial settings. There are all sorts of lifting devices on hand to aid the millrights, jobsetters, tool and die persons, pipefitters, and the many other skilled tradesmen. There is nothing that precludes women from filling these roles except for the training that is required.

OPPORTUNITIES FOR MINORITIES

The principles and laws that govern the world of science, math, and the skilled trades take no regard for a person's race, color, creed, or nationality. Knowing this, and having a fundamental belief in its premise, the only thing that prevents people from taking advantage of employment opportunities is their own mindset. The process is not difficult to follow. To simplify it even further, recognize where you are, where you want to be, and what is it that you have to do to get there. A person must be prepared to get there. What is "there?" It is different for every person. "There" is defined as the culmination of your dream, the target that you have placed in your sights. Opportunities abound for those willing to pay the price to achieve success. As I have stated before, there is always someone, somewhere, willing to pay for what you know or what you know how to do. Connecting your abilities and skills is a matter of understanding **"job winning techniques."**

There is no insatiable demand for those individuals whose abilities lie solely in the humanities. Any rudimentary study will prove this to be true. That is not to say there is no demand, just that the demand for those who have mastered math and the sciences fare much better in terms of employment opportunities. Then again, there is great demand for labor in the service industry. What is categorized as the service industry are occupations that involve hotel, motels, fast food eateries, store clerks, and anything that deals directly with the public in a private sector format. These are honorable jobs and the work has merit. The fact remains that flipping hamburgers at "Burger Biggee" is not going to do much for one's career unless one is using those experiences to further one's short-term goals. It is not uncommon for a person to commute over long distances to get to some of the fast food places. The commute, coupled with the limitation on earnings, should be enough to encourage the worker to continue up the ladder of success.

This statement was said to me rather bluntly one day. "All that education and stuff is good for the few people that get it, but what are the masses going to do who do not have or want an education? Where are they going to work? Where are the good paying factory jobs?" I was not unsympathetic to what this gentleman was saying and I understood him. He failed to comprehend the fact that good paying jobs that require little or no education have gone the way of the dinosaur, they are extinct. There is no plot to keep minorities unemployed by closing factories. The reality is that nations are interacting in a global economy, placing a demand on productivity at decreased costs. It so happens that many of the older industrial production facilities are located in areas around big cities. These employment **"opportunities"** once served as magnets, attracting and concentrating minority workers in urban areas. As these facilities became older and the tax burdens began to rise, it made good economical sense to re-establish production elsewhere.

One only needs to have an attentive eye to discover opportunities for employment. The name of the game today is divestiture. Original equipment manufacturers are shedding themselves of affiliates in order to save money. That is a good thing for everyone. Take the auto industry, for example. The majority of the automakers have stated that they no longer want to make the components needed in automobiles. They want to buy them. That means that some other entity is needed to make them. These entities are called suppliers. The suppliers usually operate on very small profit margins and do not have the resources to train large work forces. That means they'll have to draw from the trained talent pool that is readily available. That signals **"opportunity"** for laborers and the salaried, professional staffs. It may mean relocation to another area. If indeed that is the case, you should be ready to make the move because you have read the chapter on **"The Comfort Zone."**

THE POSSIBILITIES ARE ENDLESS

If you have a desire to work for yourself, the only restraints are those you place upon yourself. There are countless numbers of examples of people who ventured out on their own and became successful. I watched an interview with Wally Amos, the gentleman who started Famous Amos cookies. He told the story of how he was walking along the beach with nothing, no job prospects at all, and little or no money. One day he got the idea to bake cookies and sell them to those visiting the beach. Well, as sometimes happens, when people have a good idea, it goes over big. His cookies became very popular. The rest is history. What do you have a desire to do? Are you good with your hands and dislike the idea of having to study in a formal setting? Have no fear. There is something suited just for you. All that is necessary is that you discover what it is. That may not happen all at once. It may emerge gradually. Things have a way of taking shape once some effort is given towards the task.

I see opportunities for self-employment everywhere. I dislike waiting in a long time to get a hair cut. Yet, when I visit barber shops, the lines are long and some of the available chairs are empty. The chairs are empty because of the shortage of barbers. This is astounding to me. Here is a profession in which people wait in line to bring you money. If you kept the doors of the barber shop open until the late evening hours, there would still be people waiting to get a hair cut. There seems to be no convenient time to get this type of personal grooming done. When I converse with the shop owners, they all tell the same story. They cannot get good help or any help at all. These barbers do very well as far as monetary compensation. With the completion of every hair cut comes a gratuity.

I have been often asked, “Do you know someone with a pickup truck? I need some light hauling done.” There have been occasions when I needed some light hauling done, too. Nothing large, just household and garden items such as sod, brick pavers, landscaping timbers, etc. Therein lies the opportunity for some energetic person, male or female, to start a small business. A brand new truck is not needed, just one that is dependable. An investment in a moving dolly would also be a good idea. It is very inexpensive to have business cards and fliers printed. This work could be performed on the weekends or during evenings. The word of this service would spread quickly by word-of–mouth. This entrepreneur would have so much business, he couldn't handle it all by himself. This could lead to expansion. A simple contract could be made to haul certain items for small businesses on a regular interval. The next thing you know, you could own a company, employing people.

****

When asked my advice on multilevel marketing opportunities, I speak very candidly about these ventures. I applaud the entrepreneurial spirit wherever it exists. However, there is no easy way to make money. If it is too easy, it is most likely illegal. Having said that, one must have a realistic assessment of what is involved in multilevel marketing. Multilevel marketing is not a 'pyramid' scheme as some would have you to believe. That is true as long as there is a product associated with the program. There are some products that are so popular that they sell themselves. Extra coaxing isn't necessary because the demand is there. In cases where the product is popular, all that is required is casual revelation of your association.

Selling the products associated with multilevel marketing and building a business by establishing an army of helpers are two different things. In order to be truly successful in one of these ventures, it takes people that you personally have signed up. That is called a "downline." The goal is to harness the energy of other people. In this manner, you receive a percentage of what they sell also. You are not going to approach strangers with this newfound money-making venture. The very first people you are going to talk to are your friends and relatives. Some people just do not like to be hustled. I am one of those. Nothing can kill a friendship like being constantly hustled by one of your friends.

You do not mind their entrepreneurial spirit, as a matter of fact, you applaud it. Who couldn't use a few extra bucks? The problem stems from them being so easily influenced by all of the multilevel marketing ventures. Sure, the people representing the products and services make it seem all too simple and wonderful. That type of badgering makes all of your relationships with other people uncomfortable. They now feel as though they have to avoid you because you will always bring up your involvement in the venture. You will glisten with enthusiasm as you tell them how much money they could be making. Another problem is that there are not enough people for everyone to make it to the plateau where the "big money" is. Everyone is trying to do the same thing you are, sign up people. You become offended because you are being avoided. You have given your friends and relatives little choice.

I respect the privacy of my friends and I expect them to reciprocate. I have purchased goods and services where the salesperson offered me a cash rebate if I were to give them the phone number of one or more of my friends. They were shocked that I would not do it. I explained to them that I did not hand out the private phone numbers of friends so that they could be exploited. Besides, when the salesperson would call them, he would no doubt mention the fact that I gave him their phone number. What would my friends think of me, knowing that I sold them out for $50.00? If the product or service is worthwhile, I will tell my friends about it and under no circumstances will I accept a gratuity. Give multilevel marketing much thought before entering into such a program.

****

At one time in my youth, I looked with disdain upon those who were commonly called "Junk Men." Those were the guys who hauled away old stoves, refrigerators, washing machines and various other items composed of metal. I thought them to be men of little learning, destitute, men who were not capable of reasonable thought. After all, they only hauled junk! If they could do something else, wouldn't they? So much for judging by appearance. There are many other such items that we discard as refuse. These men haul it away. We think that we are getting such a good deal when we place this stuff out on the street on trash day. You look around and the stuff is gone. Why? These men (I have never seen women doing it) know that there is value in that so-called junk. Some of those items contain precious metals that can be recycled. One man's trash is truly another man's treasure. Even I have stopped on occasion to retrieve something from the trash that I recognized as having value. There is an occupation waiting for someone to direct it.

TRUE STORY

In the mid 70's, a very good friend of mine asked me if I were interested in making some money. Of course I said, "Yes," to that proposition. We got in his car and drove to his parents' home in the city of Flint, Michigan. His father, a retired autoworker, had a very nice pick-up truck that had a tilting bed placed on it. His father had it specially modified. It soon became clear why he had that done to the truck. My friend and I started out early the next morning and began to drive down the alleys and streets of Flint, picking up metal objects. There was an assortment of items that we loaded into the bed of the truck. When we reached our destination, which was a junk yard, we rolled onto a very large scale. This scale weighed the vehicle and its contents. The person at the meter wrote down the weight on a piece of paper. We then proceeded to an area where we were instructed to dump the load. Men who did not have lifts on their trunks had to unload their trucks by hand. That was consuming time and energy.

Upon emptying the load, we drove onto the scale again. Weighing less than we did when we came in was the difference of how much metal was deposited at the site. We were paid so many cents per pound. The exact amount that was paid per pound escapes me. We followed this routine all day long until the evening hours. My share was $60 and I was glad to get it. My friend didn't reveal how much he kept for himself. It didn't matter. It was his father's truck and I incurred no expenses. The work was not that difficult. Then it suddenly dawned on me what was happening all those years when I thought that the junk men didn't know what they were doing. They knew exactly what they were doing. It was I that who in need of educating. My friend's father filled his days of retirement with hauling scrap metal. That would explain the appearance of affluence. Their home was well appointed. There were also two brand new Buicks in their garage.

ONLY IN AMERICA

This is the land of opportunity and everyone knows it. There are some very ingenious people in this country who refuse to sit idly by and lct prospcrity avcrt thcm. Whcrc clsc can you go in thc world and make a tremendous living, selling an idea? That is why immigrants flood this country by the thousands. It is the freedom to live for one's own sake that they seek. These are people who really know what it is to be oppressed. If they were to come up with an idea that could sell, there are very few outlets for them to sell it in their country of origin. Do you remember the idea that someone had to sell ordinary rocks by labeling them extraordinary? They were called "Pet Rocks" and the originator made a bundle of money on this idea.

Then there was the frenzy that was created over "Eating Dirt." Yes, this was dirt that you were supposed to eat. We were assured that it was clean dirt! The creators of this frenzy made a bundle of money, too. Last and foremost, portions of the Berlin Wall were sold to Americans. We all watched with heartfelt gladness at the destruction of this European symbol of death and oppression. As the advertisement stated, you can own a piece of history. "Send $19.95 and we will ship you a piece of the Berlin Wall." In actuality, it was a cleverly devised scam. Some men gathered cinder blocks, broke them up with sledge hammers, bagged the crushed block up and sold the packages as portions of the Berlin Wall. Quite some time had transpired before this scam was uncovered. The point is that you can capitalize on any good idea that you can come up with. The only thing preventing you from doing so is your disbelief.

A market can be created for goods and services that you come up with. This can be accomplished by doing what you know how to do and perfecting it. Take for instance an acquaintance of my wife and myself. This particular individual had a knack for embroidering handkerchiefs. Her handiwork was displayed at workshops and art fairs. So peculiar was her style that it drew interest from all over the city. Soon her fame spread by word-of-mouth, as one person told another and that person told someone else. After a great deal of patience, her handiwork became a bonafide business.

A long-time friend of mine began baking cakes as a hobby. His regular employment was with a transportation agency. As so often stated in the chapter **"A Job Well Done,"** you will become good at what you practice. He became so good at baking cakes that his fame spread by word-of-mouth only. One of his simpler cakes costs upwards of $100.00 and his clientele is among the who's who of the Detroit Metropolitan area. He refuses to take orders from those who are not already one of his clients. Working at his part-time trade, he made over $50,000 in three years. He did well enough to go on an extensive tour of Europe.

He is not alone; many individuals turned cooking hobbies into full-fledged businesses. The most famous of these individuals is the actor, Paul Newman. "Paul Newman's Own Olive Oil and Vinegar

Dressing" is some of the best I have ever tasted. The making of this dressing began as a treat for himself and friends. It was so good that they encouraged Mr. Newman to bottle and commercially sell it. Not wishing to retain the profits from this venture, Mr. Newman donates all of the proceeds from the sales of his products to charity.

Got an idea for a new product or gadget? Do you have a specialized skill that can be capitalized on? Do you make trinkets and doodads? Do you enjoy doing yard work, such as landscaping? There is your job, at your fingertips. One area of astounding growth is in home day care. Many parents prefer the home setting to that of the traditional day care operations. I know of a number of individuals who started out taking care of one or two children in their homes. Their home-based businesses grew by word-of-mouth into major operations. The cash flowed like rivers. It was hard work, but what good things come without hard work? Ventures such as this fit one of the criterions for success. It has a constant source of customers. Businesses that revolve around births, deaths, and eating will always have abundant opportunities.

Some Good Advice

Avoid, like the plague, working for a friend, no matter how attractive it may seem. There will invariably be deterioration in the relationship. You may end up losing the job and your friend. Specifically, cases where the friendship was in place prior to one of the individuals being placed in authority over the other. Working for your friend or going into business with your friend can kill a relationship like nothing else. It takes individuals of outstanding character and stamina, sustaining professional attitudes, and workplace demeanor, for the situation to work. How many people can sustain those requirements?

All relationships have boundaries or borders, which place limits on how far you will go for that person. You can only hope that the amount that you would extend yourself to assist your friend is the same amount that they would do for you. There has to and will certainly be a point in the relationship where the borders will be defined. Some event will happen, your fault, his fault, no one's fault, which will cause the two of you to establish that border. Nothing will be said, it will be an inferred border. Perhaps you will be spoken to in a manner that is surprising to you. If he or she determines that you should be reprimanded, will it be done in private or will you be openly embarrassed before your colleagues? If it is done in a public setting, he will no doubt apologize to you later, although in secret. You will, without doubt, forgive him because he is your friend. However, you will still be scared by the altercation because there was public humiliation. That which is incorrectly done in public should be corrected in public, but it won't be.

A person should have the mindset of being fiercely loyal to his boss, executing his or her instructions, once a decision has been made. That can pose difficulties when there are serious differences in opinion as to how to handle certain situations. You will have to do what was required of you because as Colin Powell stated, "If you take the King's ransom, you must do the King's bidding." There is bound to be a point at which the situation is going to become unbearable. The new boundaries of the relationship will be drawn and they will be substantially different than before. The boundaries will be determined by which person has the authority, power, and prestige. The extent to which you would extend yourself for them will not be the same as that displayed for you. When these new boundary lines are drawn, it will surprise you how narrow they are.

It is a fact that when you work for a friend, you are subordinate to him or her and he or she will laud it over you. In not so subtle ways, he will let you know that he is the boss and you aren't. There will be a lack of respect shown to you, sometimes in front of other people. You may receive mundane tasks that you know are beneath you. You will perform them because he now has your livelihood in his control. That is just another way for him to let you know that he is on top. The friendship has turned into something else. The working relationship now has preeminence. Little jabs and cutting remarks may be made from time-to-time. These things can be very upsetting.

It has been said that the people who are close to you are the ones who know how to hurt you. They know your weaknesses and where you are vulnerable. A situation may arise called "diverging interest," a circumstance in which something is profitable for your career, but is not in the best interest of your boss. In fact, it is in his best interest to block your path of exit. How will you handle that? The very best thing to do is not to allow it to happen. Only the most respectful and articulate professionals can balance a working relationship of this kind. It can be done, but it will be difficult.

Your friend has been bugging you for as long as you can remember to go into business with him. Because the two of you have been friends for so long, it is assumed that all will go well. There are several problems that can arise from this seemingly innocent proposal. Both of you feel strongly that your ideas should take precedent. Which two people see things exactly the same? In any relationship, decisions are never split along the lines of 50/50. At best, the decisions are made along the lines of 51/49. It stands to reason that if the power were shared equally, no decisions would be made. The one who has the more overbearing or dominant personality is going to be the person who assumes that leadership role of 51%.

It could be a factual statement that one of you actually does know more than the other. If one is willing to acquiesce to the judgment and leadership of the other, then the problems are likely to be minimized. The down side of this is that sometimes you will have a good idea. Because the dominant one among you is used to having his way, there will be a tendency to dismiss the ideas of the other because of the "corruption factor." What is the corruption factor? It is that adage, "Power corrupts and absolute power corrupts absolutely." When your ideas are continually rejected, some hard feelings will arise no matter how close the friendship. It happens in the closest bond on earth, husband and wife. Why can't it happen with good friends? It does happen, and with great frequency. Your good friend can become your worst enemy. He knows your secrets. He knows where you're vulnerable. How does he know? You told him! **Keep your friends as friends and business as business. You will maintain the business and the friendship.**

More Good Advice

If you plan to send out resumes in response to ads that appear in newspapers or some other venue, it is a good idea to purchase a spiral notebook and some adhesive index tabs. As you respond to the ads, you can paste the clipping in your spiral notebook, making sure they are in alphabetical order. The adhesive tabs will assist with the alphabetizing. There are cases when an advertisement may indicate the hourly pay scale or salary range. When conversing with a prospective employer over the phone, the notebook will become a handy reference tool. If you are sending out a large number of resumes, it is difficult to keep track of what you sent to whom and when it was sent. It is equally as difficult to remember what it was the advertiser indicated he needed. Notes can be placed on the pages, indicating the dates and responses received.

OPPORTUNITY REFERENCE

Employment Web Sites

To access the following information, the reader must use a computer, modem and an Internet Service Provider. Training on how to use the Internet is beyond the scope of this book. For more definitive usage instructions on the Internet, the book, ***Resumes In Cyber Space*** will prove to be a valuable learning tool. The following information was gleaned from the ***World Wide Web Yellow Pages, 5th Edition*** Career & Employment section. For a complete listing of web sites and job listings, this book is a valuable resource.

JobHunt

http://www.job-hunt.org

- This web site provides online job search resources and services. "JobHunt" contains a collection of links to job listings, companies, newsgroups, recruiting agencies and resume banks.

Jobs & Careers Online

http://www.servonet.com/jobs

- This web site contains an online listing of classified advertisements. The advertisements are broken down into categories, which include administration, finance, sales, education, medical, dental, technical, and more.

JobSmart

http://www.jobsmart.org/index.htm

- This web site is maintained by the Bay Area public libraries. This site is a good source of information for job seekers in Northern California. JobSmart provides access to career guides, information about resumes and salaries, job advertisements, job hotlines, and job fairs.

OPPORTUNITY REFERENCE

Employment Web Sites

Adams Media Publications

http://www.careercity.com

- This web site contains information on employment in various cities of the country.

JobWeb

http://www.jobweb.org

- JobWeb is a huge collection of links to resources on the Internet. There is information about jobs, the job search, human resources, and career planning.

NACCB Online Job Board & Resume Bank

http://www.computrwork.com

- This is a free service provided by the National Association of Computer Consultants Businesses. They are devoted to helping individuals find technical jobs and contract opportunities. This web site allows you to post your resume to their databank and search their online board.

Intellimatch

http://www.intellimatch.com

- A highly sophisticated approach to job searching and resume posting. It is a structured database that allows you to enter all your skills and areas of expertise. The employer is then able to perform a search on those keys.

OPPORTUNITY REFERENCE

Employment Web Sites

Tech Careers

http://www.techweb.com/careers/careers.html

- A web site for employers and for those seeking employment in a technical field.

Top Jobs USA

http:// www.totalhr.com/thr

- A searchable job database that also provides links to other Internet career resources.

Women In Technology International

http://www.witi.com

- A web site that has career information for women interested in technical careers.

Job Factory

http://www.jobfactory.com

- A searchable database of 245,000 job opportunities, 9,285 employers, and 3,167 job lines.

Green Thumb

http://www.greenthumb.org

- The Green Thumb organization is America's oldest and largest provider of mature and disadvantaged worker training and employment. Their mission is to strengthen the nation by providing disadvantaged and older individuals with opportunities to learn, work and serve others.

OPPORTUNITY REFERENCE

Contract Employment Agencies

Contract employment agencies literally number in the hundreds. There are entirely too many to name for this publication. However, the best source for an exhaustive listing of contract firms and their employment specialty is a publication called the ***Contract Employment Weekly Directory of Contract Service Firms.*** This directory is published yearly by **C.E. Publications, Inc.** There is a fee for this directory. In addition, C.E. publications publishes a weekly magazine that has up-to-date information on where the "hot jobs" are, domestic or international, what the duration of employment is, and how much is being paid on an hourly basis. This magazine is called the **"Contract Employment Weekly."** In addition, the magazine informs the prospective contract employee if there is any overtime being paid, travel benefits (per-diem), and which contract firm(s) is doing the hiring. With a paid subscription to the **"Contract Employment Weekly,"** you will receive the ***Contract Employment Weekly Directory of Contract Service Firms.*** This publication is well worth the money for anyone seeking to explore the opportunities that lie within contract employment. You may make inquiries about this publication at:

Contract Employment Weekly
P.O. Box 3006
Bothell, WA 98041

Phone	425.806.5200
Fax	425.806.5585
E-mail	publisher@ceweekly.com
Website	http:/wwwceweekly.com

OPPORTUNITY REFERENCE

Contract Employment Agencies

The following is a sampling of the information that can be gleaned from this publication.

ABBTECH SERVICES CORP.

E-mail: abbtech@cais.com

- Abbtech is well established in the Mid-Atlantic region, serving a variety of Fortune 500 companies and providing a wide range of computer and technical skills.

  Washington Office

  Dulles International Airport, P.O. Box 20098

  Washington D.C. 20041-0012

  Phone 703.450.5252

  Fax 703.406.9261

  Baltimore Office

  P.O. Box 18525

  Baltimore, MD 21240-0525

  Phone 410.766.5454

  Fax 410.766-4544

ADECCO TAD TECHNICAl.

E-mail: resume@adavancedrd.com

Website: http://www.adecco.com

- Adecco is a topnotch employment search firm. They perform searches for qualified individuals for their clients. Their client list is very long, too long to mention here.

  ADECCO TECHNICAL CENTER

  5442 East 25st Street

  Columbus, IN 47203

  Phone 800.748.2342 Fax 812.372.5742

OPPORTUNITY REFERENCE

Contract Employment Agencies

ADVANCED R&D INC.

E-mail: resume@advancedrd.com

Website: http://www.advanceddrd.com

- AR&D has earned a reputation for being one of the most dependable sources of technical personnel in the industry.

  Advanced R&D Inc.
  Central Offices and Central Recruiting
  P.O. Box 540747
  Orlando, FL 32854-0747
  Phone 800.365.6023 407.894.0111
  Fax 407.894.0115
  Dedicated Resume Fax Line 407.894.0103

AIM EXECUTIVE STAFFING SERVICES

- AIM is one of the largest full-service human resources consulting firms. Aim reviews each candidate's background to match him or her with the proper assignment. Automotive, CAD/CAM, chemicals, data processing, electronics, heavy machinery, iron & steel, manufacturing, technical welding, and more.

  AIM Executive Staffing Services
  1760 Manley Road
  Maumee, OH 43537
  Phone 419.893.2400
  Fax 419.893.2491

OPPORTUNITY REFERENCE

Contract Employment Agencies

B&M ASSOCIATES

E-mail: resume@bmanet.com

- B&M offers opportunities in engineering, information systems, design/drafting, manufacturing, administration, technical writing, and multimedia. B&M Associates have many offices. Contact the corporate headquarters for an office near you.

  B&M ASSOCIATES
  Corporate Headquarters
  18 Commerce Way, Suite 5000
  Woburn, MA 01801-1006
  Phone 800.487.2967 617.938.9120
  Fax 617.932.3930

BASELINE ENGINEERING

E-mail: baseline@ble.com

- Baseline offers opportunities in engineering, information systems, design/drafting, manufacturing, production support, technical writing, and computer programming.

  BASELINE ENGINEERING
  1046 West Taylor, Suite 200
  San Jose, CA 95126
  Phone 408.243.7700
  Fax 408.243.0384

OPPORTUNITY REFERENCE

Contract Employment Agencies

CDI CORPORATION

E-mail: cdihq@voicenet.com

- CDI is one of the largest contract employment agencies in the country. They have offices scattered throughout the United States. They offer employment in many technical areas. Contact the corporate headquarters for an office near you.

  CDI CORPORATION
  Corporate Headquarters
  1717 Arch Street, 35th Floor
  Philadelphia, PA 19103-2768
  Phone 800.562.5463
  Fax 800.684.6838

INTERIM SERVICES, INC.

Website http://www.interim.com

- Interim Services, Inc. is a leading staffing service provider with 700 offices in North America, Europe and Asia. It provides staffing and consulting solutions in technology, legal, accounting, human resources, job search and outplacement, clerical, administrative and light industrial.

  Interim Technology
  Corporate Headquarters
  823 Commerce Drive
  Oak Brook, IL 60521
  Phone 888.948.6252
  Fax 630.574.3076

OPPORTUNITY REFERENCE

Contract Employment Agencies

MANPOWER TECHNICAL
Website http://www.manpower.com

- Manpower Technical is a division of Manpower International, Inc. Manpower is the world's largest contract employer with offices in 38 countries. Manpower has opportunities in a variety of technical positions. Contact the corporate headquarters for an office near you.

  MANPOWER TECHNICAL
  Corporate Headquarters
  5301 North Ironwood, Department D1
  P.O. Box 20533
  Milwaukee, WI 53201
  Phone 800.558.6992 414.961.1000
  Fax 414.961.7336

WESTERN TECHNICAL
Website http://www.westaff.com

- Western Technical offers technical opportunities in computer aided design, computer operations, data control, lab technicians, and a host of others. Western Technical has many offices throughout the country. Contact the corporate headquarters for an office near you.

  WESTERN TECHNICAL
  Corporate Headquarters
  301 Lennon Lane, P.O. Box 9280
  Walnut Creek, CA 94598
  Phone 800.872.8367 510.930.5300
  Fax 510.934.5489

OPPORTUNITY REFERENCE

Material In Print

Are you working presently or would like to become employed in another city or perhaps another state? Adams Media Publications prints a series of books that detail the job market in a number of larger populated areas of the country. These books are published every year and can provide you with a picture in time of the job market in the area in which you are interested. Subsequent research can then be done by acquiring the classified advertising section of their local newspapers for up-to-date information. The titles of the Adams Media Publications include:

The Atlanta Job Bank
The Austin / San Antonio Job Bank
The Boston Job Bank
The Carolina Job Bank
The Chicago Job Bank
The Cincinnati Job Bank
The Cleveland Job Bank
The Dallas-Fort Worth Job Bank
The Denver Job Bank
The Detroit Job Bank
The Florida Job Bank
The Houston Job Bank
The Indianapolis Job Bank
The Las Vegas Job Bank
The Los Angeles Job Bank
The Missouri Job Bank
The Northern New England Job Bank
The New Mexico Job Bank
The Pittsburgh Job Bank
The Metropolitan New York Job Bank
The Phoenix Job Bank
The Portland Job Bank
The Upstate New York Job Bank
The Seattle Job Bank
The Tennessee Job Bank
The Greater Philadelphia Job Bank
The Virginia Job Bank
The San Francisco Job Bank
The Metropolitan Washington D.C. Job Bank

OPPORTUNITY REFERENCE

Material In Print

The Great Jobs Ahead

by

Harry S. Dent Jr.

A Hyperion Publication

A comprehensive guide to surviving and prospering in the coming work revolution.

Temp By Choice

by

Diane Thrailkill

A Career Press Publication

A guide to temporary employment agencies and benefits of working as a contract employee.

When It's Time To Look

"Being entirely honest with oneself is a good exercise."
Sigmund Freud

When is it time to begin your search for another job? With some helpful hints from this segment, it should become clearer. The quote from the renowned Austrian psychoanalyst, Sigmund Freud, was used to remind the reader to be honest with himself when the signs are present. What signs, you ask? Signs that you should begin your search for another job. As I have stated in other chapters, you should always be looking for a better job. Looking, not necessarily because of discomfort where you are presently, nor because of dissatisfaction with what you are doing, but be prompted by the desire to continually improve your lot in life. There is no need for you to leave a job because you think there will be no problems on other jobs. Each setting has its own unique set of quirks that can drive you up a wall. It becomes a matter of what you can tolerate and for how much money. I can tolerate a lot of headaches for a lot of money. I am not willing to tolerate a lot of headaches for an amount I feel is not commensurate with the responsibility, nor should you. In addition, looking for another job does not necessarily mean leaving one company for another. It can entail looking for a different position within the same company or business.

The search should begin long before the final decision is made to leave. From my 25 years of experience, in conjunction with input from knowledgeable supervisory personnel, I have compiled what we have collectively decided are significant signs of impending adversity. They are not being offered as the only signs to be looking for. It would be ludicrous for me to claim a "know-it-all" status within the limited print space allotted to me. It is not humanly possible to state every cause or reason to begin the search for another job. One should not have as a philosophy, "I'll leave if things get rough." Sometimes a little patience and persuasion can bring about a change. Leaving the job should not be the first resort but the last. Having said that, there are all sorts of variations and combinations that can give you the same message: it's time to leave.

A POOR APPRAISAL OR PERFORMANCE REVIEW

It is customary in some business circles to provide each employee with a regularly-scheduled review of his performance. This review can take place on an annual or semi-annual basis and is usually conducted by the person who directly supervises you. The verbiage on these reviews differs very little from one company to the next. You are usually given the opportunity to rate your own performance in a number of categories. You are also asked to reveal your weaknesses as well as your areas of strength. One must be creative when describing to one's boss how one is weak in certain areas. This is self-incrimination at its best. You are asked to rate yourself in the categories which may appear in a vertical column. Typical categories are, **Gets Assignments Done On Time, Anticipates and Receives Instructions, Provides Useful Input, Works Well With Others, etc.**

Along the horizontal axis are the ratings. They may appear as: **Outstanding, Meets or Exceeds Requirements, Adequate, Needs Improvement, Poor Performance,** etc. Do not give your boss ammunition to use against you. He must rate you in the same categories as you have rated yourself. Give yourself a good overall rating.

A poor review or appraisal, in itself, is not enough to prompt you to begin your search for employment elsewhere. A serious disagreement with your boss on your appraisal can bring about friction. This can and often does happen. This is especially true when your boss hasn't a clue as to what you do. It becomes evident when he asks you, "What do you do all day? You don't look that busy to me! I want you to write down your daily activities and keep a log." There are many things that can take place behind the scenes when an assignment is given. They may not always be visible to the casual observer. Nonetheless, they must be accomplished first before the main tasks can be taken on. "The fruit must be peeled before it is eaten. Peeling the fruit doesn't count." The originator of this quote is unknown.

For example, take an administrative assistant who is given the task of making travel reservations for his boss. The location to which this person is traveling is also hosting a convention. This fact is unknown to the boss. Moreover, he doesn't care. It may take several hours for the administrative assistant to arrange travel accommodations that meet the stringent requirements of his boss. In this case and ones similar, the peeling of the fruit can be quite difficult. Let's say you are given a last minute assignment. It involves making presentation materials for a meeting that is to take place the next day. This is no ordinary presentation. It is comprised of 147 pages, all in color. It just happens to be 4:00 PM and the color laser printer is out of toner. Not every office supply store supplies this special cartridge. Not to be outdone, you drive across town to buy the cartridge. You stayed extra late to complete all of the color transparencies. The presentation goes on without an impediment.

These are the sort of unseen events that are true to life and exemplify the notion of "things going on behind the scenes." Everyone wants to be appreciated for what they do. Even though this appraisal is subjective, it has a direct bearing on the compensation that you may be receiving in the future. The compensation is the reason we go to work. When you have done your absolute best and receive an unsatisfactory appraisal or review that is not satisfactory, it is time to look. There are, of course, exceptions to this. If you have been in place for a period of time and your boss is new to the location, time must be allotted to allow for his proper evaluation of you. A proper time period may be six months to a year. It is expected that a new boss will defer an evaluation until a sufficient amount of time has passed. Your new boss can also draw on the records left by the previous one and come to a conclusion as to what to expect from you. Your appraisals should be a permanent part of your work history. By law, you are allowed to view them.

CHRONIC INADEQUATE COMPENSATION

Working for free, without some sort of compensation, is not virtuous. It should be avoided in the same manner as accepting government assistance as a way of life. A person should be paid for his labor. A contradictory tone has not been sounded here. This author wrote earlier that offering to work for free could be used as a method of convincing an owner or manager of a business to hire you. This was giving of your time and effort as a means to gain employment in a case where you would otherwise not be considered. Working for free is not the same thing as volunteering your labor as a good will gesture.

Most of us work for one purpose and one purpose only, the money. We therefore expect to receive that monetary reward which is fair and just. What is considered fair and just differs from person to person.

There are few things that can be as disheartening as not being adequately compensated for your efforts. This is very common: someone is being paid more or the same as you and they do not perform as well. If the person is a colleague with whom you are friendly, you may choose to ignore the situation. In cases where the relationship is not a close one, it may be intolerable. The question becomes, how do you get more money? You must make your case in terms which your management can understand. What you do not want, and should not accept, is the run around or flimsy excuses. If you are represented by a union, your compensation is determined by the contract. Trying to get an unscheduled raise could be an exercise in futility. Your chances of getting a raise are much better in instances where you are an [At Will] employee. A strategy must be developed, a plan "A," a plan "B," and perhaps a plan "C," all revolving around what you are going to do if you do not get your increase.

How do monetary differences break down? On a 40-hour work week schedule, a one dollar an hour raise amounts to a 40-dollar-a-week raise. Fifty cents an hour amounts to a 20-dollar-a-week raise. Does the thought of someone making 40 dollars a week more than you ruffle your feathers? Only you can answer that. In a real sense, it depends on how much you are presently earning. I counsel people in this manner. There will always be someone making more money than you, whether they deserve it or not. The issue must be narrowed down to differences in the compensation in terms of thousands of dollars, not hundreds. My attitude about this was placed in its proper perspective because of my love for sports and the insane salaries that athletes receive.

I include entertainers in this group also. Nonetheless, it is common to find an athlete in a particular sport earning several million less than someone with similar statistics. Now that is something to make a fuss over! This cannot be stated where the athletes are compensated with prize money. Professional golfers, track & field, tennis players, (pool and bowling are not sports), come to mind. In these cases, it is truly a pay-for-performance type of compensation. They are rewarded according to how well they perform.

If someone is making $20,000 more than you, that is a case requiring attention. The greater the disparity in terms of thousands of dollars, the more you had better scream for adjustments. If adjustments are not forthcoming or promises are made of something being done at a later date, it is time to look. Discretion should be exercised in some cases. There are instances when a company could be in financial difficulties and all spending is severely curtailed. A pay increase may be construed as not being in the best interest of the company. You know that your request for increased compensation has hit a brick wall when your boss begins to complain about not receiving his raise or bonus. There are instances where a company or business just cannot afford to pay any more for labor than what they are paying.

In either case, you have to make a decision. We all have options and it is better to leave a company or business rather than to remain there and be a disgruntled employee. Being disgruntled affects your attitude towards your employer and colleagues. Your **"attitude"** will always affect your **"performance."** There are a couple of good questions you have to ask yourself. They are, "How much will it take for me to leave?" and "What are the benefits of staying?" The increased wages received at a new job could be offset by a longer distance to travel to work. A longer distance can also translate into a longer workday.

TRUE STORY

I recently became involved in a situation where an employee of one of my clients requested a pay increase. I was familiar with the work that the employee was performing and the job requirements. In order to protect the identity of the individual, he will be referred to as "George." I was asked by the department's manager to provide input as to whether an increase was merited. He provided me with George's employment history, which included a chronology of past pay increases. I had a closed door meeting with George as a neutral observer. I let it be known that I was without bias and had no interest other than that of mediator. "Make your case for a raise," were the words I spoke to him. He began by making a comparison of his performance and the wages paid to his predecessor. His next point was that yearly increases were the norm (George made an assumption here) and it had been a year since his last increase.

When he had finished, it was time to burst his bubble. He was not going to receive an increase. After examining all the data that was before me, I determined that the rate he was being paid was adequate. I am quite sure he thought his reasons for requesting an increase were valid. Although he was a good employee, he was not the most skillful in the department. An increase was not merited merely because of time since the last one. Furthermore, it was not his place to tell management how to run the company. If he felt that he was being treated unfairly, I would understand and support his decision to leave.

It was true that his predecessor was paid more, but that person was overpaid. For clarity's sake, this overpaid person will be referred to as "Frank." Frank applied pressure to management for more money in the middle of a very important project. It was the thinking of managers that Frank would quit if his demands were not met. The project would have been placed in jeopardy. I was asked to give them a recommendation and I plainly stated that it was imperative to retain him at that time. After the project was completed, I would present to them alternative options for Frank's replacement. Placing management in a position of "Give it to me or else," is not a good thing. It often backfires. In Frank's case, it did.

NO ROOM FOR ADVANCEMENT

This is not a hard one to uncover. When you inquire with company officials or a business owner how you fit into their long-range plans for the business and they have no answer, it's time to make plans. It should be quite obvious to anyone who is paying attention what the possibilities are for advancement. This is especially true in small companies or businesses. Take a look. If all the slots are filled, then there is no place to go without someone either quitting, being terminated, or some expansion taking place within that entity. You should always be looking towards the next step. That is what will help to keep you motivated. Management uses the prospects of forward movement as a tool to keep the best workers enthusiastic about their jobs. Some have referred to this as dangling the carrot in front of you. If there are 10 people qualified and vying for one promotional slot, it stands to reason that there will be many disappointed individuals. They all could make the case for the promotion. Management will then give the proper signals that you could be the next one to get promoted. The key words here are "could be." You may not mind playing this game when you are younger, but when one gets older, one becomes less tolerant of these types of games. What really determines who will get the promotion is covered in the section entitled **"Politics."** When you are not moving forward, you are not merely standing still, you are going backwards.

NO ATTENTION BEING PAID TO THE THINGS THAT CONCERN YOU

There is perhaps nothing that concerns employees more than money. After all, that is why most of us work. For companies and small businesses where the monetary compensation is not meted out at regular intervals, an employee has to rely upon the word of his supervision or the owner. Promises are made all the time about when you will receive an increase in pay. When working for the [job shops] many years ago, we made it a practice of getting our raise when we came in the door to start working. There was no guarantee of anything else. A promise is only as good as the person making it. Occasionally, a promise will be made in good faith but circumstances beyond a person's control will prevent the fulfillment of the promise. However, if you are constantly being put off and given an assortment of reasons why you have not received or will not be getting a raise, take that as a visible sign to start looking.

This also applies to the promises made concerning perks and equipment that enhances job performance. Those are promises like:

- Being the next one to get an office, moving from a cubical.
- Being the next one allowed to go on vacation.
- Being the next one to get a new computer or peripheral.
- Getting a piece of equipment repaired or replaced.

They are acting as if what you are doing is not important until they are in need of your output.

EXTERNAL PRESSURES

These are not the normal types of pressures that come with almost every job. They are things that affect your quality of life at home. A person can withstand a lot of turmoil on the job as long as they have peace in their home. When the quality of life at home is stricken and begins to suffer, one should carefully contemplate what one's next action is going to be. Nothing affects the quality of home life as much as a traveling spouse. A husband and wife are a team. When one of the team members is absent, the other has to pick up the slack. There are usually things that men attend to in a household that are separate from those of the women. Both genders are capable of doing each other's tasks, but it becomes a matter of what they are comfortable doing. Anyone who has traveled a great deal on behalf of his job, can attest to the fact that it is not always pleasant. Especially when the children and/or spouse is left at home. There you are:

- Sleeping in a bed that is not your own, and an uncomfortable one at that.
- Eating food that is not always prepared the way you like it.
- Having to focus on the job at hand, while being mindful of home.
- Getting calls from your spouse reporting that something isn't working properly.
- Getting calls from your kids reminding you of their game or musical that you promised to attend (kids do not forget those things).

All this while having to deal with people who are not cooperating. Add to this, a boss who is chastising you because you are staying longer than was expected. Forget the fact that the longer stay was required to ensure that all was done properly. What is foremost in the boss' mind is the expense report that you will turn in. So what if you stayed over a weekend? What does your boss think, that you were having fun? Your boss never commented about the outcome nor was he able to comprehend what it took to get the job done. What the boss continues to focus on is the fact that you stayed longer than was expected. That can be extremely disheartening. When you return home, you get the report from your spouse of all the things that went wrong. Each child had after-school activities that required a parent or guardian to get them there. Normally, you would assist with the ferrying of the children. However, the job demanded that you be somewhere else. Your spouse wants to know how much more traveling you expect to do. This kind of thing can reek havoc on a marriage. The spouse may be torn between the career advance that may be ahead and his or her family.

YOUR WORK IS CONTINUALLY BEING GIVEN TO SOMEONE ELSE

In the building that houses one of my clients, there are several administrative assistants. I came to befriend one admin in particular because of her outgoing nature. After being employed with a company for a little over a year, she was summarily dismissed. Not being familiar with her work habits, I made inquiries with some of the other admins who knew her. I asked, "Why did they fire Betty?" (That is not her real name) This reply came from a very well seasoned and insightful admin: "What was wrong with her, that she couldn't see the signs that her last days were eminent? Her boss was having his work done by all the other admins in the building. He didn't care which one, as long as it wasn't Betty. Betty was content to sit at her desk all day and play solitaire on the computer."

She was absolutely correct in her assessment of the situation. Betty should have been discerning enough to recognize that something was wrong, even though her boss wouldn't tell her so. Her boss should have been respectful enough to inform her of his displeasure with how she was performing. Since he didn't, Betty should have taken charge of the situation and made inquiries. Betty was not merely dismissed. It was a dismissal in the rudest of manners. She was told at 2:00 p.m. that she was fired and to be out of the building by 3:00 p.m. There was no time given for her to make alternate arrangements. Moreover, I doubt she would make use of her previous employer as a reference. That was not a good thing.

INTERNAL PRESSURES

I'll give a real-life example of what internal pressures are. A new Coney Island-type restaurant opened very close to my client's office. The decor and its location have an attraction that is difficult to resist. It is owned by a very well-known family and part of a chain. I, along with some other gentlemen, decided to go there for lunch. We arrived early to avoid the noon time rush. To say that the service was poor would be a gross understatement. We waited for 45 minutes to get our orders and then they were wrong when we received them. Deciding to forget having them returned to the kitchen for correction, we returned to the office hungry. In protest, one of the gentlemen refused to leave a tip. I talked him out of it. I explained to him that the waitress was not responsible for the cooks' mistakes. She wrote down exactly what was asked for and was totally dependent upon the competence of the cooks to place the correct order on each plate.

Looking at the numbers of people who were in the restaurant for lunch and given the size of the restaurant, only the most organized staff could have contended with the crowd and done well. I am quite sure that we were not the only patrons who were disappointed. A passing statement by the manager was enough to confirm that he knew there were problems. It had to do with the momentary popularity of the restaurant. After the lunch time peak, the traffic was normal. However, patrons usually take out their anger on the individual they see as a representative of the establishment. Because some wait staff at restaurants depend upon gratuities to supplement their wages, they can be made to suffer because of a poor performance from someone else.

In this example, what is the waitress to do? She is the one receiving the dirty looks and complaints of "Waitress, where's my food?" No doubt she has asked the cooks to pay closer attention to the orders because a number of them have been wrong. I would guess that the cooks do not care. They are bombarded with food orders and if some are wrong, so be it. What will complaints to the manager do for the waitress? Nothing. Good cooks are harder to find than wait personnel. Is this example, and scenario, realistic? You bet it is! This waitress would fare better at a restaurant where the lunch time crowd is more sedate and upscale. The meals would most likely cost a bit more but her gratuity would be larger. The patrons would be in less of a hurry. The waitress can take her time and treat the customers with more cordiality. The cooks could take more time to get the orders right. The waitress would no be longer be looked upon with disdain. Now she is a great waitress.

You know when you are not receiving the support that is needed to get the job done. Requests have been made by you to acquire a new piece of equipment or a replacement part, is perhaps, additional labor to help with the load, etc. All requests have fallen upon deaf ears. This occurs very often when companies are in cost-cutting modes. Managers are looking for all kinds of ways to reduce the costs of doing business. In some cases, it could be a matter of trying to "one up" the next guy, so they can receive praises from the boss. The law of diminishing returns comes into effect. You can reduce costs only so much and still function properly. If the boss is rewarded in proportion to the amount of money he saves, it is not in his personal interest to make the work place better for you if it involves spending money. This is the sort of politics that is difficult for a worker to deal with.

If reports are not out on time, projects are not completed, and performance quotas are not met, your management is more than willing to allow you to take the blame. However, they'll step to the front to receive credit for the good things that are done. What about a boss who is fond of assessing blame when he should be focusing his attention on fixing the problem? These types are every workers' nightmare. I recall a boss who was a design room supervisor at General Motors who would not allow his staff to take the blame for errors and mistakes. His philosophy was, "I'm in charge. If something goes wrong, it is because I didn't give good directions." He was a rare individual indeed, not looking to save his own skin.

These examples, and variations of them, can be applied to many situations. One should expect to bear the burden of blame when things go wrong and one is in charge. When you are made to be responsible for things that go wrong and do not have the authority to make corrections, it can be extremely frustrating. It borders on being nonsensical. Changes must occur in cases such as these because your performance can diminish as well as the monetary compensation related to it.

DIVERGING INTERESTS

What does "diverging interests" mean? It describes a change in the employment picture. The change could be brought on by a merger, or a retirement of an individual who had your best interest at heart. This describes the situation I faced at General Motors prior to making my decision to depart. When I was first employed by G. M., my best interest and theirs coincided. What was good for the company was also good for me. Due to the pressures brought on by the influx of foreign automobiles, G. M. had to enact measures that would make it more competitive. General Motors was then, and still is, the highest cost producer of passenger vehicles. It had to reduce the man-hours it took to produce a vehicle and reduce the numbers of employees on its payroll. At the same time, G. M. was faced with dwindling market share. Assembly plants were closed to consolidate production, thus reducing costs. Divisions that were not directly related to automobile production were sold. There was also a merger that eliminated many promotional opportunities.

Sensing the change in the wind, I could see that G. M.'s best interest and mine no longer coincided. What was good for them was no longer good for me. The divergence began. There was a merger of two divisions. The new division had a different philosophy and the new culture was one that was difficult to adjust to. My objectives and the strategies that I had developed to reach those objectives endured a major setback. What was clear to me was the fact that I had to leave my comfort zone (working for G. M. is comforting) and find a new place of employment and a new comfort zone. When there are mergers or takeovers, the core values of a company or business can change. It can go from being people-oriented to profit-oriented. In certain businesses, it is solely the people who make the company or business profitable and not a product. This is true of any service industry. It is the quality of the people who are employed that make the difference.

LACK OF ENTHUSIASM FOR YOUR WORK

Do you dread Monday mornings because you must return to work? Are paydays and Fridays all you look forward to? Is it your belief that just good enough is good enough? Maybe it's time for you to find another job. You are going to spend the majority of your life working. Why not be doing something that you like or even love to do? All it takes is work. Work at finding what it is that you would like to do that, at the same time, will afford you sufficient income. Your lack of enthusiasm can be driven by constantly being given work that is beneath your capabilities. It is not only a matter of the money you are being paid. You want some satisfaction from the work you're doing. For instance, you could perform the most mundane tasks and be successful. However, you want to be used in a manner that is fitting. The menial tasks your boss gives you is almost insulting.

I am mindful of the dreadful experiences of one administrative assistant who was one heck of a worker. She was expected to service a staff of 10, seven engineers and three managers. To begin with, this was an impossible task. It was made even more difficult after being inundated with mundane tasks such as faxing documents, mailing letters, and making photocopies. The fact of the matter was that these men walked by the fax machine and mail drop-off on their way to her desk. They could have just as easily done it themselves and would not have had to wait. Each of these men acted as though the administrative assistant was dedicated solely to him, and his work was all she had to do. The woman became a nervous wreck because her overall performance suffered greatly. My advice to her was to begin the search for another job. She had the skills necessary to land another one quickly. That is exactly what she did and she was successful!

I whole heartedly agree with Dr. Edward Deming, the author of *The Deming Principals of Quality.* He stated that "work should be fun." Donald Englehoff was an employee whom I had the pleasure of working with in one engineering group. Don was labeled as an idiot, malcontent, and a loafer. He was none of those. He was, however, somewhat disrespectful to our boss, behavior that I did not condone. Don was a very bright individual and demonstrated his ingenuity and analytical skills when presented with a difficult problem. Don was bored and disgruntled because he felt that he was not being used in a manner fitting his abilities. At the time, there was not much that could be done as far as transfers were concerned. Eventually, Don went to work for another boss and there was an unbelievable transformation in his outlook. He told me that he got along great with his new boss and loved his job. All he needed was a change of workplace.

I know what it is to have a job that you love doing most of the time. As a Development and Test Engineer for the now defunct Cadillac Motor Car Company, I truly loved my job. The work was important and the support I had from my management was tremendous. Those people allowed me to fly (figuratively speaking) and I paid them with jobs that were well done. There were some days when I would rather have been somewhere else. Those days were few and far in between. The hardest thing that I had to do in the morning was get out of bed. Once at work, it was time to have some fun. It should make perfectly good sense that a job that is liked will be performed better. When you no longer have that zeal for what you do, why waste precious time. Remember, all you have on this earth is time and not a great deal of it. Make the best use of it. Find a job that you like doing.

PROBLEMS WITH YOUR BOSS

It is with a great deal of experience that I can write of problems with the boss. Always keep this in mind. No matter what the problem, **NEVER, EVER, BURN A BRIDGE BEHIND YOU!** You never know when you may have to re-cross that bridge. Making disparaging remarks about your boss is tantamount to bridge burning. When you are being treated with disrespect by your boss, it is fitting and proper to have a person to person meeting with him. Not to berate him, but to express your concerns regarding his treatment of you. One administrative assistant recounted to me the statement that her boss made to her. He said that he had higher expectations for her than she had for herself. That was quite an insult when you think about it. How did he know what expectations she had for herself, having never asked her?

You can become entangled in the inter-company business squabbles that involve other people. It is your expectation that your boss will back you up and not retreat when the going gets a little rough. The accusations begin to go around in a vicious circle with no end in sight. All you want is some support from your boss. He is sending conflicting messages to everyone, including you, by remaining silent. You are being told one thing while persons in other areas are being told a different story altogether. You are thinking, "It shouldn't be this hard to get a job done." When your boss will not stick up for you, it is time to look around for something else because he will not fight to get you a raise either.

It is also tough to maintain the proper attitude when you are constantly hounded by your boss. What is worse than a boss who doesn't plan things well? It is a boss who plans everything at the last minute. The poor planning on his part has now become an emergency on your part. After all, he have you to bail him out. You have become the fireman who has to constantly put out the fires that he creates. This type of boss adds a lot of stress to your life and can sometimes cause you to harbor bad feeling towards him. It is Friday afternoon and you have your Saturday all planned. Your entire family is looking forward to an outing. It just happens that it is going to be a beautiful day, one of only a few. Here comes the boss with another last minute emergency that requires you to come in on Saturday. What are you going to do? Refusing to work is not a good thing!

I have had several administrative assistants tell me what upsets them the most is being asked to do things that fall nowhere within their job description. Number one on that list was going to get the boss coffee. Taking care of the boss's personal matters such as picking up his laundry from the cleaners, running errands for him on their lunch hour, and making purchases with their own money, came in a close second. That is one of the reasons why a job description is so important. It removes most of the ambiguity concerning what is and what is not your responsibility. Most of the tasks mentioned here can be placed under one heading, a lack of consideration.

Behavior becomes ingrained in humans and as we age, it is more difficult to change the way we behave. When asked to do something that makes you feel queasy, you would like to say no but there is the underlying feeling that you will fall into disfavor with your boss if you do not do it. That makes for a very uncomfortable working environment. Rather than make a fuss about doing these menial tasks, plan your escape. You must plan a strategy to escape. The word escape sounds harsh but that is exactly what you must do.

"My boss doesn't listen to me." How many times have I heard this statement? Too many to number. There are very few people who choose not to give input into the daily affairs of their workplace. I tend to think that those who give no input do not care about the work they're performing. When you care, there is pain involved. You want to be listened to. Moreover, you want your suggestions and concerns to be addressed. When it appears that you are not being listened to, it makes you feel less important. We all need to feel that we are needed, thus reinforcing the notion that we have value.

I counsel in this manner. Do not become so concerned that your attitude and job performance is affected. The boss is still the boss and he does not have to react immediately or positively to your suggestions or concerns. As a consultant, I am paid for my advice and the direction I give. I make sure that the information I receive is reliable so that my output will be equally as reliable. I have told some bosses point blank what should or should not be done. Sometimes they adhere to my suggestions and at other times they do not. When an event occurs as I foretold, nothing need be said by me to reinforce the notion that I was right. They know it. However, they chose to reject my advice and that is their privilege. That is what I am paid to do, offer advice and direction. It is not cast in stone that they have to listen to me. Refrain from taking this type of rejection personally. It is a sign for you to begin your search for another job.

The regular workday is bad enough with your boss piling the work on you. You do not mind working hard. You prefer that your boss set the example and work hard also. It becomes difficult for you to take your boss seriously when he has his feet up upon his desk while rehashing his golf game. At the same time, you are told how behind the department is, how much work there is to do. Your boss says to you, "We all have to pitch in and do a little more." On the other hand, your boss realizes that you are constantly bailing him out of jams. Your reward, a nice merit increase or bonus. That had better be the case. If not, start looking. Gratuitous pats on the back should not cut any mustard with you.

How about this one? You are never given the entire story on anything, just spoon-fed pieces of information as your boss feels you need it. What happens? You get to a point when a decision has to be made and your boss is nowhere to be found. Something has to be done. You are now in a very precarious position because if you do nothing, there is the possibility of error for lack of action. If you do something, there also exists the possibility of doing the wrong thing. What was wrong with your boss giving you the background and providing you with "what if" scenarios? The answer to this question is, nothing! By handing you only bits of information, your ability to think for yourself is hindered.

Why wouldn't a boss want his employee to be able to think for himself? The answer to this question can range anywhere from being insecure, to being a bad boss. When something goes wrong, (it usually does when information is not disseminated) you are left feeling incompetent. You have every confidence in your abilities to handle workplace problems. However, your boss has a convenient scapegoat to blame for mistakes, you. He will not fire you or have you transferred. That will require him replacing you with someone else, someone who will not endure being made to feel incompetent. If it sounds like I have been there, it is because I have.

Another tactic that is common is management having one employee in conflict with another. The reason why is not as important as the solution to the problem. Two people cannot share a computer, a desk, and other items that are normally thought of as exclusive to one person, not if they expect to get their work done. Peripherals, such as a printer, a copier, a fax machine, a stapler, etc., can be shared because they are seldom used, therefore not considered to be exclusive. When the duties of worker "A" depend upon the execution of the duties of person "B," that in itself can present a problem. One administrative assistant was responsible for compiling a month end report for her department. Her boss suggested that she work through lunch and stay late in order to have the report done by the next morning.

It seems her boss promised the higher-ups that it would be done. All would have been fine except for the fact that her computer was marginal at best. It was on its last leg and could not handle the massive software package used to generate the report. The computer technician who could have given her aid was working on another task that this same boss had given him. Yes, a deadline came with that task, too. Frantic cries for help were made to the technician, "Peter (not his real name) is going to have my butt in a sling if I don't have this report done on time. You could take ten minutes to help me."

"I can't stop and help you. That's not a ten-minute job. You're having file conflicts that will take a long time to fix." On and on the conversation went, with tempers escalating. Here you had two employees, both eager to perform and please their boss, but they were pitted against each other. The report was rendered on time but with great anguish. The problem with the computer was revealed to her boss many weeks prior to this incident. His reply, "Work with what you've got."

This boss had high expectations but would not provide the proper tools with which to work. There are many others like this. Why tolerate these kinds of behaviors if you do not have to? You can certainly "Find a Better Job" if the **"Preparations"** have been made to do so.

TRUE STORY

All of us have personalities that differ. At times, these differing personalities bring us into conflict with other people. Such was the case with one of the bosses I had. This person, who shall remain nameless, was on my case from the start of work to the end of the workday. There was no pleasing him, even though I tried earnestly. As I look back on the situation, it was not his fault that I did not meet his expectations nor was it my fault that he was somewhat unreasonable. At the heart of the matter was a serious personality clash. We were from two totally different backgrounds and ideological perspectives. It was incumbent upon me to find a way from under his supervision without upsetting anyone.

I made an appointment to see his boss. I made sure that it was after returning from vacation. I could be confident that he would be in a benevolent frame of mind. I explained to this executive that Thomas (a fictitious name) was an excellent employee and was quite knowledgeable in the matters that concerned our department. He was an employee who had over 25 years of experience. It was not a good strategy to go in complaining that Thomas didn't know what he was doing. I further explained that we were having a personality conflict that was causing us both a great deal of discomfort on the job. The company was not getting the best output from either of us. When you go in to a boss with a problem, always have a solution. He has enough people giving him problems to solve. He will be more receptive to your verbiage when you have a solution or possible solution.

In this case, I had found an opening in another section of this executive's department. He would not be losing my services. I paved the way by asking the supervisor in that department if he would allow me to become a part of his group. He was very receptive to this proposal. Best of all, there was nothing he had to do, as in filling out paperwork. The executive was also receptive to this idea and further elaborated that there was a time in his career when he had a boss that he did not get along with. I would like to believe that I was successful in this case because I did not indulge in name calling and made no disparaging remarks about my supervisor. I could have possibly burned several bridges had I proceeded in that manner.

CONFLICTS WITH A CO-WORKER WHO HAS BECOME YOUR BOSS

Not everyone gets along on every job despite all of the sensitivity training that has gone on for several years. Let's face it, some people do not like others for all sorts of reasons. Trying to force them to get along only makes matters worse. Minus some heartfelt religious experiences, there are going to be some people who will abhor the very air you breath. I have seen bitter enemies work in the same area for many years. It makes everyone uncomfortable. It becomes your worst nightmare when this person now becomes your boss. One of three things may happen. He may want to keep you in his department to make your life miserable, he may have you transferred to a department of his choosing, or you may opt to leave on your own and find a spot for yourself. The latter is the preferred and smart choice. Don't even think about staying around!

GENDER BIAS AND LACK OF RESPECT

You can tell when your boss does not respect you. His body language can reveal it. Does your boss walk away from you when are you trying to talk him? Does he fail to look up from his desk when you are in a conversation with him? Does he refer to you as "girl?" If so, you have a dinosaur for a boss. It is usually male bosses who are of a certain age and era who cannot handle the influx of women or minorities into the workplace. The disrespect can run deeper than vulgar jokes and sexual innuendo. At its heart is a contempt for your gender. The good news is that these types of men are being rapidly removed from our workplace. You know when you are being insulted and demeaned. One administrative assistant was constantly being referred to as "My girl" by her boss. This woman was a middle-aged mother of three. She was hardly a girl. This was a term that was used in a pejorative sense to enforce his dominion over her. Sometimes a simple heart-to-heart talk with your boss can correct things of this nature.

Despite the gains that have been made in the last decade, the treatment of men and women in the workplace is not equal. The differences in pay and treatment are more noticeable in jobs where the educational prerequisites are less important. Although I am not a fierce advocate of organized labor, unions do tend to bring an equalization of treatment and pay among male and female workers. In some occupations, women are constantly having to prove themselves because their competence is not assumed as it is with men. When things reach a point where you can no longer tolerate what is going on, make the only right decision. Rather than make a bad name for yourself by being labeled a troublemaker, it is more beneficial to you as an individual to leave the company or business. Seek employment elsewhere. Easier said than done? Of course it isn't easy. If it were easy, everyone would do it. The good things in life seldom come easily. They come through hard work and perseverance.

If respect is a byproduct of authority, then the lack of authority means there will be no respect. This happens with jobs that one would call token positions. You have the title but lack the authority. If you are paid a considerable amount of money, perhaps being in a token position does not matter to you. However, bear in mind that if the token position carries no real authority, there is no real need for the position. If there is no real need for the position, the job can be taken away as easily as it was placed before you. This means a great deal when you are not being paid a large amount of money and there are no contractual employment agreements.

RACIAL, ETHNIC OR CULTURAL BIAS

There is nothing inferior or superior about any person of any gender of any race, due to their birth. There is a theory that if all people are afforded the same opportunities, most will excel at the same level. That is assuming there are no external forces promoting one while demoting another. To my knowledge, I have never been discriminated against in the workplace. That is not to say that discrimination does not take place. The question becomes, "How are you going to handle it?" What steps will you take to remedy the situation that you are in? Some conflicts that are labeled as discrimination and reported to the Equal Opportunity Commission as such, are nothing more than personal conflicts. They are conflicts that transcend race, color, creed, or nationality. In a perfect world, there would be no discrimination. One cannot allow discrimination to be used as an excuse for not succeeding.

No excuse is good enough for not putting forth the effort to succeed. If enough effort is put forth, a job can be found where the employer has no concern about your race, ethnicity, or handicaps. All he wants to know is, "Can you produce for them?" I stress this fact, there is always someone willing to pay you for what you know. You must find him. Don't wait for him to find you. Do not harbor bitterness nor condemn entire races of people because of the actions of a few or one. Focus your energies towards obtaining a better job.

THRIVING ON CHAOS

Order and disorder cannot co-exist. There are those individuals who seek after and pursue a more perfect way. They are not perfect but they pursue perfection. They are some of the most misunderstood people around. Those who converse with them come away with the false impression of superiority. They love knowledge, seek after it whole-heartedly and have little or no tolerance for those having opinions that are contrary. Those with this frame of mind find it difficult to work in environments where the staffs routinely conduct their business with unprofessional conduct. Confusion reigns when management, by omission or commission, ignore good suggestions on improving processes and workplace procedures.

The frustration is compounded when you make decisions based upon the knowledge you have at hand and the decision is berated. There are mishaps that could have been avoided if only your suggestions were heeded. What is ahead of you? More of the same. The company seems to thrive on chaos. If you can prosper in that setting, continue therein. If you find yourself quoting the cartoon character,

Popeye, "I had all I can stands and I can't stands no more," it's time to develop a strategy for a better job.

YOU ARE NOT AMONG THE ANOINTED

In every job, there are what I call the anointed. These are the individuals that have favor with your boss and your boss's boss. When information or news comes down the pipeline, they hear about it first. That way, they can react quickly if an action is called for. By the time you hear the news, it is old news. If there are any perks that are available such as overtime, sports tickets, theater tickets, availability of the company fleet vehicle, they are at the front of the line. The anointed are the exceptions to the rules and regulations that companies have in place. There will be reasons why they are exempt from the rules and regulations. You are not among the anointed and have no hope of joining them. You cannot anoint yourself. Sound like sour grapes? Not really. Some of this cannot be helped. Everyone has their favorites and within large companies, there will be many of those who are anointed. Remember, there is no such thing as equality or equal treatment. If you are the boss and, within your group, there is a person with whom you have had a friendship for many years, there is a natural tendency to favor him. You know him well and he also knows you.

Within one of my supervisory positions, I had such a person; a person with whom I had attended many sporting events socially when we were colleagues. His father helped form my career in its infancy. This gentleman moved to California and we hadn't seen each other for 10 years. We worked well together because there was no pretending. We had a thorough understanding of our expectations of each other and I could count on him to execute my instructions when I was not present. When difficulties would arise, he would not only present me with the problem but he would offer me solutions to the problems. I wrote of these types of individuals in the chapter **"A Job Well Done."** Bosses love these kind of employees.

Generally speaking, this individual watched over things for me when I was not present. I anointed him! That is not to say that I treated the other employees as stepchildren. Quite the contrary. I made a concerted effort to make sure that they all received what was coming to them. If they presented me with disciplinary problems and/or were untrustworthy, they were held to a different standard. What is the solution? Try to become one of the anointed somewhere else. The remarkable thing is that the very person a boss would like to get rid of can be an individual another boss would like to have working for him. These differing opinions of the same person happen all the time, thus giving credence to the declarations of Dr. Edward Deming, that everyone wants to do a good job. It is up to management to find out what they are good at and motivate them.

JOB WINNING TECHNIQUES

"There is no harm done when trying and failing. There is great harm done when we fail to try."
Author Unknown

One key factor in obtaining the job of your dreams is understanding the specific needs of the employer. Obtaining this information is not difficult. All that may be required is a little research or study of the products produced or the services rendered by that company. For most job openings, the requirements are posted in the advertisements. If not posted, a phone call is the next best thing. Do not procrastinate. There are people out there looking for the same thing you are and the job is not going to wait for you.

SEND OUT RESUMES ON A REGULAR BASIS

Follow the lead of many executives and celebrities. You do not see them sitting on the stool of do-nothing. They are always looking for a better job and so should you. Many of them could do nothing and still survive off of what they have already gathered. Once you have determined what it is that you would like to do, watch intently for advertising and job postings. Visit your local bookstore and obtain out-of-state newspapers. Ignore the crime statistics and horoscopes and head for the classified ad section. Send a resume to every listing for employment that interests you. Send them to the ones that don't interest you, too. You never know what can happen. I made it a practice to send out resumes every six months to selected areas of the country where I would consider moving. I am still getting calls from faraway places. Am I bothered by this? No. That was the point of the exercise, to get a reaction. More substantive issues regarding resumes is covered in the chapter, **"Preparation."**

DO NOT OVERSTATE YOUR ABILITIES

In your zeal to get the job, do not overstate your abilities or your area of expertise. In this day and age, people with computer skills are in demand. This means that if you have on your resume that you have a working knowledge of databases, spreadsheets, presentation software, etc., your prospective employer will expect you to be able to perform at the level you claimed. You will not be afforded the time to learn those functions, nor will you be able to "wing it." Your deficiencies will be discovered shortly after you are asked to do something. There have been cases when I have given tests to those interviewing for jobs. Their resumes looked very impressive. I could not wait to add them to the staff of my clients. Giving them a test beforehand saved me from a great deal of embarrassment.

Not only were the resumes of these individuals sent to oblivion, the contract firms that recommended them were viewed in an unfavorable light thereon. The names of these people are not likely to be forgotten. It is a very small world.

THEY WHO MAIL EARLY GET THE JOBS

Have your resume ready by tailoring it to a given advertisement. Most people can take their basic resume and have it reflect various workplace experience with minor editing. Jobs often evolve into something entirely different than what they were in the beginning. Therefore, it is not deceptive to tailor a resume to suit the task at hand. When reading ads for help in Sunday newspapers, you must have a quick turn-around time in sending your resume off to the advertisers. That means the resume must be in the mail or ready to fax on Monday. When it comes to landing a job, they who mail or fax early get the jobs. You are not the only person seeking a job, nor are you the only person who has seen the posting. When my clients post an opening, they are bombarded with responses from job seekers.

If the advertisement is in a national newspaper, it is even more acute to get your resume in the mail the same day or the next. When conversing with one job seeker, she asked for advice about her resume. The job she was interested in appeared in a major Detroit Metropolitan newspaper's Sunday edition. It was Wednesday and she not only didn't have it in the mail, she didn't have it updated. Because the advertisement was posted by one of the major automobile manufacturers, it would be no stretch of the imagination to say that hundreds had already responded. Interviews were no doubt scheduled. I would say that some prospective candidates were being critiqued and the selections narrowed down to maybe four or five by Thursday. The job posting was for persons with skills that were not rare, thus increasing the likelihood of the position being filled early.

One note: some advertisements that appear in national newspapers are out of date before they arrive at the newsstands. When asked, "Would it be a good idea to subscribe to one of the national papers that only advertise jobs?" I often reply, "It can be a waste of money. By the time all the information is collected from across the nation, the post may be filled." For the common person, local newspapers from the area give a better flavor for what jobs are available.

DO NOT BECOME DISCOURAGED

You may not obtain the job of your dreams immediately. There may be rejections due to many things. One might be the stand-by answer, "You lack the experience." You may have to take a lesser-paying job to gain experience before someone will give you a job in your field of choice. Be prepared to get to your goal in an incremental manner, taking jobs that will eventually get you to your destination. You will no doubt learn a great deal with each subsequent job. The knowledge that you have gained will be invaluable. Doing this involves making use of a predetermined plan and strategy.

DON'T TAKE NO FOR AN ANSWER

"No" does not always mean "no." It only means "no" if you let it! When there is a specific person whom you must talk to and he's always busy and cannot take your call, go see him in person. Many times [HRM] people use their office staff as a buffer to screen individuals. It is more difficult for someone to [blow you off] when he is staring you in the face. Such was the case when the now defunct Cadillac Motor Car Company was being dissolved. In actuality, the division was absorbed into the Flint Automotive Division to form a brand new division. The FAD was a much larger division as far as the number of personnel was concerned. Thus, the joke became "The Big Fish swallowed the Little Fish." Many of the personnel at Cadillac went scrambling for other jobs because they did not want to be swallowed by the Big Fish. Some individuals persistently tried to obtain a job at the General Motors Truck Division. This story was recounted by an engineer who sought employment at the Truck Division. He said, "The person in charge of personnel would not take my calls. No matter, I got in my vehicle and drove over to their office and waited to be seen. I was eventually seen and was told by this person that it was, 'Hands off all Cadillac people.' I was told that they would like to have me on board but they were prevented from employing me. The directive came from the General Manager and it does not get much higher than that. The point is, I did get to see the person I was after."

Another job seeker expounded on one of his experiences, one in which he would not take "no" for an answer. For the sake of clarity, I'll call him Rudolph. Rudolph began by explaining to me the job posting procedures for that company. All job openings below a certain level were to be posted on a bulletin board in plain view. In this manner, it was thought that the selection process used to fill the positions would be fair. Anyone could apply for any job. This particular job posting was one that Rudolph fit perfectly. He wrote down all the information that was pertinent and began to plan a strategy. A mistake was made on the document listing this particular job. The name of the assistant chief engineer was listed as the person to contact. Usually, an engineering group manager was listed as the person to contact. An assistant chief engineer was several levels above a group manager. Nonetheless, Rudolph had the name of the person to see about the position. That proved to be more difficult than he expected. As Rudolph stated, "You do not go to the office of the assistant chief engineer and ask to see him out of the clear blue. A person at that level is tied up in meetings all day. So what? I wanted to see him and I would not take 'no' for an answer. The receptionist in the outer corridor called his office continually. It became apparent to her that I was not leaving until the assistant chief engineer saw me. He had to come by me sooner or later. I asked that his administrative assistant be told that I had some information to relay to him."

While being seated in the outer office, the receptionist beckoned Rudolph. The assistant chief engineer's administrative assistant wanted to speak with him. "What is the nature of the information?" Rudolph replied, "The information is for his eyes only."

"Then you'll have to wait." And wait Rudolph did. For three hours he waited in the lobby. It was near the end of the day when the phone rang. The receptionist looked up at him momentarily. Rudolph could read her lips as she was saying to someone, "Yes he is." Rudolph surmised, the assistant chief engineer's administrative assistant was asking if he was still waiting.

Rudolph said, "If I wasn't going to take 'no' for an answer, I had to be prepared to wait." Thirty minutes after the phone call, the administrative assistant came out to greet him. "Mr. Automobile (that was not his name) will see you now." Into the office he went. Rudolph came right to the point. The information that was for the eyes of the assistant chief engineer was about Rudolph. The folder contained his resume and other credentials that qualified him for the position that was posted. After a short and pointed sales pitch, Rudolph was informed that the job posting was a mere formality. The person who was going to fill the position was chosen before the job was posted. It was someone within the same department who was more qualified than he. That is a common practice among large and small corporations. The posting is done to give the illusion that everyone has equal opportunity to get the job.

This was a case of discrimination. It was the type of discrimination that is practical. What better person to pick for the job than one who knows the product, and all the people and places involved? Rudolph was applauded by the assistant chief engineer for his stick-to-itiveness. Rudolph was told that if there had been another opening within his department, he would have given him a job on the spot. The assistant chief engineer said, "Anyone who displayed that kind of eagerness to work for me should not go unrewarded."

What do both of these incidents have in common? If your answer is, the individuals didn't get the jobs they were going after, you would be missing the point. The correct answer is, they didn't take "no" for an answer. The message that this sends to a person in charge is quite clear. He interprets it as, you want to work for him. You are willing to do what it takes to get the job. Who would not want to employ a person with that kind of tenacity? The chances are that if he placed you in charge of a project, you would see it through to completion. When bottlenecks arose, as they often do, you would not accept defeat. That would be taking "no" for an answer.

PRESENTING A GOOD RECOMMENDATION

A good recommendation from a previous employer is always impressive. The letter should accompany the resume and should be on hand prior to the interview. When I am interviewing a prospective candidate and he has provided me with a written recommendation, he has a "leg up" on everyone else. First, I am going to examine the letter for its content and status of the originator. A low- level supervisor is not sufficient. I want the letter to come from someone of substance and authority. Having the letter prior to the interview will allow some opportunity to call the writer on the phone. Some marvelous, lofty words written on letterhead can be deceptive. I, as a rule, I do not give recommendations. On the occasions that I have given them, the recipients have merited the recommendations. I make the assumption that other managers, like myself, are selective in their praise.

MAKING GOOD CHOICES

When you send out resumes, you are advertising yourself for a job. Do not be surprised if someone answers your ad. If called for an interview, go to it. If the job meets your pre-established criterion, accept it. One mistake that some people make before or after accepting the job is placing their potential employer in a precarious position. How so? By announcing things such as, "Oh by the way, my family and I are going on vacation next week. I hope this doesn't cause a problem." Of course it can cause a problem. You were hired to perform a needed task. If your services were not needed, you would not have been asked in for the interview.

Not being ignorant of the fact that there will be some disappointed people, the issue becomes, what is more important, a vacation or the job you want. If tickets have already been purchased, you can have them reissued. Cancel the vacation and take it later. There may even be some benefits that the company can offer that were not previously available. Many companies offer their discounted group rates for hotels, rental cars and airline tickets to their employees. Making sacrifices are a part of everyday life. We organizc things in a stack as to the level of their importance. In a case such as this, it would seem prudent to forego the vacation.

There are exceptions to this. It all depends on your bargaining position and whether or not you are dealing from a position of strength. When you are negotiating from a position of strength, your prospective employer is likely to be more flexible to your request for leave. How can you determine if you are negotiating from a position of strength? The question can be easily answered. Did you seek out the employer or did the employer pursue you? If the latter is the case, you may have some bargaining strength. If you sought him out, your position may be tenuous. He is likely to get someone else to replace you if you insist on taking the vacation. I am speaking of replacing you by not employing you.

NAME DROP

There are a variety of messages left on my voice mail. The ones I pay the most attention to when sorting through them are those individuals that invoke the name of a person that I know. I have left instructions for friends and acquaintances to have their person call me. As the message begins, they name drop, "Hello, Mr. Stokes, I was speaking with 'Joe Doaks' and he told me that I should call you regarding …." I am guilty of forgetting the names of the persons though. This is not a tried and true method. To make it more fool-proof, actually get to know someone who is close to the individual that can make it happen for you. Make what happen? Make the door of opportunity open for you, that's what. Get to know the secretary of the individual. Under no circumstances should you contact family members of the person you wish to see. As should be the case, people can be very protective of their families. Invading their privacy for the sake of a job will not get you the job, but it will get you into some major trouble.

BE CLEVER BUT NOT DECEPTIVE

You have to get yourself noticed by the person who can make things happen for you. Find out information about this person's outside activities. It is a safe bet that they are not a closely guarded secret. Become involved in that civic work, recreational activity, volunteer group or other organizations for which this individual has passion. You may not care about the activity in the beginning, but it is possible that you may gain some fondness for it later. All of the fervor surrounding golf is not due solely to love for the activity. There are many people playing golf because it gets them noticed by the people that can make things happen for them. This is not only a good **Job Winning Technique,** it is also a good **Strategy.**

It is not a good idea to send gifts or offer money to persons working in personnel offices. Besides it being construed as an outright bribe, many companies are instituting "zero tolerance" policies. A "zero tolerance" policy is one in which no gratuities of any kind are to be accepted by the employees of that company. Any violations are met with the "death penalty" for that employee. The death penalty is the immediate termination of that person's employment. Your gift would be a threat to his livelihood and he would be smart to resist your overtures.

OFFER TO WORK FOR LITTLE OR NO MONEY

I am not completely sold on this idea, but somehow it strikes to the core of even the most coldhearted individual. This technique should be used only in professions where "getting your foot in the door" is half the battle. These types of jobs are those that can be found in television and radio broadcasting. Something radical has to be tried in order to give you the opportunity to display your skills or learn the trade. I loved listening to Bruce Williams when he was on the radio in our area. Who is Bruce Williams? He is the man who has done everything at least once. He is the Michael Jordan of practical knowledge and has a syndicated radio program. I recall him telling of a young lady who wanted to work for him so badly that she took the job for little or no pay to prove herself. Her words were, "No one can outwork me." Who would not give a person a chance after she has said that to you? This should not be done to land a job that involves strenuous labor. We have laws against slave labor.

TAKE IT, DON'T SEND IT

Companies place advertisements for positions on the radio and in the printed press. When the openings are aired via the radio waves, they often give you a choice in method that you may use to send them your resume. When you are instructed to fax or mail your resume, mail it. As part of my function for a major client, I make both recommendations for hiring and termination. I frequently receive resumes from individuals. The ones that are mailed are much easier to read and comprehend than those that have passed through the strain of a telephone line. I am faced with a choice of two individuals to fill one position. One of them faxed to me their resume and the other express mailed or Fed-Exed it to me.

I ask you, which one has impressed me the most, all other skills being equal? The correct answer is the one who mailed me their resume. I may call both individuals for an interview. However, I already have a preconceived idea of the character of the person who faxed to me their resume. One must remember what the whole exercise of sending a resume is all about. You are trying to win a job by imploring someone to give you a call. Prior to a formal introduction, there is no other way to give a prospective employer an impression of you. If you are not given a choice and a fax number is all you have, then by all means fax your resume. If the company gives its name, you have a lead that can be taken to retrieve its address. You can then mail your resume. A nice, clean, crisp resume looks pretty good compared to one that has passed through the ringer of a fax machine.

Better than both of these techniques, personally handing someone your resume gives you a jump on everyone else. It is a little known fact that if you hand someone your resume, upon accepting it, they must give you an interview. The same cannot be said when your resume is mailed or faxed to the location. Many [HRM] personnel are not aware of the fact that they do not have to accept the resume from your hand. I learned that from Gary Kulkis, the ex-Cadillac guru of [HRM]. They can refuse to take it just by saying, "I don't want it." That is the down side of this technique. But why not take advantage of the ignorance of some HRM'ers. How impressed would someone be if they knew you caught a plane, train, or drove a long distance to hand them a resume? Very impressed, I would think.

PROMOTE YOURSELF

What can be more important than promoting yourself? Why not look the part you want to play? This can be easily accomplished by having some business cards printed with the job title you presently have or the title that you are seeking. You can also make use of business cards by presenting them with your resume. There are resume folders that have a pre-formed slot cut into them for business cards. When I was sending out resumes, an exercise that was performed every six months, that was the method I used. The responses were overwhelming. I still get calls from [headhunters] to whom I sent a resume years ago. They want to "update their files," as it was told to me.

- Solicit newspapers from other cities, close by and afar. Scour the classified advertisement section for employment opportunities. Send resumes to all the addresses that fit your plan. For that matter, send some to those that do not fit your plan. They may know someone who has need of you. This should be done at least once a year.
- If you are computer literate, you could generate your own web page and have it posted by one of the many internet service providers. If your internet service provider will not host your web page, find one that will. Why pay for something and not get full service? You will want to be linked to one of the many

search engines so that anyone doing a search can easily find you. A search engine is a software mechanism developed to help find the information that you are looking for in that universe called the internet. Your resume must be available within your web page. Any perspective employer can then print out the resume.

- Make up a flyer of brightly colored paper and list your job qualifications. Post these flyers, with permission, in the entrance of supermarkets, libraries, gas stations and home improvement stores. Business owners and HRM'ers shop and purchase commodities, too. You never know who will see your advertisement. I engaged one college student as to how he obtained his summer job. His response was, "I posted flyers everywhere. The only problem was I got more responses than I could handle."

If your local newspaper has a classified advertisement section for "Work Wanted," place your ad in the paper if the cost is not prohibitive.

ATTEND JOB FAIRS

What has become increasingly popular are job fairs. A job fair is a single or multiple-day event where many companies and businesses come together in one locale to do recruiting. These fairs are announced many days beforehand and the advertisements are placed in all news media forms. You must come ready and prepared to "take care of business" when at a job fair. All sorts of opportunities await you there. For the most part, jobs are waiting for those who are prepared for them. There is a chapter devoted to the topic of preparation.

DO SOME CRUISING

Many communities have what are referred to as industrial rows. That is an avenue or boulevard where many small businesses and manufacturing facilities are located. Riding down one of these industrial rows will reveal many "Help Wanted" signs hanging in front of the buildings. With a handful of resumes in your hand, you'll be ready for impromptu interviews. The message you are conveying to the persons in charge is, you want to go to work immediately. That is a good thing. Do some cruising on the weekends or in the evening before darkness arrives.

HOLD DOWN THE GLAMOUR

This is an area that is geared towards the female reader and its message can be easily misinterpreted. When presenting yourself for a job, do not make yourself look too glamorous, especially if you can discern that men will be working in the department. Very large companies have personnel departments that are in charge of acquiring personnel for the requesting departments. There is no doubt that you will be among many candidates applying for the job. The personnel department's job is making sure that you meet the minimum requirements for employment. The final decision may be made by the department's manager. Any savvy manager, male or female, can examine your **"presentation,"** and determine whether it will be a distraction.

This is not to say that the perspective employment candidate should appear like "Rebecca of Sunny Brook Farm," but she should not look like "Elvira" either. Modesty should set the tone of dress and appearance. Everyone's judgment of modesty is different. However, there is that look which can appear so disruptive that it could send the wrong message. To be more explicit, seductive attire is definitely out of the question. With all the emphasis being placed on sexual harassment and proper workplace behavior, managers are at their wits end trying to maintain an environment conducive to work.

If I am a manager of an office environment where the genders are mixed, I have to consider workplace stability. For instance, two female candidates are applying for the same job. Their resumes, skill levels and ages are relatively close. One of the candidates is slightly overweight and unattractive. The other candidate is very attractive and sports the figure of someone who works out often. This is surmised because her clothing is clinging and too revealing. Who gets the job? You guessed it, the slightly overweight, unattractive woman. Her invitations to lunch by single males on the job will be few, if any. Lunch dates translate into lost productivity, especially on Fridays. There will be less talk among the men concerning dating during business hours. Overall, the distractions will be fewer and more work will be done. We all know that dating in the workplace is quite common and can lead to all sorts of personnel problems. When workplace romances fizzle, they cause untold personnel problems.

THE INTERVIEW

You will go through all the pain and toil of these exercises for one thing, an interview. That will be your opportunity to promote yourself without being ridiculous. I am very skeptical of someone saying that he was chief of staff at an engineering firm when he was only 25 years old. I equate age with experience. There are, of course, exceptions to this. If indeed he was chief of staff, what does that say about the firm he was with? I have interviewed people who have done everything except design the space shuttle. They were so great that the only reason the shuttle Columbia blew up was because they hadn't worked on it! I can't get these people out of my office soon enough. The goal is to provide enough information so that the interview can come to no other conclusion except that you will be an asset to their company or business. Remember, just as your resume has a limited amount of time to affect its reader, so does your appearance at an interview. You are being critiqued from the moment you enter the room.

There are certain things that you must do before the interview. Prepare to wear clothing that is not provocative or too sedate. For a male, a shirt and tie is the absolute minimum. More impressive would be a darkly-colored or gray suit. If a suit is not available, a darkly-colored blazer with a white shirt will suffice. Needless to say, that all of these items must be clean and free from offensive odors. That includes household odors. Care must be given to where you place the clothing the night before. If your household is having a fish fry, you do not want your apparel to become contaminated with the odor of fish. You will become desensitized to the odor, others will not.

- Make sure your clothes are neatly pressed.
- Polish your shoes.
- Cover up any tattoos.
- Get a hair cut and trim your beard if you have one. Be neatly groomed.

For females, a conservatively-patterned dress or a darkly-colored gray, blue or brown business suit is preferable. Needless to say, the clothing should be clean and free from stains of makeup and other cosmetic paraphernalia.

- No low cut or provocative clothing.
- No high-heeled shoes.
- No excessively long slits in the skirt.
- No excessive makeup.
- No flamboyant hair styles.

Do not schedule multiple interviews within hours of each other. You must make allowances in case the person you are meeting is delayed by other matters. If he is running late, you do not want his lateness to affect your next interview. One professional recounted the antics of a person who not only arrived late for the interview, he asked if the interview was going to take long. She abruptly told him that the interview was not going to take long at all. She said, "Its over right now." It is a very wise thing to make allowances for something to happen. Traffic accidents, railroad crossings, flat tires, and a host of other things can cause you to become delayed. If I am the interviewer and you are late, there will be no excuse that is good enough. It is far better to reschedule the interview than to arrive late. The reverencing of time is a good habit overall. I always make sure that I allow myself sufficient time to attend to any unforeseen mishaps.

Before arriving for the interview, have a note pad and ink pen ready for note taking. It is the policy of some progressive companies and small businesses to have several persons involved in the interviewing process. In this manner, items or issues that escape one person may be discovered by another. This process can take several days, with each interview being scheduled for some date in the future, or they may all take place in the same day. Some companies and small businesses also have the employees that you will be working with interview you as a team. There are a whole host of potential conflicts that can be avoided by using this technique. If you are a dud, chances are you are not going to be able to deceive everyone. As a whole, a company or small business that would take that kind of care to ensure that their employees are cooperative and can get along would be a good company to work for.

This is the interview process in a nutshell. Arriving early, perhaps 15 minutes before the scheduled time, will afford you the opportunity to calm yourself and rehearse your thoughts. Have prepared questions to ask the interviewer, perhaps questions regarding the company and its policies that you have not discovered. This is assuming that you have already done some research into the company and have a conversational knowledge of what services or products it provides. Remember, a firm handshake is a sign of confidence. The interview is more than just a question and answer session. It is where the company is sizing you up. A good interview will not guarantee you employment, but a bad impression from a interview will most certainly mean you will not get the job.

For this reason, you must sell yourself. Companies and small businesses are depending more and more on the interview and not what is contained in a resume. What is written on paper can be misleading or deceptive. The likelihood of this is lessened greatly when the person is before you and having to recite things orally. The interview is exactly the same as an oral examination. You are being examined to determine how well you speak and listen, how you respond to the questions that are being asked of you, if you stammer before your retort, your posture, your poise, and overall mannerism. Companies and small businesses want to know what you can offer them and why they should employ you. Be ready to answer some unusual questions such as these:

- "Tell me about yourself. What have you been doing with your life?"
- "Besides the possible increase in pay, why are you interested in working for us?"
- "What are your long-term and short-term goals?"
- "How have you contributed to the success of your previous employer(s)?"
- "What ideas do you have to help make us more competitive, productive, and profitable?"
- "What do you consider to be your weaknesses and how do you plan to improve on them?"

Be prepared to answer these types of questions as honestly as possible. Some questions will not have a simple answer, so rehearse the answers so that it will appear as though they were spontaneous.

There may be a period in your career in which you have undergone numerous job changes in a short period of time. This is not due to your being terminated, quite the contrary. You have accepted a better job each time. There are times when a particular segment of the market is hot. Why not capitalize on it? To someone viewing the dates and duration of employment on your resume, it may appear that you are unstable, a job hopper, not willing to stay one place for any length of time. Be prepared to explain why you have changed jobs so frequently. Focus on being positive, not negative. Do not say things such as, "I left there because I could see that it was not going to be a nice place to work." Frequent job changes of one year or less in certain professions is not a good thing. It sends the wrong message.

Do not assume that the interview will be cordial. You may be asked slightly provoking questions as to determine how you will react under pressure. It is when we are placed under pressure and duress that we discover what we are truly made of. As a very wise woman named Bonnie Demings once said to me, "When you are placed under pressure, what's in you is coming out, albeit good or bad."

Once you have accepted an offer, it is not proper to continue the interviewing process. Bartering for a better position or more money will not endear you to the company with which you have an agreement. It may result in the employers rescinding their offer and damaging your reputation. It is indeed a small world. You cannot predict who you may come across at some later date. They will remember what you tried to do.

PROFESSIONAL COURTESY

What is professional courtesy? It is giving the proper acknowledgement to your job and the person you work for. Every job requires certain protocol when personal issues arise. We all have them from time to time. That is a part of being an adult and living on earth. Things happen in life. It is how we handle ourselves when these issues arise that determine our level of professional courtesy. Most of the time, issues that require our attention also require time away from work. As it was stated to me by one manager of a department of a Fortune 500 company, "If someone needs a day off, I'd like at least a one day notice. If he needs three days off, I'd like to have a three-day notice, if possible. If he needs a week off, a week's notice is not asking too much. I think that is a reasonable policy. It gives me time to prepare for his absence."

An emergency is something that occurs without prior warning. Something just happened and it requires immediate attention. Those who have small children know this all too well. No person in authority wants to be told at the last minute, "Oh, by the way, I'm going to be off for three days. I forgot to tell you." That manager is not going to be thrilled at this last minute declaration. It may cause him to have to fill your spot with a temporary employee. That takes time to arrange.

This story was recounted by a school administrator who was familiar with the incident. One elementary school aide was going on medical leave. Out patient, non-emergency surgery was required. What this employee neglected to do was inform the school's principal of her pending absence in a timely manner. Instead, a note was written and given to the secretary to pass on. It was recalled by the principal, "I see her every morning before school starts. She could have told me days ago that she was going to be off. I would have accommodated her. Now I've got to try and fill her spot in one day. That's a tough thing to do."

It was the desire of this school aide to move up to the next level of employment for the school system, **"a better job."** The goal for most aides at that level was to become a paraprofessional. All promotions required extensive evaluations and a letter of recommendation from the school's principal where one last worked.

Would this aide be likely to get a good recommendation from the principal in charge? Perhaps this one incident was not enough to prohibit a good recommendation from the principal. A person becomes good at what they practice. What if there had been other acts construed as being unprofessional? Remember, you are always looking for a better job.

SEASONED CITIZENS

If you are a seasoned citizen, there is no need for you to consider yourself unemployable. Quite the contrary, you have a lot to offer a small business or company. First, there are the many years of actual workplace experience that you can use to your advantage. This is experience that is hard to come by and is difficult for a younger employee to emulate. The elderly employee can also act as a mentor and counselor to the younger employee. There still exists some respect for the elderly and with that, a savvy employer could place an elderly worker among the younger as a moderator on the job.

As a seasoned citizen, there are other distinct advantages that you can capitalize on. Perhaps you have been in the same home for a long time and do not have the pressure of making large mortgage payments. This will allow you to work for less money, thus making your employment cost effective. An occasional visit to a fast food eatery bears this out, as more and more franchises are hiring the elderly instead of younger workers. The elderly are dependable, they'll show up on a Saturday morning for work whereas younger workers consider Friday night as party time. So what if they are scheduled to work the next day. They will call in sick and have no regard for the wages that they are losing. Some employers I talk to complain vehemently about the lack of dependability of younger workers. Offering more money in exchange for faithfulness seems to have little or no effect.

Along the same line of thinking, being older usually means no young children at home. That can translate into no lost days of work due to children who are sick. Sometimes the children aren't really sick at all. They will feign illness just to stay home and have mom or dad all to themselves for a day. This is a ploy used occasionally when siblings compete for the attention of their parents. Having no young children at home also means that there is no need to leave work early to attend parent-teacher meetings, school concerts, and other school-related activities. Lost time from the job means lost dollars for your employer. Another advantage you'll have is that you can be flexible in your working hours. There is no pressure placed upon you to be at home in the evenings.

What about an appreciative spirit? This has to do with **"attitude."** There is something about age that tends to bring on a sense of civility, or at least it should. Rarely have I seen an elderly worker expressing adversarial opinions, bad attitudes, and overall poor demeanor. By being flexible, cooperative, and appreciative, I am not stating that the elderly worker should be a doormat for his or her employer. It is my contention that the elderly have something to offer and they should exploit their offerings. All citizens can be productive until they are no longer physically able to withstand the rigors of the workplace. But who can place an age limit on this? There are many elderly workers who are able to contribute well into their 70's. These are just a few of the things that you, as a seasoned citizen, can use as leverage in obtaining employment.

STUDENT WORKER

The student worker has a distinct advantage over his older counterparts. He has employment attributes that are similar to those of the seasoned citizen worker. This is especially true if the student worker happens to be living at home. The student can work for a smaller wage because he does not have the responsibilities of caring for a household. Being able to work for the established minimum wage makes the student very attractive. Usually, entry level jobs offer the minimum wage to persons who do not have a great deal of experience. This presents an **"opportunity"** to get some experience.

Small business owners are individuals who know at the end of every day whether they have made or lost money. The cost of labor is paramount in this equation of profit versus loss. As a student, you can offer a flexible work schedule, assuming that school will not be interfered with. Bear in mind that you, as a student, are at the very beginning of your workplace adventure. Every job should count as a good work experience. Therefore, focus on making it possible for your employer to say about you, "They were jobs well done." In this manner you can ask for, and should receive, a letter of recommendation from him after your employment period has ended. An accumulation of these letters make a powerful statement to whomever will employ you next. I have hired persons on their letters of recommendation more so than what was contained in their resume. I examined who the letters of recommendation were from and counted them as qualified to make a judgment about the individual.

Some Good Advice

At the interview, do not ask about policies governing smoking. Avoid the subject of smoking at all cost. It is a sign that you will be losing time due to an uncontrollable habit. There are very few buildings, if any, where smoking is permitted. This necessitates the smoker to exit the building to indulge. Exiting the building means that you are being unproductive for the amount of time it takes to smoke the cigarette and return to your workplace. For that matter, do not smoke a cigarette before going into an interview. To anyone who is sensitive to smoke, you will reek of smoke. For a woman, it presents a horrible conflict, the stench of cigarette smoke mingled with perfume. If you have to smoke, wait until all interviews have been completed. Smokers can add to the difficulties of managers trying to make for equitable treatment of their employees. The many breaks that smokers take during the day can add up to a large amount of time. Non-smokers will want an equivalent of amount of time to indulge themselves.

****

Do not use the interview as a forum to declare your complaints, criticisms or grievances against those who employed you. Have nothing but good things to say about previous employers. Even if it is difficult, say things that are complimentary. The interviewer is not interested in all of the injustices you have suffered. He is not going to make right all of the bad things that have come your way. Even if baited and asked by the questioner, do not follow that lead. Stay focused on the purpose of the interview. It is not a gripe session. The interview is an opportunity for you to sell yourself. It is not about what they can do for you but what you can do for them.

STRATEGIES FOR EMPLOYMENT

"Let no man think more highly of himself than he ought to think."
Romans 12:3

Of all the people that I have known in my career, there are very few of whom I can say, "I owe a debt of gratitude." One such person is Gary Kulkis, a personnel director at the now defunct Cadillac Motor Car Company. Anyone can teach you academic lessons. There are very few qualified to teach on the interactions between people in the corporate setting. Gary Kulkis was such a person. Gary was not the most popular person among the United Auto Workers. He was the one given the responsibility of representing the management of Cadillac in labor disputes. He was also the one responsible for handing out disciplinary measures when necessary. It was a game between he and the union. Gary played the employment game very well. Perhaps that is why I liked him so much. He knew how to play the labor management game, and I wanted to learn something.

One of his favorite sayings was, "You want to always deal from a position of strength." A position of strength can be very easily defined. When you are interviewing or applying for a job where the positions are few and the candidates are numerous, the interviewer is dealing from a position of strength. He will weed out all those except the most desirable ones who will proceed to the next stage. However, when the jobs are plentiful and employers are competing for a limited talent pool, those being interviewed are dealing from a better position. Not a position of strength, but a better position. Those individuals with advanced degrees in the sciences are more likely to be the ones dealing from positions of strength when applying for jobs.

Gary told me of a situation where the candidate being interviewed was a graduate of a very prestigious university. This young lady had her stuff together, slang term meaning that she was dealing from a position of strength. She had offers from many of the Fortune 500 companies upon graduation. She made this fact known to Gary. There was something about G.M. that attracted her. The young lady negotiated the amount she was going to be paid and wanted a company car also. Gary was a shrewd and experienced negotiator and admired her boldness. Knowing where you stand is a must when developing a strategy for employment. That is why a strategy for employment is so vital. There are Gary Kulkis' out there.

There are many people who do not realize just how important it is to continually plan their careers. When they lose their jobs or are amidst adverse working conditions, then they begin to make a frantic search for other work. It is always easier to get another job while you have a job. Not only does this place you in a position of strength, it can also be used as a strategy for better employment. That is because there is no pressure to take a job that is unsuitable. Taking a suitable job does not mean that it is the last job you will ever have. It is merely a stepping stone towards something bigger and better. You must always look out for number one, and you are number one. If you don't, no one else will. Target the job you want, then develop a strategy for attaining it. A strategy is a plan that examines where you are, where you want to be, and plots the course on how to get there. It can be revised along the way as things change.

****

Before we begin to develop a strategy, there are some self-help items that will serve you well to remember.

SETTING GOALS

Set goals for yourself. When you set a goal, that is the equivalent of a having a target. You know when you have hit the bullseye on a target and you know when you have missed the target. What is equally as important is being able to measure your progress and how far you are away from success. One important thing about a goal is that it cannot be so lofty that it is beyond your reach. I qualify this by saying that every goal is achievable. It may take several steps to get to the final prize. The goal that is set should not be looked at as being reached in one giant step. That is what is meant by "being lofty." When you are an infant and lying flat on your back, you don't begin to walk right away. The first thing you must learn to do is crawl. After learning how to crawl, you then begin to learn how to walk upright.

There are countless numbers of stories of people who took jobs to learn the business that they were interested in starting. They then used that knowledge and started their own. They started out with a plan to reach a certain goal. Then they developed a strategy to accomplish the goal. They planned their work and worked their plan. Do not be afraid to take some risks. You have everything to gain from taking them. Keep your goals before you so that they may be seen. In this manner, you will be constantly reminded of them. They can be placed on the ceiling over your bed so that they are the last thing you see before you go to sleep and the first thing you see when you awaken.

It is also advisable to discuss your strategic plan with your boss. In this way, you will discover what long-range goals he has set for you and what you need to do to achieve them. Some companies give their employees annual reviews which in theory takes place on the anniversary date of hiring. This event can be used as a forum to discuss your personal objectives. There may exist an opportunity to integrate your goals with those of the organization to which you belong.

"You have to do more than work hard at life to succeed. You have to work smart. That means first and foremost, you need a plan. All of us need a strategy, a design, a map if we're to realize our potential in life. The secret to reaching any goal is to first define the goal, then work out a logical, practical plan for attaining it." These are the words written by Mort Crim. Mr. Crim is a television anchor, radio broadcaster and creator of the internationally syndicated radio series, "Second Thoughts," and author of the book, *Second Thoughts*.

KEEP YOUR EYES ON THE GOAL

Always be mindful of what the goal is. As the motivational speaker, Les Brown, says, "It's not over until I win." You must also adopt this saying and embrace it. There will be disappointments along the way. That is a fact of life. That does not mean that you have to give up. When things do not go as planned, treat them as a temporary setback. In doing this, that is all they will be, temporary, with no permanence attached to them.

LEARN TO HOLD YOUR PEACE

This is something that is easier said than done. There have been many situations that placed me in between the proverbial "rock & hard place." In one case, I was severely chastised for making a decision that saved an individual from being ridiculed by his boss. Not knowing the facts and caring what they were, this individual proceeded to embarrass me beyond belief. My first instinct was to retaliate in like manner. A cooler head prevailed and I thought about executing my plan. A rapid, terse response could have hurt me more than it could have helped me. I had a strategy that was unfolding. In addition, making a scene would not have been a good witness for me. The people who knew me within the building would have been surprised at any uncontrolled outburst. My credibility and image would have been damaged. When speaking in anger, it is easy for something to proceed out of your mouth that is counterproductive to your plan. Something along these lines could be uttered in the heat of anger, "Well I was planning to leave anyway," or announcing, "I quit" before you are actually ready, and are not beneficial to you. Giving your boss or other person in authority a "piece of your mind" is not a good thing.

DELUSIONS OF GRANDEUR

This describes people who feel they are more important than they actually are. They inwardly feel as though, "They can't do without me." That is one of the worst mistakes that a person can make, to feel as though he cannot be replaced. Everyone can be replaced, from the executive level down to the rank and file. I learned this lesson while working for General Motors and Chrysler. I watched many talented people offer letters of resignation. They were never refused. That is not to say that their presence was not missed. Every individual brings his own uniqueness to a job setting. However, if he leaves, the companies carried on. Therein lies the strength of large corporations, their size. These giants have momentum that carry them on, even when an individual person is no longer present. They have systems that are in place and people learn the systems. When a person leaves, the system does not leave with them. They are replaced by individuals who learn the system.

The lesson is, have a realistic assessment of your abilities. Do not use the threat of departure as a strategy for employment or monetary gain. There are very few individuals who can use this tactic and be successful. Woe be unto him or her who outwardly express the sentiments that he or she is irreplaceable. Having this feeling of confidence inwardly because of superior performance is not all bad. It is that outward expression that can be detrimental to your employment health. If I were an employer and an employee stated that he could not be replaced, steps would be taken. I would clandestinely seek his replacement to maintain a position of strength. His postulate would then be tested to see if it has merit.

TOO GOOD TO BE TRUE

One has to be careful of offers for employment and the benefits attached as offered by contract or permanent recruiting agencies. The old adage, "If it sounds to good to be true, it usually is," comes into play. A strategy of working out of state or a foreign country can be one that yields substantial monetary gains and experience. The monetary gains are temporary, but the experience is permanent. The experience can be parlayed into even better employment when one returns to native surroundings. However, some recruiters do not reveal all of the facts. It is not what they tell you that counts, it is what they don't tell you that can get you into a very precarious situation. Family considerations should be paramount in one's decision to work away from home. Nothing can cause more havoc in a marriage than when one of the partners is habitually absent. When there are young children involved, the situation can become even more untenable.

There are constant openings for technical people in oil producing regions of the Middle East. The wages paid to those working there are unbelievable. Because I am acquainted with some individuals who have sought employment there, I am familiar with the facts. You are given a place to live and a food allowance. In some cases, the wages earned are free of U.S. taxes. There are certain rules that govern this particular benefit. One individual signed a contract to work for one year and was told he could come home to the U.S. every six months at no cost. Coming home prior to the scheduled time is not permitted for any reason. If a person decides he must leave, the contract is voided and he will not receive the amount agreed upon. One should know all of the pitfalls before embarking on foreign ventures.

Foreign assignments are ideal for single persons who are adventurous. They are less comfortable for those persons with families, young or older. There are cultural differences that can also make overseas work assignments less comfortable. There are things you may take for granted as being O.K. or assume are meaningless, such as the wearing of short pants, the exposing of hair by women, and certain hand gestures. The next thing you know, a commotion arises. The consumption of alcohol is strictly forbidden in some countries. You may be restricted to a compound or certain areas during non- working hours. Recruiters seldom tell you these things until they feel you are committed to the assignment.

After all, they are paid a fee for delivering workers to foreign locations. It is not in their best interest to reveal all of the bad stuff.

The situations can be more pleasant but less profitable in the European countries of Germany, Italy, France and the United Kingdom. These areas are more tolerant of Anglo-American customs, habits and idiosyncrasies. By far, there have been more individuals taking advantage of the **"opportunities"** to work in Europe than in the Middle East.

Just as there are foreign job recruiters, there are domestic job recruiters that scour the country for people with specific skills. The same care and discretion must be exercised when entertaining thoughts of working out-of-state. There have been numerous cases of individuals packing up and moving possessions to locations thousands of miles away. They were not there for too long before they discovered that the grass wasn't so green there after all. When you are in a location foreign to you and have expended considerable financial resources to get there, it isn't always possible to turn around and come back. You are bound to meet other disgruntled people with tales of woe.

One individual was lured away from his home state, and a steady job, with an attractive offer out-of-state. "The money is too good to turn down," he was reported as saying. The wages being offered there were far above anything being offered in the area. The location of the job was four hours away from his family. Commuting during the week was out of the question. Only weekend visits with his family would be possible. The good job that was to be six months to a year in duration was found not to be such a good deal. Instead of cutting his losses and returning home, a job was taken that was eight hours away. This job was taken because of the promise of one closer to home being offered later. If four hours away was unfavorable, eight hours away was intolerable.

There was one problem with returning home. All local positions were filled. Special arrangements could have been made, but only if a substantial pay cut was taken. Every dollar-per-hour decrease is 40 dollars per week, computed on a 40-hour work week. Remember, if a job sounds too good to be true, it usually is. There can be no substitute for the careful deliberation of **"opportunities"** that are away from home.

The following are examples of what I consider to be bad strategies.

OVER STEPPING YOUR BOUNDARY

There are many ways to overstep your boundaries. What is at the heart of the matter is your desire to work for someone else. You have espied an area or department where you would like to transfer. The plot thickens as you think of ways to ingratiate yourself with the manager or supervisor of that area. What you want to happen is not likely to happen. A good manager will not interfere in the affairs of another manager. They would not look favorably upon someone doing that to them. Your desire to better yourself and move on is to be applauded. It is how you accomplish that goal that counts. Work through the proper channels that are established. If there are no proper channels established, do not employ deceptive techniques, like going behind your bosses back and orchestrating things. That amounts to bridge burning. Don't burn bridges!

USING GENDER OR RACE AS A STRATEGY

Gender should never be used to secure a better job or position. The exceptions are positions that are thought to be exclusively female. There are enough legitimate problems in the workplace without artificially creating some. The absence of females in a small company or business does not mean that discrimination is taking place. The absence of females could be attributed to something as simple as the job being too strenuous or distasteful. It is understood that more and more women are taking jobs in traditionally male occupations because of the need for money. We concede that there is an increase in the numbers of single-parent households headed by women. What is objectionable is any person being placed in a position merely because of his or her gender. The qualifications necessary to perform the job should be the primary concern, not the politics of gender.

The same can be said for using race as a strategy. Not only is it working less and less, it should be offensive to any rationally thinking person. You do not want to be excluded because of your race and you do not want to be preferred because of it. This message can also be derived from the great speech given by the late, great civil rights leader, Dr. Martin Luther King. It was his dream that men and women would be judged on the content of their character. It would be ludicrous for anyone to state that racial discrimination is a thing of the past. The recent disclosures of discrimination at Texaco prove that there are still those among us who judge people by their pigmentation. What is also true about this great country of ours is that if you are wronged, there is a remedy. Unlike many other countries, the American people have a sense for what is right and what is wrong and hate injustice with a passion. Righting the wrongs may take some time in certain cases, but corrected they will be. Being of the mind that everyone is against you is a definite strategy for continued failure.

Much has been said concerning the subject of affirmative action. There are those who benefit greatly from all of the discussions, both pro and con. If one were to examine the issue analytically and not emotionally, a more rational debate could take place. Why are we so eager to pay the high cost of going to a professional sporting event? Because there is no affirmative action policy in place. We have an expectation of seeing the best-at-what-they-do perform. The owners who pay the salaries of these athletes are not going to allow that sort of politics to influence them.

You pick the sport or activity, the crowds come to see those who are the very best. We only wish that we could do what they do. They make it look so easy. That is because they have honed their skills to perfection. Would we pay the high dollar figure to see the inferior perform, even though it may be politically correct? I think not. The howls of indignation would be deafening if that were the case. In theory, the same can be said for the workplace. What is needed are people who have honed their skills to perfection, no matter what they are.

If I were asked if I would use a friendship or acquaintance to get a job, the answer would be yes. Would I use a relative? Yes. Would I ever use the circumstance of my birth to gain an advantage over someone else? Absolutely not. What is the difference? The difference is in the nature of the politics that make up the examples. There are some politics that are so local, they only affect a few people, if any. Having a preferential policy and hiring a friend or relative is that kind of local politics. Then there is that brand of politics that affects the entire structure of our country. It divides us into factions that war against one another. There is nothing local about it. I wrote in the chapter called **"Politics,"** that affirmative action and preferential treatment are the same thing. Their outcomes are the same, but the compositions of the motives differ.

All people at one time or another have been discriminated against. No race or nationality can claim to be the sole recipient of mistreatment from their fellow man. All men, absent of moral fiber and a humanistic base, are capable of inflicting atrocities upon other humans, even those of their own race. As previously stated, you do not want to be excluded because of your race and you do not want to be preferred because of it. Using race as a strategy to get a job is not a good thing.

THE BROTHERHOOD

It is never a good idea to criticize your boss to other bosses. In your mind, you are using the conversation as an opportunity to explain how dumb your boss is and how smart you are. In the mind of the boss listening to you, the boss you would like to work for is an entirely different thought. He is thinking, "If I get this person in my department, he will no doubt belittle me the same way." No one wants a person like that working for him. Here you are, wondering why no one is chomping at the bit to get you. The word is out on you. One very talented engineer with whom I had worked, was indeed his own worst enemy. It was embarrassing how he openly criticized every decision his boss made. There were even times when this criticism was displayed in the presence of his boss. I could discern that other people were taking note of this by there querying looks. He was never promoted and couldn't figure out why. That type of ridicule was considered insubordination. There are three things that will bring about your termination with General Motors if you are a salaried employee and not represented by a union. Those things are stealing, fighting, and insubordination.

Bosses are a group that bond together just as any other group of people. They all have similar problems and concerns. It is the equivalent to the neighbor's child complaining to you about how terrible his parents are. You, being a parent, will automatically take the side of the other parents. The damage that can be done is irreversible, as you will have attained the label of "back stabber." You should always be seen as supporting your boss. That is what will make you attractive to other managerial personnel. If you take their ransom, do their bidding.

****

That's enough of things that you shouldn't do. Now it's time for some things that you should do in the form of developing a strategy for employment. The very first thing that you should do is determine what your real worth is. That can be done by finding out what others are earning while performing the same job. From there, you can make a rational decision whether to continue in the same field or go on to something else. The economic laws of supply and demand can affect your strategy. If there are sufficient numbers of individuals who can fill vacancies created in any market, compensations are held down. The reverse is also true. If there are not enough qualified persons to satisfy the need, wages and other forms of compensation escalate accordingly.

The following examples are given to provide a basis for formulating your own strategy for getting a better job. There are many variations that can evolve from these examples. It is not possible to expound on every possible [permutation].

FIND A MENTOR

A mentor is described as being “a wise and trusted counselor or teacher.” If you have worked for any length of time in the [real world], you no doubt have come across someone who displayed the wisdom of his years. A mentor can be someone who helps to guide you through the bureaucracy of a high school, college, trade school, corporation, skilled trade, or business. He is someone you look to for advice and guidance. This person can be male or female. Those of us who have been fortunate enough to have had mentors, have benefited greatly from their counsel.

There are some who say, “I got where I am all by myself.” That is not possible to do within any company or business. They had a helper whether they recognized them as such or not. The only setting in which a lone individual can make it by himself is if he starts his own business. Even then, he needs the patronage of other people. Sometimes there are individuals who have worked in that business for a great amount of time. They then share their knowledge with the new business owner. That person has been mentored.

Experience is by far the best teacher, and mentors are usually people who love to impart their knowledge and wisdom to eager listeners. I have sought out mentors in every setting that I have been in. On one occasion, I solicited a high level executive within General Motors to act as my mentor. I phrased my request in such a way as to make it difficult for him to refuse me. A mentor can not only help plan your strategy, they can also aid in it being executed. It is hoped that you leave one place of employment for another setting. If you had a mentor in the former place, you'll also need one in the new location.

BUILD ALLIANCES

I have stated over and over again, no man or woman is an island. You cannot get to where you want to go by yourself. I often tell the crude story about two men stuck in a hole, each desiring to get out. The hole is just deep enough to prevent each from rescuing himself. As individuals, they cannot help themselves. If they form an alliance and help one another, then they both can prosper. What does it matter which one gets out first? The weightier matter is, they both will get out of the hole.

We become obsessed with the idea that if we help someone, he will be ahead of us. What does it matter if he is ahead of you? It should be your goal to form an alliance with someone whom you see as a [fast tracker]. Why waste time and energy being envious or jealous of the prosperity of someone else? Will these feelings enhance your position one iota? When you see that someone has the favor of management and is rising quickly through the ranks, hitch your wagon to his if you can. The last thing you want to do is make an enemy of someone who can one day freeze you where you are. I have talked to many low-level managers in various disciplines. They all say the same thing. Their careers would be further ahead had they paid attention to the political winds. Instead of coming to the aid of the [fast tracker], they became his or her detractor. That behavior profited them nothing.

You think that this doesn't work? Look around you. When politicians, corporate executives, athletic coaches, etc. begin to forge their way ahead, they bring certain individuals with them. They are individuals that have demonstrated their competence in their respective fields. It stands to reason that those closest to them will be the people they have known the longest. Time and energy was sown into their success. You may be the person at the base of the hole. However, when the individual whom you are supporting gets to a position where he can help you get out of the hole, he will. If the saying is true, "You are known by the company you keep," then keep good company. Build your alliances with those who are as conscientious as you or as you would like to be.

KNOW YOUR FIELD

When developing a strategy, know the culture of the organization of which you belong or hope to belong to. All corporations and even some small businesses have a culture. The culture is the makeup of that organization or entity that sets it apart. It is important for you to know how the company or organization thinks in order for you to develop a productive strategy. As outlined by Jay B. Barney and Rickey W. Griffin, there are various types of organizations.

There are Large Profit-Seeking Organizations, Start-Up Profit Seeking Organizations, Small Profit-Seeking Organizations, Government Organizations, Educational Organizations, Health Care Organizations, Interest Group Organizations, and Religious Organizations. It matters not which one you choose to work for, they each have a culture that is peculiar to them. Whatever strategy you develop, it must include an understanding of the culture of that organization.

There are times when a person just does not fit the mold of the place where he is. It can be compared to being a small fish in a big pond. In cases such as this, looking for a smaller company to work for can be a good strategy. Large companies do not tend to be solely dependent upon one individual for certain tasks. They build in redundancy for that very reason. A person can achieve a change in status just by working for a smaller company. In that way, you may be able to take on more tasks, thus increasing your value. Increasing your value to the company or business should translate into a better job and greater compensation. You are still a small fish but the pond is smaller, too.

TYPICAL SCENARIOS

You do not consider yourself just a secretary. You would rather be referred to as an administrative assistant. It has a better connotation attached to it. Besides, your skills are far beyond that of the average secretary. However, that was the only opening within the department for which you now work. You took the job because you needed the money. The manager you work for, manager "A," drives you up a wall. He is unorganized, makes decisions spontaneously and is forgetful of the things he feels are not important. Without you though, he would be lost. He thrives on chaos, but you bring order to his chaotic department. He dumps work on you by the ton. So much work that you have to do some of it at home. If you didn't take it home, you would be at the office late at night. Manager "A" is a rising star in the company because he gets the impossible done, even if it is at the last minute. Under his guidance, the department is now showing a profit every month.

You are approached by another manager we'll address as manager "B." Manager "B" is soliciting your services to help out with his department. Your skills in word processing, spreadsheet formation, charting and graphing, and overall competence, prompted him to request your help. In addition, manager "A" volunteered your services. Manager "B" has put in a requisition for a secretary, but there is no money in the budget for one this year. After a lengthy conversation with manager "B," you discover that the work he wants to give you is more to your liking. It is the kind of work that a technical analyst would do. A technical analyst's classification is a level above yours. One major problem is that you are already overloaded with work. What do you do? Remember the title of this segment, **"Strategies."**

You accept the added burden with a strategic plan for getting your classification changed later. You have to provide a business case to substantiate your claim as being qualified for a classification change. A better opportunity than this will not present itself. To make time for the added work load, no longer do the faxing, copying, and general office hopping that eat up valuable time. Explain to those who ask you to fax things that they walked by the fax machine on their way to you. Show them how easy it is to place their documents into the memory of the fax machine and then walk away. Politely refuse to make copies for them when they can make them for themselves.

What will hurt your case is excessive chatting and visiting at your desk by your colleagues. Let them know that your added burden does not provide for frivolities. Work through your lunch period. Not by skipping lunch, but by eating at your desk while working. Document everything that you are doing by using a daily diary. One of the personal planners will be sufficient for this purpose. You now have ammunition to use when you make the case for a classification change.

It will be difficult for them to refuse you when you provide them with the documentation. Remember, if you didn't write it down, it didn't happen.

MOVING WITHIN RATHER THAN OUT

Care and discretion must be exercised in the quest to seek out a better position within the same company. As discussed in the chapter called **"Politics"** there are many candidates who qualified for too few spots. It is the politics that will invariably make the case for those who will become the anointed. Getting to the next position takes a plan and a method to execute the plan. There are several things that can happen to you on your way up the ladder, the worst of which has to be working for a boss with whom you have conflict, albeit blatant or veiled. Your boss is the person who can make or break your career. It can be easily done. All that has to be repeated often enough among a variety of the managerial staff is that you are a troublemaker. It doesn't have to be true, just placed in the minds of these persons. There could be friction between you and your boss due to a serious personality conflict.

One thing to remember is who holds the reins of power, and it is not you. You must stay focused on your mission, to get a better position. Simply stated, it's called keeping one's eyes on the prize. That cannot be accomplished by reacting in a manner that is not suitable. The first step is to get out from under the supervision of the boss with whom there is conflict. That can be accomplished in several ways. The absolute worst way would be to perform poorly for him. That would provide tangible evidence of your inability to perform up to expectations. The poor performance would be recorded in annual or semi-annual reviews.

Poor performance can be reflected in your compensation or lack thereof. The best way is the one that makes the least amount of waves, (as in don't make waves). If the company you work for has a policy of allowing internal transfers, apply for one. In most cases, there will be an area provided on the transfer form where you are asked to give a reason for requesting the transfer. The prudent thing to do is place non-offensive verbiage in this space. Attacking your boss may send shock waves through the company. His or her ire will then be aroused and a defensive posture will be taken against you. If you are thinking along the lines of, "I am away from him, so it doesn't matter what I say," you would be wrong. You are going to be working for a new boss. What is he to think of you? The objective should be to get away without ruining your chances for future employment.

MAKING THE CASE FOR A BETTER JOB

It is normal for a person to aspire to improving himself. Especially when he can see the benefits of doing so. To be specific, if you are an administrative assistant, the position you may want next is that of a technical analyst. The question is, how do you get there from where you are presently? You must form a strategy to get there. A strategy could be to take on more work, doing that to assist a manufacturing engineer for example. You would be learning the verbiage, the needs of [tooling shops], and the person to contact. You would then write down everything you did during the day in order to construct a log book. After a sufficient amount of time has passed, you could then make the case for moving into a technical analyst's position. In order to support your claim, you would then produce your log book. This is a sample strategy and can be adapted for use in a variety of positions.

What if you are not employed in an office setting and are just a general laborer looking for work? The following are some examples of the strategies that can be developed. Your strategy should be simple to devise. However, it may take time to materialize. If you are an assembly line worker in a factory, your strategy for a better job should revolve around becoming a foreman. You begin the execution of this strategy by learning every job associated with your general assembly area or group. If you start out on a janitorial job as a general laborer, your goal could be to be the crew foreman or to start your own janitorial service company. By working for the janitorial service, you have the **"opportunity"** to learn everything there is to know about the maintenance and care of buildings.

Are you interested in the construction trade and want to learn to acquire the skill to build homes or start your own business? What better way to do this than to become a general laborer on a construction site. That, at least, gets your foot in the door. If you have to work for less than desirable wages, consider it as paying your dues and an educational experience. In the meantime, become a sponge. Learn everything you can about the trade. Work as a framer's helper, then a brick mason's helper. The same examples can be applied if a person is interested in becoming an electrician or plumber. Both of these professions are what are referred to as skilled trades. As such, training and testing is required to receive a Journeyman's Card. This card allows you to work anywhere in the country. Your chances of getting into a skilled trades school are enhanced when you have made the proper contacts. The proper contacts are made by working in the industry and learning the jargon of the trade. This is employing a strategy for better employment.

****

When you are a good employee, you know it, your colleagues know it and so does your management. In your day-to-day interactions with colleagues, your feelings about working for a company will be expressed by you. If there exists a situation where you feel that the compensation received is not equivalent to your performance, you are going to do what most people would do, complain. It could also be a lack of promotional opportunity that has you contemplating some sort of action. What action, you may not be sure of at the time. Companies are always looking for good people. It is a fact that companies that compete in the same market, love to take employees away from each other. You receive a phone call from one such competitor. You are being offered a new job. Through the grape vine, they were made aware of your disgruntlement. They are offering a substantial pay increase.

There are many things to consider with this new proposal. Are there any conditions (strings attached) to the offer? One common offering is not an immediate raise, but one in 30, 60 or 90 days. The reasoning is, they'll need time to make the case with the personnel people. Credibility is everything. Another thing to consider is the proximity of the new location to your home. Extra travel time must be compensated for. What level are you coming in at? Although you may be getting an immediate raise, the possibility exists that the level being offered to you is not attractive. Overall, the total package must be considered worthwhile before departing for pastures thought to be greener. Ask yourself this question: Who fulfills the promise if the one who made the promise is no longer in that position and has moved on?

You approach your management with the news that you are being courted by a competitor. You attempt to make your case for a raise from them. "I'm wondering what can be done for me. I would like to stay where I am but what they are offering is pretty good." This scenario is realistic and happens with great frequency. You have not initiated the contact, the contact was initiated by another party. What if you were the one who initiated the contact? You have devised what you think is a clever scheme. To be more explicit, you would like to stay with your present company and get a raise. You begin to make phone calls to other companies to use as leverage against your present employer. It is not a good idea to use the offer of a new job as leverage for a better position where you are presently. This could backfire on you at some later date. Some managers have long memories and are not very forgiving. If I am your boss, I'm encouraging you to take the position because I will always have to be in a position of strength.

I have seen this happen in the midst of a very important project. The individual was turned down for a raise because he was already above where he should have been. What he suffered from was a severe case of self-adulation, thinking that he was more valuable than he actually was. He had a part to play in the project, but he was not irreplaceable. People make major mistakes when they think that they cannot be replaced. Everyone can be replaced, especially in large corporations that have systems in place. The system doesn't change, although the people may. The new person just has to learn the system. This person did indeed receive his raise. The situation left a very bad taste in the mouth of his employer because it upset the wage compensation distribution for the entire department. After the project was finished, he was dismissed without explanation. They were merciful in that they gave him three days to find another job.

Some Good Advice

There are many things that can compel someone to begin a search for another job. Perhaps the most important reason is money. You have made several requests for an increase in compensation and have been denied. The reasons for the denial are immaterial. Having begun the search for a new job by contacting a prospective employer, make certain that it is what you are looking for. Once having made the commitment in the form of a verbal agreement, do not renege on your decision because of a counter offer from your present employer. Employers can play games too. One game that you should refuse to play is "O.K., I'll stay." What is the game of "O.K., I'll stay?" It's simple really.

You made your request known. The management decided that you were not worth the increase. Some other employer decides that you are indeed worth the compensation being offered. The two of you have agreed on a start date. All that is left is the task of informing your present employer. He may be shocked at the news that you are leaving in two weeks. A few phone calls are made. Your boss calls you into his office and asks you one question and one question only. "What will it take for you to stay?" Your reply should be, "I have made a commitment to another company and my word is my bond. I have to leave the company and there are no hard feelings on my part. I see this as an opportunity that I must seize." Who can be angry with you after uttering that? Instead, your reply is, "The new company has agreed to pay me…." Now your boss agrees to pay you the exact same amount and you reply, "O.K., I'll stay."

Several things have happened now that you have changed your mind, and none of them are good. One question to ask yourself is, if you were not worth the money prior to making arrangements to leave, what makes you worth the money now that you have arranged employment elsewhere? Aren't you the same person, possessing the same skills and work ethic? Your present employer has lost some respect for you because it is known that your word is no good. This decision has also angered the new prospective employer because arrangements were made to add you to the payroll. One should always remember that one job is a stepping stone to another, increasing in stature and compensation along the way.

Burning bridges along the way is not advisable. You never know when you will have to return across that bridge.

Returning across the bridge is a metaphor for renewing old contacts. It could be as simple as meeting with a former boss and asking for employment. It could even be a case of later meeting the person you once broke your commitment to. The statement, "It's a small world" is commonly used for that reason. You never know when or where you will meet up with someone from the past. It is desirable that the circumstances surrounding the meeting be amicable. The last thing you want to see at a job interview later on is that very same person. That interview is over, although it may not be verbally expressed.

More Good Advice

Never reveal your strategy before your plans are well underway. There are vindictive managerial types who will not sit quietly while you plan your escape. They may ask you to leave before you are ready to go. That may be fine with you if you are awarded severance pay. Your premature departure can then be treated as a paid vacation. What if there is no semi-golden handshake? Then it's out of the door with your pockets empty. In an ideal world, those who would be saddened at your departure would be happy that a career move was made for your betterment. That is not always the case, as some have discovered too late. I adhere to the old saying, "Loose lips sink ships."

Sometimes your departure is taken personally rather than just as a move to better one's lot in life. If you are employed within a small company or business where there are no formal guidelines for promotions or transfers, it is in your best interest to be careful to whom you reveal your plans. A boss or coworker going nowhere may be jealous that you have made plans and are headed for something good. They may seek to damage the deal. In most cases, a coworker is not in a position to interrupt something of this nature that has been set in place. The same cannot be said for a boss. Some people cannot tolerate seeing other people's lives blessed. Tragic but true.

BE PREPARED FOR FAILURE

What are you going to do if your strategy does not work? I'll tell you what you are going to do. The focus of your attention will be on developing a new strategy. There is no guarantee that you will succeed upon your first try at doing anything. Failure can be painful and disappointing. As you may remember, when trying to ride a two-wheel bicycle as a child, there was some pain involved. The pain came from your contact with the ground after losing your balance and falling. That did not deter you from accomplishing your goal. You could see the elation and expressions of joy on your friends' faces while riding their bikes. You were determined to do the same. There were no thoughts of quitting, no matter how many times you fell. You knew full well that if you continued to try, you would eventually succeed. The examples of success were before you. Your friends riding their bikes was proof that it could be done. They were no smarter or gifted than you.

I love to give analogies when trying to convey a message. Sometimes the analogies are long-winded, but pointed. I counsel in this fashion, that finding your place in the job market is like searching for oil in an oil field. There is abundant proof that there is oil present below the ground. You see your fellow prospectors hitting the jackpot. If you do not strike oil on the first try, drill another hole. If on the second try you do not strike oil, drill another hole. If you stop drilling, you are guaranteed not to strike oil. Continuing to drill provides you with the best chance at success. What is the point? DO NOT GIVE UP! From your failures, develop a mental library of "Lessons Learned." In this manner, you will refine your technique and hone your skills. In a given situation, you will know what works and what does not work. That is what developing a strategy is all about.

Do not waste valuable time treading on the same turf, trying to make something work that won't. This is not the same as giving up. Giving up means you stop trying. What I am speaking of is something entirely different. It would be equivalent to a door-to-door salesman not having success selling expensive vacuum cleaners in an impoverished area. His or her lack of success is no reflection on the quality of the product he or she is selling. He or she must move to a different area in order to increase the chances of success. The most simplistic strategy is this: if you want to get somewhere, stay in the presence of people who are going somewhere.

GETTING ALONG WITH PEOPLE

"Follow after the things which make for peace..."
Romans 14:19

Who can debate that getting along with people is a difficult task? I happen to believe that it is an art form that can be learned. For me, getting along with people comes easy. I happen to love people. To me, the greater the variety, the more interesting the environment because each person adds something unique. What does it have to do with getting a better job? The answer is one that is complex in explanation but simple to understand. There are certain individuals who don't care whether they can get along with others. Those persons are business owners and those who are independently wealthy. The rest of us who work for a living must contend with the attitudes, moods, and idiosyncrasies of those around us as we attempt to get our work done. We are not independent but dependent upon one another for our existence. Make no mistake, it is people who will make things happen for you. It has been my experience and teaching that nice guys (and gals) finish first. You may not win every battle, but over the long haul, you'll win the war. It is being a bit unrealistic to insist that we all like each other. That would be a mandate impossible to fulfill. We do not have to like one another but we do have to work together. Asking that we be cordial and polite is not unreasonable.

Being difficult to get along with does at least two things if not more. It severely curtails your ability to become employed somewhere else. It puts you on the list of people to get rid of when the opportunity presents itself. Who would recommend you for a job when it is widely known that you are the type to be avoided? What may happen is that a job could be found for you to get you away from where you are presently employed. The premise being, to let you become someone else's headache. Secondly, it hinders your ability to receive and transmit information. People have a tendency to avoid those who are unpleasant and migrate towards those who are. I have discovered cases where vital information was withheld from certain individuals because of their general "nasty" dispositions. They do eventually receive the information but it is not given in a timely manner. That is not a good thing.

As one of my college professors once told me, "You can't choose who you work with. Your boss does that." That statement was in response to my complaints about a group project that I was to begin working on. The class was not allowed to choose the individual members of each group. That was done by the professor. I wanted to pick the individual members who I was going to be working with on the project. My goal was to be allied with individuals who would do their share of the work. I had worked on enough group projects where that was not the case. There were individuals who did practically nothing and shared in the group project grade of "A." After the first or second project, you learned your lesson and tried to get the composition of the group placed in your hands.

The statements of my professor were right on target. In real life, you may work with people whom you really do not like. Who can account for personality conflicts? Perhaps you are too tall or too short for someone's liking. The reasons are as numerous as stars in the sky. You may dress in a manner that some feel shows them up. One secretary that I know of was hated because she wore her fur coat to work in the winter months. The other secretaries felt that she was showing them up and was being paid considerably more than they were. I knew this woman personally and knew of the circumstances involving the fur coat. The coat was a gift from the estate of a deceased relative. She wore it to work because there was no place else to wear it. Personality conflicts arise out of all kinds of frivolous things.

Know this for certain, you cannot avoid conflicts, they come with the people. You are not going to leave one job and go to another where conflicts do not exist. I have been through the gamut of people who did not like me for all sorts of reasons; that was unfortunate. We did have to work together and I was going to act in as professional a manner as possible, even if they weren't. There are some people who have the ability to make your job an absolute chore. Your thoughts are along the line of, "It shouldn't be this hard to get a job done." One cannot act in a cowardly manner to avoid conflict. You must be willing to confront individuals when oversights or mistakes have been made. It is how the individual is approached that can make the difference in whether the conflict will erupt into something greater. To avoid this, do not personalize the problem. Portray it as a misunderstanding that can be resolved and do not assess blame. If you sense that the individual is being offended, offer an apology and clearly state that it was not your intention to injure. Stay focused. That is the mission ahead of you. Knowing what your goal is and not being deterred by obstacles revolving around personalities is vital. No one said that it was going to be easy. Time eventually runs out on difficult people. Soon, their reputations will precede them, and guess what? They're finished. Always treat people the way you would like to be treated and you cannot go wrong. It is a written law that we reap what we sow.

You always want to be known as a person who can get things done not by strong arming and intimidating people, but by persuasion and endearment. Compelling people to want to do things for you is by far the preferred method. Establishing a reputation as a person who gets things done will have the [headhunters] ringing your phone off the hook. The people with whom you have worked in the past will help to spread your prowess. They are doing the same thing you are, looking for a better job. Therein lies the fulfillment of your goal of getting a better job. This is how you get things done. Realize first that it is people who are going to help get things done for you. You are not an island and you cannot do everything yourself. You need people to help you. Your disposition and your treatment of your fellow human beings play a major role in becoming successful in your endeavor.

One of my clients had a very capable individual in his employ. Although thoroughly versed in many functions of the department, this individual was not liked. He was abrasive, short tempered, and moody. If you think that being liked is not important, it is important to be liked by the right people. This individual had many good ideas and made verbal suggestions that had merit. In order to get your ideas acted upon, you have to be in a position to influence people. One cannot be influential when one lacks the interpersonal skills that are necessary to build alliances.

SHARE YOUR KNOWLEDGE

The most beloved people on any job are those who willingly share their knowledge. To pinpoint them further, they are those who give assistance without an arrogant delivery, not making others seem inferior. One should always be mindful that knowledge did not come about by spontaneous generation. From the boiler operator in the bowels of an office building to the chief executive officer of a Fortune 500 company, someone had to show each person what to do. They were not charged for the instruction they received. Neither were you. So, freely you have received and freely you should give. You make yourself a valuable commodity when you have established a reputation for helping people. You will be known as someone who can be called on in a time of crisis to provide guidance.

Furthermore, there is a residual effect to being helpful. Bosses will invest money in you in the form of more training. The more you are trained, the more valuable you become. The more valuable you become, the easier it is to justify increases in your monetary compensation. Get it! In addition, you are aiding your department or company by helping to build redundancy in their system. The system will be able to function in the absence of one or two individuals. This is one of the most logical ways to merit salary increases. It is preferred over demanding increases because of time served on the job. Time spent on the job is not necessarily a determinant for monetary compensation.

Don't hoard information. Doing so is self-defeating. Some misguided individuals think that keeping information to themselves makes their jobs secure. It does the opposite. It provides management with an incentive to place you elsewhere, someplace where the dissemination of information is not necessary. It also causes people to work around you, keeping you out of the informational loop. Why would they do so to you? Because they know that you hoard information. This can cause a great deal of strife and animosity among those who are in need of the information. Management now has to deal with the conflicts that arise out of this turmoil. How will you defend this position of isolation?

Cooperation is an employment strategy. I have long ago determined that my position would be one of sharing knowledge. I can always get more knowledge. Helping someone to perform better should give you a sense of fulfillment. Sharing your knowledge will also give you an incentive to acquire more by continuing your education and training. One should be increasing one's knowledge base until the day that one gives up the ghost and dies. Sharing your knowledge is a good thing and, as previously stated, can be used as an employment strategy.

SHARE THE GLORY

When you are working on a project with one or more persons, share the accolades that may come from **A Job Well Done.** Unselfish acts such as this tend to promote harmony within a department or group. Bosses love it when they do not have to deal with interdepartmental problems that arise from personal conflicts. Everyone likes to be a part of the winning team. Avoid placing yourself at the front of the group, even if you did all of the work. Chances are that who did what is already known. You will be thought of as a good person for not claiming what was rightfully yours, the glory. Search out those who need help on projects and who are in a tight squeeze as far as time allotted for completion. Be a "Team Player." What does being a team player mean? Don't be greedy. Let other people share in the success. Do not allow it to be "I," but let it be "we." There have been cases when I included individuals as giving assistance when they had very little to do with the project. Not having an inflated ego, I could allow room for them. What I gained was an ally, a person who would come to my aid the next time I really needed him. That is an invaluable tactic that should be considered also as a strategy. It is far better having people to work with you than against you.

DON'T MAKE ENEMIES UNNECESSARILY

In the pursuit of your daily activities, you are bound to upset someone. It cannot be helped. People are the most marvelous creatures on the face of the earth. They are also the most unpredictable. Reactions to conflicts are not always based on logical thought. There are some conflicts that can be resolved without hard feelings when the individuals involved are intelligent and reasonable. Misunderstandings happen for all sorts of reasons. Lack of communication has to be foremost. When you are forging ahead on the job or on a career path for greatness, know this, you will have enemies. There will be individuals who are dead set against you making it to the level where you want to be. Do not be deterred by them.

- Allow every knock they give you to be a boost upward.
- Perform good deeds for people without an expectation of reward. Good things will happen for you.
- Be "Wise as a serpent and harmless as a dove." Your enemies are not going to help you. Work at placing yourself in a position where they cannot hurt you. There is no better way to do that than to be at a level above them.
- Don't despise them, pray for them.
- Avoid using people in an obvious manner. You will be seen as being manipulative.

MIND YOUR OWN BUSINESS

There you are, a new person to a job or department. A well-meaning person comes up to you and says that he is going to show you the ropes. He begins to give you the scope on everyone as he sees it. He sees it as fact though. Be wary of misguided individuals. You will be assuming their prejudices. You can only know a person through first-hand experience. Reserve judgment on these people until you get to know them, then form your own opinions. There are individuals whom I do not have high regard for, but my wife does. I came to know them first. Rather than prejudice her feelings towards them because of our disagreement, I didn't tell her about it. These people had done nothing to her. Why should she be made to assume my experiences?

How often does this type of thing happen in an office environment? Office environments are singled out because of the need for cooperation in a close setting. Cooperation between parties is absolutely necessary. Two individuals have become smoking break buddies or perhaps their friendship is much deeper. The break gives them a chance to discuss office problems. One of them begins to tell of the conflict he is having with another person. The friend becomes sympathetic and decides to shun the offender. What's the point? Something that I have reiterated over and over again, you are always looking for a better job. Care must be taken not to do anything that can hinder your objective.

You cannot predict where someone's career will take them. That person whom you have decided to shun because of your friend is now a level or two above you. He now is in a position of strength and can have influence on what happens to you. You have made an enemy unnecessarily. Some may say that this hypothetical scenario is too absurd but I have seen this happen. You wonder why your requests are hitting a brick wall. Maybe someone is blocking them. Taking on someone else's fight could be a career killer. That does not mean that it is a job killer. The best advice is don't become embroiled in squabbles that do not concern you.

Avoid becoming distressed because of what you see others doing or not doing. I was in the office of one of my clients and was engaging the administrative assistant in a conversation concerning some billing procedures. Her boss's office was adjacent to hers. His office was vacant with the light off. In walks a person who happens to be at the same level as her boss. He charges into her boss's office, turns on the light and then shuts the door. This gentleman then began to use the telephone. The administrative assistant became incensed at this trespass and cried out "What is he doing in my boss's office?" Being in tune with the situation, I said to her, "What do you care? He is at a much higher level than you are and you never know whom you may be working for one day. Do not damage a relationship before it starts." Quizzing a boss about the meaning of his intrusion would not be a smart thing to do. He will not have you fired but he will not forget how you overstepped your bounds. Bosses love to be treated with respect. Don't we all?

****

Pay attention to what you should be doing and not the actions of others. This is easier said than done, especially when it appears that they are being rewarded for their frivolity. It is easy to ask yourself, "Why am I knocking myself out? They are getting paid and I am doing all of the work." Know this, the antics of those not performing to the level of expectation are not going unnoticed. It takes time, but the good guys (and gals) always win. There is a law that sees to it that we get the good that is coming to us. This same law sees to it that we get a return on the bad that we hand out. It is called, "The Law of Sowing and Reaping." If a situation arises which necessitates staff reductions, you want to be one of those whom management cannot do without. I have met a few individuals of this caliber who did not have a professional status (non-degree).

Regardless of the commotion around them, they stay tuned to their objective. Various methods were used to accomplish this. Sometimes headphones would be used to listen to music or other radio offerings. Occasionally, the individual would get up and walk away from his assigned work area if the frivolity became too intense. Whatever method is used, one has to stay vigilant and forever focused on the goal, continued and better employment.

MIND THE BUSINESS OF OTHER PEOPLE

There is no big secret in getting along with people. Everyone has needs and desires. Finding out what the needs are of other people is paramount in your quest for getting what you need or desire. Within the automotive community, there has always been some friction between the engineering and manufacturing sectors. Both disciplines are after the same results, a quality produced vehicle that is affordable. They are, however, sometimes at odds as to how to achieve this goal. Engineering is concerned with the design and functionality of the vehicle. At the manufacturing end (assembly plants), the concern is assembling all the parts in a manner that is efficient and inexpensive. Engineers are notorious for designing things that meet their criterion but not those of the assembly plants. In some cases, engineers are humorously considered as the enemy.

In my many visits to the plants, I was easy to spot because of my shirt and tie. Irrespective of my appearance, I had a mission to accomplish. I needed to acquire some parts for a design review that was taking place that afternoon. This was no time to get all the proper forms signed. The mission was not originally mine. It belonged to a fellow engineer. When the engineering group manager told him that the parts were needed for the meeting, he said, "You need a shipper request to get parts out of the plant and it takes seven days to get one." Indeed it did take a shipper request to get parts out of the plant. It only takes seven days to get one if you are not adept at dealing with people. I told the engineering group manager that I would take care of retrieving the parts for the meeting.

I was mindful that I was going to a place where I was considered a friend. I do not believe in the practice of "fighting fire with fire," but rather, the "fighting of fire with water." Water takes the heat out of the flame. Without heat, the fire will be snuffed out. Now, consider this situation. I have volunteered to go into an assembly plant and remove parts without the proper paperwork. Moreover, it is in an area where I was totally unfamiliar. The people whom I needed to do most of the work for me were bargaining unit employees. What was I to do? I believed in my own principals. Not knowing the specific needs of people whom I didn't know, I thought of what their primary need would be, food! So I ordered a pizza and took it down to the assembly plant.

I took the heat out of the flame before it started by explaining to the shipping clerk that I did not have the proper forms ready. I would get them and bring them to her later if given the opportunity. Further, I told her that I needed her assistance in helping me to help the company. That gave her a feeling of importance. It was a comforting stroke and we all need those kind of strokes. I then presented her and her colleagues with the pizza. She instructed me to go get the part and she would make out the shipper. Walking along the assembly line, I found the part that I was looking for. When I returned to the shipping dock, the shipper was completed. I was handed the documentation necessary to give to the security guard at the gate. Now I was a hero to my boss, having saved the day.

Lesson Learned

People can make things happen for you. Mind the business of other people. Find out what the needs and desires are in their lives and satisfy them first. They will reward you by helping with your needs and desires. Discovering the needs of those with whom you work can be easily accomplished. Be mindful of the people who are experiencing misfortune, such as a death in the family or an illness. Pay a visit to the family or at least give verbal acknowledgment of the situation. As previously stated, you cannot make it alone. You need the help of other people. In order to enlist their help, you will have to do your homework beforehand. Building your list of acquaintances is both a strategy for employment and an act of getting along with people. This can be done by breaking bread with your colleagues or attending events together after work.

QUERY YOUR FRIENDS AND TRUSTED COLLEAGUES

It is difficult to assess one's own disposition. More clearly stated, you cannot see yourself. Nor can you determine how you are perceived by other people. For this, you need the help of friends, relatives and those who work closely with you and whose opinion you respect. These are the individuals who can tell you if you have an abrasive personality, lack discretion or are impolite. They can also inform you if your interpersonal skills are not up to par as far as manners and personal grooming are concerned. These are all characteristics that may not be shared with you unless someone is asked to do so. I conducted an informal survey of this type. It was a requirement for some graduate studies. You will be surprised at what those with whom you interact everyday think about you.

AVOID CONTROVERSIAL DISCUSSIONS

Nothing can disrupt the harmony of the workplace like discussions involving politics and religion. These are issues that people feel passionately about, and that passion can lead to some pretty heated arguments. This is not to say that the arguments will result in violence, but productivity will be hurt by this behavior. Being a controversial person in matters that do not concern work will place you on the list of undesirables. No boss wants someone in his department who disrupts the flow of work. There are places and times to engage your colleagues in these types of discussions. They can take place during lunch or breaks but not during the time in which business should be conducted.

There was one young lady who considered her workplace a fertile field for Christian evangelism. It was the normal procedure for this company to use temporary employment agencies as a screening mechanism for future employees. The candidate would be on-site for a period of a year or so. That would give the company ample time to evaluate the behavior and habits of these individuals. If they noticed that the person was not performing in a manner suitable for them, they could do one of two things. They could refuse to hire the person, or they could have the person recalled by the temporary employment agency. Either one of these is not a good thing. When you get an opportunity to better yourself with a good job, wisdom and prudence should be exercised. Because she and I had friends common to us outside of work, we became friendly.

In a manner as politely as I could, so as to not offend, I attempted to give her the benefit of years of experience. Her colleagues did not want to be preached to, nor did some of the senior men want to be told that they could not curse around her. I admired her distaste for profanity, but there is such a thing as freedom of speech, even if it is offensive speech. The entire office staff could not change their habits just for her. She felt that it was a display of respect for her as a religious woman. My retort was that, "Respect is earned and not granted by being commanded to do so." How was I to make her understand that proselytizing would not be seen by all as a noble undertaking?

She had placed herself in a precarious position. She needed to have steady employment to support her family. She was the head of a household that consisted of four children. This company had a policy of having the group that you were going to be working with aid in the evaluation of prospective employees. She was going to need a recommendation from the very people whom she was offending. All of my attempts to council her failed. I did not want her to squander a golden opportunity. She did just that. Not only was she removed from the building, she was taken off the contact list of the temporary employment agency. I saw her several months later at a shopping mall and she relayed the story to me of what happened. I didn't say to her, "I told you so." But I did tell her so!

SENSITIVITY

In this day and age of political correctness, it is becoming increasingly more difficult to make a casual remark, joke, or otherwise express an opinion without offending someone. There is some speech that is so vile, contemptible, and repulsive that it cannot be dismissed as, "I was just kidding around." The focus here is not what we say to other people. But what they say to us and the process of getting over it. In my youth, I was susceptible to the wounds that resulted from name calling. I would complain to my father about what the kids were calling me. His reply was, "You are only as big as what you allow to bother you." That was not comforting to me at the time. However, over the years I put his saying into practice and learned how to overcome those who knowingly or unknowingly uttered insulting or vulgar speech.

I have noticed that minorities and women sometimes have their guns cocked. What does having your guns cocked mean? It describes a situation in which you are expecting the worst from people. You prepare for the worst by displaying the posture of the Warner Brothers cartoon character "Yosemite Sam." He is commonly depicted as having both guns drawn and uttering, "Back Off." When this type of attitude is taken, everything is offensive, even when it isn't meant to be. When your guns are cocked, there is the feeling that those who are not like you, or not part of your group, are the enemy. You are unyielding and ready for conflict.

There was a purchasing department at General Motors that was notorious for its "Tell us what you want and get out" attitude. There were two women who primarily displayed this attitude. Granted, they were under a lot of pressure and had positions that placed them under scrutiny, scrutiny that their male counterparts did not endure. One day I had to go and see the worst one of the two. As I entered her cubical, she looked at me with "THE LOOK." Her colleagues were gazing at me too. I did the only thing I could think of. I put up two fingers in a split "V" demonstration and uttered the word "Peace." They burst into spontaneous laughter and the ice was broken.

DON'T PLAY GAMES

Have you ever noticed that people play games with one another? It can aggravate you to no end when someone purposely is deceptive or beguiling. You have asked a question in good faith. The person being asked knew what your intent was or knew what you wanted. However, you did not pose the question perfectly. So your question was answered erroneously. You find out later that the situation was not as reported. Do not get angry nor plan to get even. You cannot predict where every individual you work with will end up. You may not even know the extent of their network. Bad seeds have been planted and it may yield a crop unfavorable to you. When you play games with people, you are disrespecting them. One thing I have learned is that all people want to be respected, no matter what their level of education or social/economic status.

This is especially true of the elder worker when he works alongside someone younger. The younger person may have a tendency to point out the mistakes of their elder, albeit grammatical or otherwise. I have seen a situation in which a younger worker so belittled the elder, that the elder quit in the middle of a cooperative project. The result being, the younger worker had to complete the entire project alone. No one was going to be hired to assist him. In addition, the younger worker was made to explain why he antagonized someone to the point of making him walk off the job. This elder worker was well liked by all and was a very conscientious employee.

The practice of game playing will one day get the player in trouble. I have always made a practice of handing out good because of the biblical truth found in Galatians 5:16, "Whatsoever a man soweth, that shall he also reap." Modern day translation, "What goes around comes around." The originator of this saying is unknown, but of a truth, what you hand out comes back to you. When it comes back like a boomerang, it is always greater than what you handed out. Knowing this, it behooves one to treat people with respect, to be helpful and respectful so that one will be respected and helped in a time of need. It matters not whether you like them or get along with them. When it comes to performing on the job, don't play games.

****

Perhaps I have become somewhat hardened because of the environment in which I have trained for so long. As a whole, automotive designers are just like everyone else who has a skill. There is a marked difference between being skilled and educated. I equate true education with civilized behavior. I have worked among some very uncivilized but talented individuals. Revealing weakness would be used as a tool against you. For some reason, these individuals derived joy from making a person squirm. I was in a field that was almost completely dominated by white males and my presence was considered an intrusion into a sacred domain. No matter, I wasn't going anywhere. So I had to learn to ignore the racial epithets and continue on. This was a monumental undertaking during the late 70's when Alex Haley's series, "Roots," was airing on television. I was made the brunt of many cruel and vicious jokes.

However, I had a strategy for getting a better job. That strategy involved learning all that those men had to give. It stands to reason that they would be more willing to help someone they liked rather than a person they did not like. I could not accomplish this goal by alienating myself from them. I made it my mission to put them to shame instead. I fought fire with water by taking the heat out of the flame of racial bigotry. Some women are experiencing this very thing in many fields of work that were once the bastions of the white male. One has to understand their fear and deal with it along those lines. It is possible to become too sensitive. That is the point where I feel we are today.

Supposedly, all sorts of harassment is going on in the workplace. As is the case concerning most issues, things tend to get exaggerated and painted with a wide brush. Everyone who claims harassment is not being truly victimized by it. On the other hand, one can gain respect and accolades for holding one's own in an environment that is unfriendly. Place yourself above the fray. Do not run to the boss about things that are said that are out of place. Handle it in a manner in which you place yourself above the person(s) involved. This may be easier said than done, but people will take notice of your poise and character. One must always remember that getting that better job is perhaps 20% of what you know and 80% of who you know. A lot of good jobs are never posted. The notice goes up after the decision has been made as to who will fill the position. I have participated in that very thing. You want the right people to know you and take notice. Not being overly sensitive and having a degree of tolerance is a **"strategy"** for obtaining a better job. So if you are thin-skinned, thicken it.

TRUESTORY

It was one of the most frightening work experiences I have ever had. It was the clash between myself and the card-carrying Ku Klux Klan member, James Fenny. I wrote of my tenure at a small contract design firm called Special Engineering in Dearborn, Michigan in the chapter called **"Attitude And Performance."** When James Fenny was placed on contract, the room supervisor placed him at the drafting board in front of me. His specialty was tooling design. Good tooling designers were hard to find. One had to be fast as well as good. Mr. Fenny was a journeyman tooling designer in that he lived in his car and would travel to wherever the next job was. His home state was Kentucky.

James was polite enough in the beginning. His personal hygiene was not the best. In fact, it wasn't any good at all. He did have a tendency to embark on political discussions. Fine, I could tolerate that also. The one thing that did bug me about him was his insistence on knowing the ethnic origin of all the people in the room. This led to a tirade about how Adolph Hitler was a truly great man and that he never had Jewish people killed. That was enough for me. I had to put a stop to the defaming of an entire race of people. I politely asked him to stop making those remarks to me about other races. That led to an explosion of his temper. The room was fairly quiet when he shouted at me, "How dare you correct me, you ____________." Then a series of racial slurs proceeded out of his mouth. Now the entire room is looking at us as he declares, "I won't sit by a ____________." (some more nasty stuff was uttered).

No one was more shocked than I as he erupted like a volcano, only this was without warning. He began to throw his belongings into a box and he moved several boards away. As if that were not enough, he erected a barrier to block his view of me. The barrier was made of boxes and large sheets of cardboard. He did not notice that all were gazing upon him with astonishment. His next task was to solicit those who would be sympathetic to his cause. He had to show his credentials, his KKK card. This guy scared everyone. The management called me into the office and asked me if everything was going to be all right. They could not dismiss him. He was in the middle of the project and he was very good at what he did. He was skilled, not educated. I assured them that there would be no problem as far as I was concerned.

The next three months were very uncomfortable. I could see this grown man, every bit of 60 years old, peering at me through the cracks in his barrier. I made sure that where he was, I wasn't. On the occasions when nature called, I used the executive's restroom. There was no way that I was going to take the chance of being trapped in the men's room with this guy. James Fenny completed his project and told some of the other designers that he was leaving the state. Before Mr. Fenny departed, he thanked me for being so nice to him. I kid you not! I was asleep in my car during the lunch period. My head was against the window of the door on the driver's side. Mr. Fenny began knocking on the window. I awakened abruptly and saw him. I thought my heart was going to pound its way out of my chest. He beckoned me to roll down the glass. I hesitated, then rolled it down about an inch. "I just want to say thank you for being kind."

"That's O.K.," I said sharply and rolled the window back up.

Mr. Fenny left the state and no one ever heard from him again. I will never forget Mr. Fenny and his peculiarities. Yes, **"getting along with people"** is an art form.

POLITICS

"Work before pleasure, but neither before politics."
Author Unknown

It has been said that life revolves around three things: love, the antithesis of love (which is war) and politics. At the heart of many issues in our lives is politics. Understanding this fundamental premise will bring you answers as to why certain things happen. In my youth, I thought that politics was all about political parties and the disputes between them. The political parties were basically Democrats, Republicans, New Age, Green Peace, Libertarians, Communists and Neo this or that. In these instances, politics was all about the method by which a select group of people set out to redistribute resources that belong to others. That is what is called pure politics.

It matters not what political party you espouse or general philosophy you follow, everyone can at times be political. With an abundance of workplace experience behind me, I have learned that politics is about a whole lot more. When it comes to the subject of employment, it can all be politics. Politics can govern who is hired, who gets fired, who gets promoted, who gets demoted, who gets the gravy and who gets the shaft. I emphatically declare that those who say they want nothing to do with politics do not recognize their actions as being political. It is still politics, whether the activities are related to religion, education, social welfare organizations, recreation or employment. It matters not if you consider yourself part of a labor union, professional organization, or non-bargaining unit. Politics is in there somewhere.

If you give a recommendation for a friend or relative to get hired, that is an action in the affirmative, a preferential action, and is political. The people that you gather with to go for coffee or lunch are grouped together in a social bond. You discuss things that other people are not made privy to. They are your friends. They certainly are not your enemies or you would not be dining with them. The clique that is formed is political. Those outside your clique are just that, outsiders.

Let's say, for example, you are the administrative assistant in a certain department. You are given assignments by two different individuals. The persons are at a much higher level than you and both told you the same story, they need their jobs done right away. The decision you'll make on which assignment to do first will be a decision based on your politics. You will consider which person's assignment will be more beneficial to complete first. You will also consider what the ramifications will be for each outcome.

If you have ever sent out a resume, you did it with the intention of impressing the recipient enough to call you for an interview. There were others who were vying for the job also. You had your resume professionally done with the hope of gaining an edge. You were attempting to influence the decision-making process and that is political. When you were in college, did you sit in the front row when your professors lectured? The idea was for him or her to associate your name with your face. You stayed after the classes were dismissed to talk with the instructors. You were staging yourself for a good grade for the class. That's political.

When you are in a position of authority and have workers answering to you, it lies within your power to solicit and extend favoritism. It is conceivable that you could make more money available to certain individuals by providing them with overtime. It may also be within your discretion to provide additional paid days off or excused absences. This would only be done for those with whom you have formed an alliance. These are tactics that were prevalent prior to the application of workplace rules and standards brought on by the organized labor movement. The unions removed this form of workplace politics.

At the heart of many awards and beauty pageants is the game of politics. You and I may look at the contestants and be unable to distinguish their beauty and talents from each other. They all look beautiful and speak well. What is the determining factor in who becomes the winner? It is which contestant, along with her supporters, engage in the best politics for the first place prize. In many cases, the winner has been decided before the contest has been conducted.

At the time of this book's writing, the annual balloting is being done by the sports writers to determine which football player will win the famed Heismann Trophy. By definition, it is supposed to be awarded to the best football player that year. Because the decision is made by the ballot box, it is pure politics. The votes of the sports writers are subjective and influenced by many factors other than who was actually the best player that year.

My baptism into corporate politics started when I was 20 years old. I approached Orin Davis very gingerly because I was not sure how he would react to my request. My problem was a simple one back in 1975. I wanted to change jobs. After a few moments of small talk about our families, I proceeded to ask him about the possibilities of him interceding on my behalf at Chrysler Engineering. The location was the engineering headquarters in Highland Park, Michigan. Orin was a member of the Chrysler team that investigated accidents involved in the shipping of automobiles.

I came to know Orin through a mutual friend. After some minor verbal exchanges of information (my work history, education and training) he said he would get back to me within a few days. A few days it was. Two days to be exact. Orin gave me an employment application and told me to return it to him personally. At the very top of the application was the signature of someone unknown to me, Dennis Fisher.

Officially, there were no openings for drafting personnel within the building. More to the point, there was not a job-posting listing the department or a manager's name for contact. Dennis Fisher's signature was the key that opened the door for me to become employed at Chrysler engineering. Haven't you heard it said that it is some of what you know but more of who you know? This was proof to me and it was politics, although I didn't recognize it. Dennis Fisher was the director of personnel. There was no one higher up on the personnel ladder than he. There are always positions open. Some have to be reserved for the children of the executives who are out of school for the summer. Those jobs were not posted and no one outside of the system could avail themselves of one.

In large corporations, I have found that there is no shortage of talented people. These corporations have structures that resemble a pyramid. At the base, you have many workers supporting the efforts of the company. As one rises through the ranks, the positions become less numerable. A supervisor should have a set number of employees under his or her immediate control. In order to justify a position as a manager, a person should have a set minimum number of supervisors. This process continues as the managerial positions become fewer and fewer.

You have a situation where there are 20 people who qualify to become managers and there are only two positions open. What is it that determines which two get the jobs? Politics will determine which two get the job. The politics may be about the color of their skin, the college from which they graduated, the fraternity or sorority to which they belong, their gender, their personal appearance, or their affiliations with other top executives. These are just a few of the things that can, and do, play a part in making the decisions about who receives a job.

Everyone is good. Those who stand head and shoulders above everyone else are far and few between. You know the ones, the individuals who are brilliant. They are on a plateau by themselves. They have gifts from God. They never studied in school and still received A's in their classes. They received a perfect score on their SAT's. They have photographic memories and do brain teaser puzzles for fun. I have met such men and women in this industry. They are the Michael Jordans and the Bill Gateses of this world. Then, there are the rest of us. We are the individuals waiting for our ship to come in. The politics of the company play a part in determining our fate. If a certain level of management or positions have an insufficient number of women, some will be chosen. If a certain level has an insufficient number of ethnic minorities, some will be chosen. The large corporations are on a quest to become completely politically correct. For someone to think that they are just the right candidate, with no one else qualifying, they are fooling themselves.

I had an engineering group manager tell me that if I were offered a promotion because I was black, I should, "Take it and run." At first, I was offended at this statement because of its underlying message. I wanted to be promoted because I was good and deserved it, not because my skin happened to be the right hue at the time. After many years of observing who got promotions and why they got them, I changed my opinion. Individuals within General Motors and many other companies had received promotions on far less substantive characteristics than skin color. The truthful ones will tell you that they had someone taking care of them. A mentor who watched over them to make sure that they got some gravy on their potatoes.

Everyone gets potatoes. What are potatoes? Potatoes are the paychecks you receive from your employer. The gravy is the perks on top of your paycheck. Other people determine who gets the perks. That means that politics comes into play. To get the perks, you have to play the game of politics. The game takes several forms and has no borders. It is international in scope.

When you see executives at high levels within a corporation, it is natural to assume that they all are smarter than you. One thinks that they have achieved their status because they are outstanding and have unique decision-making abilities. That is the farthest thing from the truth. Some of them have received their promotions to the top because of the contacts they have sustained throughout their careers. While observing them at one group meeting, I thought, "What do all of those people do? How did they get where they are?" I assumed that raw ability and talent did it. It took some time for reality to strike. They got where they were because they knew someone.

In conversations with them, you find out that some of these men are no smarter than you. They have made too many dumb decisions to be brilliant. These were decisions in which there were no consequences for their costly mistakes, except being transferred to another division. That's what usually happened. If the guy screwed up in a major fashion at one division, transfer him to a different one. He'll perform better there. Yeah, right! If an inquiry was made as to where these guys went to school, you would soon discover that a great number of them were graduates of the same schools. Women and minorities in these executive positions are not afforded the luxury of making mistakes. They are held to a much different standard of scrutiny. That alone brings added pressure. However, if they want to play in the big leagues, they have to be able to hit curve balls.

Another discovery is that some of these gentlemen live in the same subdivision. It is logical to assume that they frequently see one another. Thus, when a man or woman is excluded from participating in an informal meeting being held at a health club, country club or some other private establishment, it becomes de facto preferential treatment. There are a whole host of combinations and permutations to this story. Thus my contention that the process is called affirmative action for minorities and a process of preferential treatment for non-minorities. Affirmative action and preferential policies are the same entity. Preferential polices benefit whites and affirmative action policies benefit blacks and other minority groups.

All people, irrespective of race, gender, creed or nationality, are comfortable with people who are like them. This is thought to be racism and is usually labeled as such. It isn't racism. It is human nature and has to do with our **"comfort zones." "Comfort zones"** have their own form of politics.

Let's say for instance, you take a job in a new department or company where you and the staff are unfamiliar with each other. Let's go even further and say that the existing staff resents your being among them. You are considered an outsider and they have firmly established this notion. You can sense their ire as you move around the workplace. There will be a ring leader in the group making sure that you remain ostracized from the main body. Your job will be made more difficult than it ought to be. Any mistakes made will be highlighted and made to seem more disastrous than they really are. You may not get faxes or messages that are sent to you. These are the acts of small-minded individuals and this behavior is called workplace politics. Mostly, it stems from professional jealousy.

How are you going to combat this type of behavior? By establishing your own group of trustworthy individuals. You will need good press to combat the bad press you may be receiving. It is important to verbally promote those who will advance your agenda. What agenda, you say? We all have an agenda. It could be as simplistic as placing yourself in a position to get a bigger raise. Or, it could be that you have created a backlog of work so that more over time will come your way. It is through the use of politics that our agendas are carried out. Your agenda may be to become the next president of the company. You will be making decisions and forming alliances in the hope of getting your agenda forwarded. That is called politics.

When an executive has the opportunity to choose a person to fill a position on his staff, is he going to choose an unknown entity? Isn't it more realistic that a golf partner, a fraternity member, a school buddy or a member of his parish, church or synagogue will be chosen? I have seen executives intercede in securing jobs for the sons and daughters of their colleagues. When the jobs become available for students out of college for the summer, doesn't it make sense to you that the sons and daughters of these elite individuals are going to have positions secured for them first? If I were an executive and my daughter needed a summer job and wanted to work at the company where I was employed, I would use every bit of influence I had to secure a spot. I would do it without hesitation. Would I do it for a friend's son or daughter? Of course I would. You would too.

It is nearly impossible for large corporations and businesses to operate without politics edging things along. Politics are too deeply ingrained into the system. For example, in one automotive group that I am familiar with, one of the high level executives retired. Not long after his retirement, his son was placed in charge of a group of engineers. The requirements for heading up the group had been clearly established. This person did not meet the criteria. Several members of the group murmured about the appointment. In their eyes, the logical choice would have been to choose one of them. At least three of them were eminently qualified. When I received the details of what happened, I knew that it was the game of politics being played. The decision had been made and a strategy was in place to move this person along a charted path. To become disgruntled over this appointment would profit nothing. To catch a ride on this train that's going somewhere would have been a strategy for getting a better job.

****

While working for Fisher Body, it became clear that some individuals were being denied positions because of preferential policies. It was so flagrant that General Motors had to bring about drastic changes in the way compensation and promotions were distributed. To say that it was a "Good Ole Boy" network would be a drastic understatement. The annual reviews were entirely subjective, with no measurable job performance criteria. There was this unwritten rule that everyone adhered to on Fridays. It was called Fisher Friday. No other division of General Motors adhered to this rule. No matter how much overtime was being worked during the week, Friday was to be an eight-hour day. It made no difference that we worked on Saturdays. It seemed the big boss, Charles Katco, liked to golf on Fridays. So like minions, the rest of management followed suit and played golf, even if they did not like golf. Playing golf at clubs that excluded blacks put them at a distinct disadvantage. Evoking a preferential policy ensures that the person they wanted would get the position, not necessarily the person who should have been placed in it.

At times, it is difficult to determine a businessman's and company's political ideology. That is why it is common for a businessman or company to contribute to both campaigns of opposing candidates running for an elected office. They are taking a position as being on board no matter who wins. Their allegiance is to themselves. They are in the quest for the almighty dollar, wherever it can be made. They invest their money in, and sell products to, countries that are both friendly and unfriendly to the United States. During the height of the cold war between the Soviet Union and the United States, that great industrialist, Armand Hammer, continued to do business with the Soviets. This goes back to the days of Leonid Brezhnev and was Armand Hammer's policy until his death in 1990.

When asked why he continued to do business with the Soviets, his reply was, "I'm just a businessman." He stated he had no ill will for the people or government of the Soviet Union. He left the saber rattling and the finger pointing to the politicians. The point is businesses will be placed where they can thrive. They will use the politics of the region to assure their success.

What is the message being conveyed? Do not allow the politics to discourage you. You can waste your time and effort trying to right things that are beyond your control. Understand the games that are being played and learn how to play them. One of the wisest men that I have ever known, Reverend Charles O. Miles, frequently made it a point to tell his congregation, "Your understanding will keep you safe." That is to say, when you understand why some things happen or how they work, you can deal with them accordingly. It is when things are clouded in mystery that anguish and turmoil arise. Your lack of trying to succeed should not be based on the excuse of **"politics."** The game of **"politics"** is everywhere and is played by everyone. That excuse will not be good enough.

When you see politics governing the movement of things, it can be disheartening. If you don't have the stomach for it, stay away from large corporations and companies. Look for smaller companies in which to become employed. The game of politics is being played there also, but on a smaller scale.

Wanting to be placed within a large corporate setting is a desire that most of us have had at one time or another. With the largess of many corporations is the illusion of job security. I emphasize the word illusion because no one's job is entirely secure. Everyone can be replaced. There are pros and cons with many of the working situations you may encounter. There are formalities, bureaucratic procedures, inefficiencies, and structure that accompany large corporations. One look at an organizational chart should tell you all you need to know. There is no ambiguity in the question regarding who is answerable to whom. These large corporations have synergy. This allows them to carry on when one or more pieces of the puzzle are missing.

The management is usually well-trained with upgrades to their managerial skills taking place regularly. This is accomplished with training seminars that often take place at locations removed from the surroundings of work. Persons are not thrust into managerial positions and left to fend for themselves. There is too much at stake for the corporation. Your employment within the corporation is seldom placed in jeopardy. Twice a month, or every two weeks, you are going to be paid. The down side is that it takes a lot to work your way through the morass and get to the "top." You have to define for yourself what the "top" is. Getting to the top will involve politics.

If you look at the organizational chart of a poorly-run company, you will understand why the performance is inadequate. That could be a symptom of a more serious problem like poor management skills. For management, there may be no requirement for professional etiquette. Some may even be crude, vulgar and without socially desirable attributes. These people are placed in positions that require them to be able to address the concerns of their employees. What qualified them to be where they are? **"Politics."**

Some Good Advice

A person can become engulfed in politics even though that is not his aim. It can be difficult to remain neutral when management and executives are battling over turf. Therein lies the real power of these men and women, the size of their group or number of people that are under their control. Although two individuals may have the same title, that does not necessarily mean they are equivalent in power. The larger the organization under their control, the larger their budget. That is what makes the distinction between who has the most power. It is decided by how much money they control. When disputes arise in the office or company, if it does not directly affect you, stay out of it. It takes a savvy individual to choose the correct side. From what

I have seen, very few people are good at choosing. Picking the wrong side could get you fired, demoted, or even worse, placed in a stagnant position.

This is especially good advice for administrative assistants or those in similar positions, positions where a person can easily be moved from one office setting to the next. You could end up working for the person for whom you have expressed adverse feelings. If he knows this, and most people would know, you have placed yourself in a precarious situation. Be of good service to all who call upon you, even those you do not work for. Do not become known as someone who is disgruntled. Perform tasks willingly. You will be perceived as being a team player, being cooperative, and easy to get along with. This is a strategy for better employment. Yes, it is playing politics and it is the smart way to play.

If I am a manager taking over a new position with employees reporting to me, those who are disgruntled are not likely to be cooperative. At every opportunity they will grumble, complain, and instigate dissension among the ranks. Knowing this beforehand, I would purge the area of these types and bring in people who are loyal and beholden to me. This is standard practice in pure political settings. You do not want to become one of those pegged for replacement unless that is a part of your **"strategy."** If it is a part of your strategy, it is a bad strategy. It is always desirable to have a favorable reference to place on your resume.

Another example: I am the new owner of a store or some entity that renders service to the public. If I encounter continued insubordinate opposition from the store manager or supervisor, I am not only going to replace him, it will be taken one step further. Everyone who is allied with him will be eliminated also. These are individuals who have forgotten the "golden rule." The "golden rule" states that "He or she who owns the gold makes the rules." As owner of the business, I own the gold and make the rules.

Always remember this: being smart is one thing, possessing political savvy is something else altogether. There are many smart people who go nowhere in their careers because they are too smart for their own good. Having your senses tuned into the political winds can take you far. Such is the nature and reality of politics in the workplace.

TO SUM IT ALL UP

"I have found enthusiasm for work to be the most priceless ingredient in any recipe for success."
Samuel Goldwyn

There is nothing like the feeling of being stuck in a job that you dislike. Some things we do for the love of our families. You may not even dislike the job but have aspirations to move on to something else. The luckiest people in the world are those who are doing what they want to do and are getting paid to do it. In reality, there is no such thing as luck. What we call "luck" happens when opportunity and preparation meet in the life of an individual. Searching for, and obtaining, the job of your dreams has more to do with you than it does anyone else. A better job comes from determining what you want to do with your life, not what others want you to do. A close look at the length of the previous chapters will reveal this fact. The Chapters, **"The Merits Of Work," "Dreaming And Discovery," "A Job Well Done," "The Comfort Zone," "Attitude And Performance," "Preparation," "Presentation,"** and **"Getting Along With People,"** all have to do with the individual's attitude towards himself and others. You, as the individual, have the lions' share of responsibility for your outcome in life. You must start with a good foundation, based upon the norms of society. One elderly gentlemen would counsel me, saying, "If you start out right, you'll end up right." You cannot go down the path of life doing the wrong things and hope to end up on the right side of society.

A good belief system is a must. It will provide you with stability, guidance and encouragement to keep you on the right course. Even in the face of trials and tribulations, your attitude will dictate how high up the ladder of success you will go. No one likes to be around people who are bitter. Sure, life seems to have been kinder to some than to others. Sometimes the grass just appears to be greener on the other side of the fence. I am a firm believer in watering my own grass. If you water your own grass, it will be green. Have you ever gazed upon a neighbor's yard from afar? Did his lawn appear to be greener than yours? A green lawn gives the impression of being a healthy one. The grass may only appear to be greener on the other side of the fence. Upon closer inspection, you'll notice imperfections in his lawn, too. Be sure before you leap! What is needed is a sense of appreciation, not bitterness and faultfinding. Have a grateful spirit while continually seeking to become better. As Les Brown says in his book, *Live Your Dreams,* "The fight isn't over until you win." You can make it because others have done so. They have set their sights on their goals and have refused to take "no" for an answer.

Stretch out your rod! The biblical story is told in the book of Exodus (14:13) of a potentially calamitous affair. Faced with certain destruction at the hands of those who were pursuing them, the leader of the children of Israel, Moses, was told to use the tool at his disposal. His ability to succeed and deliver his people from harm, was in his hands. It was his rod. He was told to stretch out his rod. I tell those I counsel the exact same thing. Use the talents you have by stretching your rod. The opportunity for employment is all around you. If you are drilling for oil and observe other wells adjacent to you have struck oil, is it not logical to assume that you can too? So what if you drill and the hole comes up dry, drill another hole. This is certain. If you continue to drill, you may strike oil. However, if you give up, you are certain not to strike oil. This is the summation of all motivational books, keep trying and don't give up.

You cannot get to where you want to be staying where you are. If you are already employed, be a risk taker. Leave your **"comfort zone"** despite the realness of the fear factor. If you take risks, you have the opportunity to produce works that others will admire and emulate. Creativity comes with a price. The results will always be worth the risks taken. Above all, allow yourself to make mistakes. Be forgiving of others who make mistakes. What will motivate you to get out of where you are? Life, liberty, and the pursuit of happiness can all be achieved by fulfilling one state: being gainfully employed. Being employed empowers us.

There are no mysteries to becoming gainfully employed. All that is needed is guidance. The guidance provided in this book has been proven to be sound and understandable. It is doctrine that has withstood the test of time. The message is clear. Help yourself by investing time and energy to learn a skill, one that is in demand. Everyone has worth, value, and can be a productive citizen. What type of people are companies looking for? How will the choices be made? As a reader and job seeker, you must devise a plan to accomplish your goals. This information is contained in Chapter 8, **"Opportunities And Possibilities"** Chapter 12, **"Strategies For Employment,"** and Chapter 14, **"Politics."** There is no utopia. Everywhere you go there is going to be something wrong. It becomes a matter of what conditions you can work in.

You may have to crawl before you begin to walk. This consists of taking jobs that are not to your liking, but fit into your plan and strategy for success. If there is no support or encouragement for your vision, be prepared to go it alone. That is part of the price you'll pay for achieving your goals. Remember, misery loves company and no one likes a winner except other winners. As the months go by, you'll pass the naysayers. Do not despise them, pray for them. Prayer will help to keep bitterness out of your heart.

In any job, it is the little things that matter. "He that is faithful in that which is least is faithful also in much," Luke 16:10. Performing a job well will, in most cases, result in your being given greater responsibilities. With those responsibilities come importance. You will not be able to take off work or not show up at a moment's whim. Sometimes you'll be required to come into work early or stay late, as the job dictates. Do not become known as a complainer. Your reputation will go before you. Bosses love those "I can do that" and "whatever it takes to get the job done" attitudes. Your strategy should always be one of using prior employment experiences to get you to the next level. Your preference should be for jobs in the private sector. That is where your best chances are of succeeding on your own talents. That is also the place where you can negotiate from a position of strength.

Yes, **you can get a better job**. A better job is attained by using set, pre-defined principles and rules.

QUESTIONS & ANSWERS

The following questions were presented to me from various individuals. They are a sampling of the many different situations and dilemmas that can arise in the workplace or while seeking new employment.

Q. I do not like my present job. Should I quit?

Quitting a job is not something to be taken lightly. Terminating one's employment solely because the present position is not liked does not reflect sound judgment. When one is contemplating quitting a job, consideration must be given to the alternatives. Where will you go and what will your next job be? Do you have something better firmly in hand? There should be substantive reasons for leaving. You do not want to leave a job because you find it difficult getting along with other people. You will encounter those same types of people when you get to your next job. Learning to get along with difficult people is not an easy undertaking, but it is a valuable, acquired skill.

As a professor once told me, “You can pick your friends. You can't pick who you work with. Your boss does that.” That was proven to be true. I have worked on many committees in which I had absolutely no say in the groups' composition. The desire to move ahead financially, to gain satisfaction from employment, the lack of advancement opportunities, all of these are some fundamental reasons for quitting a job. Excluded from this list are reasons such as health, both mental and physical. It is assumed that one can make a rational decision to leave a place of employment that jeopardizes one's health. There are physical attributes of employment such as toxic waste, unclean air, hazardous working conditions, etc. that compel a person to seek other means of employment. In the same respect, there are jobs that are so stressful that it is possible to send a person “over the edge.” The definition of “edge” will remain undefined.

Q. How should I leave once the decision is made to do so?

When you have made a decision to depart for what you hope are greener pastures, care should be given to how it is done. Prior to leaving, it is assumed that your new employer is awaiting your arrival. All monetary and non-monetary issues have been settled. A minimum of two weeks notice should be given to your present employer. Do not leave on a bad note, even if the situation was not a pleasant one, no poison pen letters or voice mail messages condemning your former employers. There could be a strong inclination to “Give Them A Piece Of Your Mind.” I strongly advise against these types of emotional demonstrations. I am a firm believer in not burning bridges behind you. Making disparaging remarks about your former employer is not a "good thing." Not only is it not a proper way to exit, it just isn't a smart thing to do. Bosses move from time to time also. He or she may know some of the people where you are going. It is indeed a small world. If at all possible, leave in a manner in which you will be welcomed back.

Q. How do I establish what my new salary compensation should be?

Establishing what you desire as compensation is a very smart thing to do. My rule has always remained the same: keep what I've got and get some more on top of it. Some of my colleagues have gone on record as saying that they would take less money at the next job so that they could recover it, plus some more later. I am not an advocate of taking a step backwards so that two can be taken forward. It is my personal opinion that one should always be marching forward. All of your compensation has a monetary value attached to it. Vacation days, paid sick days, paid holidays and a host of other perks have value that can be calculated. Once they have been calculated, add that total to your base pay. That should be what you seek as your new rate of compensation. There is no guarantee that you'll get that amount, but you certainly won't get it if you don't ask for it. Squeaky wheels get the grease! I have always made it a rule to get my money coming in the door. Promises of greater compensation later are worthless. What happens when the person who promised you more money moves on before the plan goes into effect? Guess what? The new person knows nothing about it, so you do not get the raise.

Q. What if my present employer counters the offer prior to my

departure?

This is a very uncomfortable position to be in and there is no set rule on how to deal with a situation like this. The general guidelines I have used throughout my career are as follows. My decision to seek employment elsewhere was based on substantive reasoning and the decision was not hastily made. Energy was expended looking and setting up for the next job. My new employers will be expecting me to show up on the day agreed upon. Preparations have been made for my arrival. I would not want to damage my reputation by informing them that I changed my mind. I come from the generation that adheres to the philosophy that one's word is his bond. New employment should not be used as leverage to obtain a raise or promotion at one's present location. I have never, nor would I ever, use the prospect of new employment as leverage to obtain a raise or promotion. Maneuvers of this sort leave a very bad taste in the mouths of management. One should not make proposals to management such as, "If you offer me the equivalent to what company 'X' is offering, I'll stay." There is a marked distinction between soliciting a new job and one in which you are actively recruited by another company. Assuming there's no acceptance of the new offer of employment, it is expected that one would discuss the solicitation with one's present employer. This is a significant factor if there is a desire to stay put. Management inquiring as to what the new company is offering and proposing a counter offer is a completely different situation. You will, of course, entertain all offers. You do not have to take them. I firmly believe that your present employers will have more respect for you if you leave once you have made a commitment. As previously stated, leaving on a good note keeps the door open for a return.

Q. What if I don't know what I want to do? How do I find out?

There is nothing magic in finding your place of satisfaction in the job market. It is a matter of applying the knowledge that you already have or can gain about yourself. The key is recognizing your talents and skills and having the courage to exploit them. I say courage because that is what it takes to move into the area of life that I call "The Undiscovered Country." The discovery I am speaking of is the discovery of yourself. We all know people who sit on their talents and refuse to make use of them. We all have talents. They are God's gift to us. What we do with those talents is return the gifts back to God. If you don't know what to do, do that which you find the easiest and most readily available to you. "Use what you've got." An in-depth answer to this question is contained in the chapter called **"Dreaming And Discovery."**

Q. Does networking really work?

Networking is the process of pooling the knowledge resources available to you. Networking is the giving and receiving, and the exchange, of useful information. It has been truthfully said that no man or woman is an island. To be truly successful in any endeavor, you will need the assistance of other people. How are you to find out if there is a job opening that is well suited for you? Someone has to relay that message to you. If the job is one that could be attractive to a variety of people, you will no doubt want to be among the first to hear about it. The question is does networking really work? It depends upon the group of people with whom you form your network. You have to surround yourself with good people, people who have the equivalent or more knowledge than you. That is how you will be helped. When information you receive comes from individuals who have credibility, it is useful. If the information comes from individuals who are without credibility, it is useless. It is better not acted upon. To do so could be disastrous. "If the blind be leaders of the blind, they both shall fall into the ditch." It has been said that "it is not what you know, but who you know" that will get things going in your favor. I would like to amend that quote. It is not who you know, but who knows of you. There is a drastic difference between these two statements. For instance, I know who Rush Limbaugh is. He is a controversial television and radio personality who has made his views and perspectives widely known on any number of issues. Having listened to him for several years, I can say that I know him. That is, I know how he will reply to the subject matter presented to him. However, that television and radio personality does not know me. Therein lies the difference. I am not known by him. Networking will cause you to be known to people, and people can make things happen for you. Some interviews may be given out of courtesy because of a common friend. If no job is available at that moment, assistance may be given at a later date.

Q. Where do you find the resources to study the industry in which you are seeking employment?

If you are considering a career change that involves embarking in an entirely new direction, it would be wise to become as familiar with the industry as possible. Rather than exhaust your monetary resources by purchasing books on the vocation, make use of the public libraries. In areas where there are large populations, one can make use of a public library's reference section. A librarian can assist you in the search for information on the business you are looking for. A discovery of what a company makes or the services they provide can also be accomplished by using the "Thomas Registry" or the "Sweets Catalog." These are catalogs that list the goods and services provided by most of the companies and businesses in the U.S. Both large and small organizations are listed. Look up the industry's products and you'll be provided with a number of businesses or companies that provide the goods or services. The libraries of all public universities have a "Thomas Registry" or "Sweets Catalog." Some libraries have both. If you have access to a personal computer that has an Internet Service Provider (ISP) use one of the search engines to find information on the company's goods or services. The names of the companies will be listed. Most of the larger companies now have web sites and have the mission statement of the company plastered somewhere on the pages.

Q. What are the advantages and disadvantages of enlisting a job recruitment agency?

A job recruitment agency is better known as an employment agency, and is an agency that actively recruits viable candidates for employment. A fee is paid to them by the companies that use their services. This is sometimes called a "finders fee." The size of these agencies vary from large to small. They exist from coast to coast. Their recruitment range has no boundaries. They will scour the globe looking for people to fill the employment slots of their clients. An employment agency is not to be confused with a temporary employment agency such as Kelly, Account Temps, or

Man Power. A temporary employment agency has, as its goal, the placement of people within a company for use on a short or long-term basis. The employee is paid a percentage of the total billing paid by the host company. If the temporary employee is hired directly from the [temp] agency, a fee must be paid to the agency. This is standard operating procedure. There are some distinct advantages to using the services of an employment agency. An agency of any reputation will have access to opportunities statewide. The larger agencies will have knowledge of employment opportunities across the nation and throughout the world. That can come in pretty handy when you are seeking employment in an area of the country where you would like to move. One disadvantage of using an employment agency is the fact that contact with the employer is made prior to your appearance for the interview (an interview is standard procedure). That prior contact on your behalf can lessen your ability to negotiate the compensation. The compensation may be fixed and presented to you as a "take it or leave it" situation. Another possible disadvantage is that a perspective employer may be looking for someone with a specific skill instead of someone who is able to wear many hats. As previously mentioned, you are not making the initial contact yourself. It is being done for you.

Q. What information should I be aware of prior to a scheduled interview?

Have, already prepared, information on the company such as the products or services that they provide. Know the history of the company, tidbits of information such as who the founder is, or was, how many people are employed in that location, and the overall size of the company. Introduce these things into the conversation. If the company has issued stocks, knowing the value of the stock shows that you pay attention to the details.

Q. Are there any techniques that set an interviewee apart during a job fair situation?

A good first impression includes a conservative manner of dress, a firm handshake, and being assertive but not overpowering. Remember, you never get a second chance to make a first impression. Bring a professionally-polished resume. You must be able to respond quickly to questions that are asked. That takes practice, so practice at home with the aid of a mirror. More on the interview and the process is covered in the chapter **"Job Winning Techniques."**

Q. I am new to the job and I am not clear as to what my responsibilities are. I seem to be doing everyone else's work. What should I do?

Get a job description outline from your boss. Your job responsibilities should be clearly defined in written form. According to Quality Standards 9000 (QS9000), each person who is designated a "classified employee" should have a job description. In this manner, all ambiguity and confusion is removed. In addition, your written job description acts as a measurable yardstick by which your performance can be judged during a review. It would be easy for your boss and your fellow coworkers to "pile on," that is, to continuously add to your workload those activities and duties they do not want to perform. If you are a new employee, there may be some apprehension involved in questioning whether a specific job falls within your boundary. It is reasonable to refuse to perform a task that is handed to you by a fellow employee. Under no circumstances would I recommend refusing to perform a task that your boss has asked you to do, regardless of your job classification. You may also ask your supervision for a handbook of "policies and procedures" if one exists.

Q. I have been promised a job description outline and have not received it as yet. It has been a month since I asked my boss for one. What is my next step?

Be patient with your management. In the eyes of a manager, a month is not a long time. Consider that your boss has many other items that must be taken care of on a daily basis. He most likely has a boss who is placing things on his plate, too. Your job description may not be on his list of priorities. There are proper and non-offensive ways to remind him of your desire to have a job description. One method that may be employed is the use of an inter-office memo. There is nothing intimidating about a piece of paper lying on a desk or in a mail slot. If you are constantly reminding your boss verbally of what he has probably not forgotten, you run the risk of making a pest of yourself. "That is not a good thing."

Q. How do you react when you are continually given work that is beneath your capabilities?

This is a situation that many of us have been in before. Rather than assume our competence in whatever area we are involved, we are told that we have to "prove ourselves." How many times have I been told that? It fails me. Nonetheless, we do have to prove ourselves worthy of the task. It is a continual process, one that is never completed. The preferred method is to approach the person responsible for your job assignments in a respectful manner that is neither threatening nor aggressive. Ask for a time when you and he can meet to discuss how you can be of greater assistance to him and the company. The idea that you should try to convey to him is that it is in his best interest to give you more responsibility and better work. It is not advisable to become boisterous or disruptive, entering into the workplace of others and complaining. It has been said that the squeaky wheel gets the grease, but not in this instance. Vehemently complaining about the work that you are receiving will not place you in a good light with your boss. Volunteer to perform deeds that are in close proximity to the activities you would like perform. Give your boss a reasonable amount of time to respond to your desires. What is reasonable? Only you can be the judge of that. However, to expect an immediate response may be construed as unreasonable. If, after having allowed him a sufficient amount of time to respond and receiving no satisfaction, it is time to move on. Moving on can mean to a new department or even a different place of employment. You will not grow by continually doing work that is beneath your capabilities. Your business should be the business of going forward. If you are not going forward, you are not just standing still, you are going backwards.

Q. What should a salary increase be based on?

A salary increase should be based upon one thing and one thing only, performance. There is a chapter dedicated to **"Attitude and Performance,"** what defines a good attitude and optimal performance. Some confuse length of time on the job and performance as being one and the same. The two are drastically different. A person can have many years on the job and not be performing at his optimum level. Should he then be rewarded for this lack of effort? Let's add to this equation, the colleagues or coworkers of that person who are performing at the optimum level. How will they be convinced that their compensation is equitable when all have received the same reward? This is the mainstay of the organized labor movement. Give everyone the same thing whether they deserve it or not. If you are what is considered to be "dead wood," you are happy that a union exists to guarantee your compensation. If you are a person who is self motivated, a person who seeks to be rewarded for a **"Job Well Done,"** it is pay for performance for you.

Q. How much is too much when asking for a raise?

That is a very difficult question to answer. A simplistic answer is, you want as much as you can get. Generally speaking, what you desire is compensation equivalent to what others in your industry or service are making at the top level. An assumption is being made here that you are an optimal performer. There are some jobs with fixed compensation. Take, for example, a person working in some sort of food delivery service, be it a restaurant, pizza parlor, or small market. The margin of profit that the owner must make is closely tied to the price of the product. The only way for you to get a raise is to produce more. Any increase in the owner's costs, without a corresponding increase in production, will cause him to lose money. The price of the product can only rise to a certain level, above which, the owner can no longer remain competitive. A different rule of compensation applies when employed by a company that expects and makes provisions for salary increases. Those raises are scheduled and structured in such a way as to provide uniformity throughout the company. In most cases, you have no say in how much you will receive. You have the option to object to how little it may be, but that may not bring any restitution or satisfaction. The question, "How much is too much to ask for?" will be answered for you after you ask for the increase. No amount is too much to ask for. However, your boss may be the person who decides how much is too much to give you. Making a reasonable request for a raise will no doubt closely resemble what you may receive.

Q. My employer verbally told me when I would be getting a raise. Should I get this promise in writing?

How do you tell your boss to put a verbal promise into writing because you do not trust that it will be kept? Then again, a promise in writing leaves little or no room for a misunderstanding. I would trust my boss to honor his word and not commit him to penning the promise. If I were a boss and was asked to do so, I would be offended. It has been my experience that bosses sometimes promise things that they are not able to fulfill by themselves. They may have every intention of granting you what was promised. That is easy to do when the boss is also the owner of the business or has the authority to grant raises. When you are a member of a large company, the [HRM] people have the final say. Their outlook is for the entire company, not an individual. It is expedient for you to be able to determine whether the person promising is qualified to bring it to pass. Basically, a promise is only as good as the person making it, written or not written.

Q. How do you work with people who are intimidated by you because of your youth and superior working habits?

This is reminiscent of the kids who would get picked on at

school because they were smart. It is not that they thought they were better than everyone else, they just wanted to do the best that they could. Today, there are still symptoms of that behavior remaining. Some elderly workers have their minds and focus on retirement. They are indeed in the twilight years of their careers. They are slowing down, coasting into that last Get-Up. Then here you come, upsetting the apple cart, not only doing what is required of you, but more. For more insight into coworker relationships, see the chapter called **"Getting Along With People."**

Q. How does a young person work with individuals who have a lot of experience and are unwilling to share their knowledge?

Realistically speaking, they probably do know everything pertaining to the job. It is difficult to be on any job for a lengthy period and not know something. Your mission, should you decide to accept it, is to learn from them as much as possible, no matter how much garbage you have to take from them. Become a leach and suck every bit of knowledge out of them that you can. You will then be able to parlay that knowledge into a better job. "Getting along with people is an art form," as stated in the chapter of the same title. Be mindful of the older worker's possible mindset. Perhaps he is worried about losing his job if you learn too much. He has needs too, the foremost of which is to remain gainfully employed. He is more likely teach you what he knows if you are not perceived as a threat to him. Do not take on an aggressive posture by speaking to him in a disrespectful manner. Be as cooperative as possible, becoming his ally, not his foe. In some cases, this could be a difficult task. I have personal experience in this area. One thing you must always do is keep your eyes on the prize and remember what the goal is.

Q. I do not have dependable transportation. What things can I do to remedy this problem?

The chances are very good that you are not the only person experiencing this dilemma. You must be assured that there is a rational solution to the problem. If given a choice, I would place greater confidence in public transportation than I would on an undependable motor vehicle. With public transportation, if the vehicle becomes disabled, the operator will have a radio to call for assistance. With your own vehicle, you can become stranded in the middle of nowhere. Another thing you could do is place fliers on a bulletin board, advertising your need for a ride. A variation of this may be to obtain a regular ride that will place you as close to your place of work as possible. Then, perhaps, some form of public transportation can take you the rest of the way. I knew of a group of individuals who contracted with a person who owned a van to take them to their place of work. Their final destination was more than 60 miles away but they were met in the parking lot of a shopping mall and rode the distance together. It was their responsibility to get to a location that was central to all. The group paid the driver on a monthly basis and the fee was payable whether they were present on certain days or not. The cost burden was shared and was not placed upon the shoulders of any one individual. There are endless variations to this scenario. What you cannot hope for in any book is to provide you with all of the solutions. That is an impossible task because there are too many variations.

Q. I am interested in becoming employed at a company that requires me to take a test to determine my honesty. Should I take the test?

This is something new that has been added to the employment scene, mostly by retail merchants. Some merchants undergo a tremendous amount of merchandise loss due to employee theft. The "Honesty Test," as it is called in some venues, is an attempt to discover which employees are prone to thievery. Although the intentions of these merchants are understandable, some of the questions on the test may require certain individuals to incriminate themselves. The possibility exists for individuals to be punished again for past misdeeds. Then again, some of the questions asked are just plain stupid. They tend to encourage one to be deceitful in order to attain the job. If it is discovered that a person answered some of the question dishonestly, the perjury could be grounds for dismissal. Consider these things when the "Honesty Test" is presented. Ask yourself, "Is there something in my past that I may not want anyone to know?" That question will help you make the determination on taking such a test. For your specific constitutional rights regarding such testing, it is advisable to consult with an attorney who specializes in labor law.

Q. I am interested in becoming employed at a company that does periodic drug testing. They also want a drug test submission to accompany the employment application. Should I submit to one?

That is an easy question to answer. If you have ever been, or still are, a user of any type of illegal substance, you need not submit to a drug test. You have a much bigger problem. The use of drugs is a serious matter. Its use in the work place is becoming more important as the liability of employers increases. Anyone driving a company vehicle at any time of the day is considered an agent for that company. It is the employer who is sued when mishaps occur and the person involved has tested positive for illegal drugs. The employer has a right to a drug-free workplace. Periodic drug testing is completely permissible as long as this is stated as a condition of employment up front. What should be objected to is random drug testing at the whim of an employer. This may occur when drug problems are brought to the attention of the employer.

Q. I am interested in becoming employed at a company that requires a credit history check. I do not understand why that is necessary. Should I submit to one?

The reason why a company would require a credit check prior to employment is easily answered. Whether you should submit to one can only be answered by you. Companies may use your credit rating to determine if you are someone they would like to employ. Poor credit ratings are sometimes thought to be an indicator of the candidate's character, judgment and how you handle responsibilities. Whether these methods are reliable or not is debatable. Your credit rating may still be used in an attempt to find out as much information about you as possible. In addition, companies would like to protect themselves against needless harassment from debt collectors. When personal finances become a problem, they can also become the problem of your employer. Your creditor(s) may seek to put a lien on your wages to recover indebtedness. These actions can place undue hardships on company payroll activities. Furthermore, most people do not read the fine print when they sign credit applications. They have discovered, much to their chagrin, that in signing the credit application, they also gave their creditor permission to contact them at their place of employment. This usually occurs when payments are slow or not forthcoming at all. This can lead to many an embarrassing situation when your boss picks up the phone and an irate creditor is on the line. In order to head off these occurrences, some companies check the credit rating of employment candidates. As for the latter part of the question, only the employment candidate can decide if allowing a credit check is an invasion of his privacy. If it is deemed an invasion of privacy, the question now becomes, "Do I want or need the job that badly?" There are times when we do things for the sake of expediency, not because we like or agree with it.

Q. I am a high achiever. What kind of company should I be looking to work for?

High achievers are sometimes known as "Go Getters." They seek to make the impossible happen. For them, employment is more than just a place to work. They must constantly be challenged. They are performance oriented. Anyone can pilot a plane in level flight. It is when the plane begins to take a nose dive that courageous will be separate from the not-so-brave. Most people do not want to wonder if they are going to get another paycheck. Their personal responsibilities may not allow them to gamble on the company and stick it out. They want a sure thing. However, pulling the plane out of the nose dive is where the opportunities lie. To that end, one possibility is to look for a company that is in financial difficulty. It is certain that people will be leaving that company in droves. There could be several suitable positions available. Have some incentives built into your employment contract, if possible. If there is no employment contract, try to negotiate some sort of reward for participating in the plane's recovery or financial stability. This is just one example of a simple premise. You should seek employment where your skills are not only wanted, but where they are needed. Therein lies the greatest possibilities for job satisfaction.

GLOSSARY

At Will: This describes a period of time that is considerably elastic. For an employee, it means the employment has no limit but can be terminated at any time.

Blow you off: A derogatory, slang term used to describe the condition of being ignored or given the brush off.

Bulletin Board: A location where information can be placed for viewing electronically. Electronic bulletin boards serve the same purpose as bulletin boards in the workplace or classroom. An Internet Service Provider (ISP) is required to access a bulletin board.

Die: A device used to shape material by punching or by stamping it. A cookie cutter is a simple form of a die.

Die Maker: A person that is responsible for the making of dies to be used in the forming of material. Die makers are skilled tradesmen.

Download: To transfer files or information from one computer to another.

EIC: An acronym for Engineer-In-Charge. This was an executive level at General Motors in the 80's where the bonuses began. This level today is referred to as Assistant Staff Engineer.

Electronic Mail: A network service that enables users to send and receive messages using their computers.

Fabrication: The process of constructing a part, component, piece or assembly by molding a shape, pouring a mold, cut-ting, stamping or roll forming it.

Fast: The informal description of someone that is quickly moving up the corporate ladder. Another term used to describe this type of person is "Golden Boy" or "Golden Girl."

Headhunter: A person that does recruiting for organizations or business looking to hire people to work for them. These recruiters are paid a 'finders fee' when they have found suitable candidate(s).

Home Page: The very first page you are taken to of a web site.

Host: A very large computer that is able to handle many users and serve as the central processing unit for them all.

HRM: An acronym for Human Resources Management. This is a fancy term for what would normally be called the personnel department.

ISP: An acronym for Internet Service Provider. An Internet Service Provider is needed in order to gain access to the Internet.

Jobsetters: A person responsible for setting up a particular machining or some other manufacturing operation.

Machine Press: A large machine that is used to stamp out parts or components.

Machine Tools: A hardened piece of high strength steel that is used to cut softer metal.

Modelmaker: A miniature or full size representation of an object that is to be fabricated by a specified method.

Modem: A device for linking computers so they can exchange information using telephone lines.

Mounty: An acronym for the Royal Canadian Mounted Police (RCMP).

Newsgroup: A segregated area where information is placed on a specific topic or subject.

OEM: An acronym for 'Original Equipment Manufacture.'

Online: A term used to describe the condition of being connected to an entity. Usually the connection is to some type of electronic equipment.

Operator Sensitive: A description of a assembly line or manufacturing operation whose quality is dependent upon which person performs the operation. Therefore, the quality of the assembly or manufacturing operation varies.

Outsource: A term used to describe the process of sending work outside of a manufacturing or assembly facility where it would normally be done.

Permutation: Any of the ordered subsets that can be formed from the elements of a set. In plain English, this means variations on a theme, subject, or tangible object.

Production Tools: The final stage of instruments that are used to form or shape placed in a facility that will produce the parts or components.

Real World: This is a term used to describe the events as they actually occur in industry or society.

Roll Form: The process of sending some type of material through a sequence of shaped, cylindrical rolls. Each roll adds additional shape to the material.

Shooters: A slang term that is meant to be descriptive of executives of a company. Another term used to describe these individuals is 'Big Shots.'

Stampings: This describes the process of forming a material by using a die in a press.

Pre-formed: This describes the process of providing shape to a material prior to its introduction to a process or use.

Temp: An abbreviation for a temporary employee or temporary employment agency. Temporary employees are also known as contract employees.

Tool Maker: The description of a person who makes high quality instruments that are used in the production of parts or components.

Tooling Shop: A location where toolmaker(s) work.

Vocations: A profession or job, especially one to which an individual is particularly suited.

Web Page: A placement of information at a particular web site. A web page can be several pages long.

Web Site: A Uniform Resource Location (URL) where information can be posted by means of Graphical User Interfaces.

Workstation: A very powerful desktop like computer that is used in industry for a variety of functions. Workstations resemble personal computers but have considerably more computational capabilities.

REFERENCE SECTION

The Professional Resume & Job Search Guide

by

Harold W. Dickhut

A Prentice-Hall Publication

Leadership, Enhancing the Lessons of Experience

by

Richard L. Hughes, Robert C. Ginnett, Gordy J. Curphy

An Irwin Publication

The Management of Organizations

by

Jay B. Barney, Ricky W. Griffin

A Houghton Mifflin Publication

Preferential Policies, An International Perspective

by

Thomas Sowell

A William Morrow And Company Publication

Labor-Management Relations

by

Daniel Quinn Mills

A McGraw-Hill Publication

Psychology An Introduction

by

Benjamin B. Lahey

A William C. Brown Publication

Thriving On Chaos
A Passion For Excellence

by

Tom Peters

A Wings Books Publication

Lifetime Encyclopedia of Letters

by

Harold E. Meyer

A Prentice-Hall Publication

Second Thoughts

by

Mort Crim

A Health Communications, Inc. Publication

The Book Of Virtues

by

William J. Bennett

A Simon & Schuster Publication

INDEX

D

E

F

G

H

I

J

K

S

T

U

V

W

ABOUT THE AUTHOR

Al Stokes is a managerial and technical consultant and owner of Hallawood & Company. His firm specializes in the affairs of small companies and businesses. Al is a graduate of Lawrence Technological University's School of Engineering. He has many years of automotive design and engineering experience, working for General Motors, Chrysler Engineering, and various engineering firms. For his clients, he has been responsible for hiring, the termination of employees, equipment procurement, and a host of engineering and managerial related activities. Al has also been certified by the state of Michigan to substitute teach all grades from kindergarten through high school. Motivational speaking and employee moral boosting is also a part of the "Full Service" offering of Hallawood & Company. Al possess a deeply rooted desire to impart knowledge. This comes across loud and clear during his lectures. He blends his interpersonal skills with insightful information. You may book Al for speaking engagements by writing to him at:

Hallawood & Company
29209 Northwestern Highway PMB 566
Southfield, Michigan 48034-1006
Phone: 248.788.2950
Fax: 248.788.3431
E-mail: hallawood@hotmail.com

Hallawood & Company Publications, Inc.
29209 Northwestern Hwy. PMB 566
Southfield, Michigan 48034-1006
Phone 248.788.2950
Fax 248.788.3431

ORDERED BY:

Name ____________________
Address __________________
____
____
City _____________________
State _________ Zip ______

SHIP TO:
(if different)

Name ____________________
Address __________________
____
____
City _____________________
State _________ Zip ______

Qty.	Title	Cost Each	Total
	You Can Get A Better Job	*$16.95	
Shipping & Handling Charges $ 0 – $ 34 = $3.00 $ 51 – $ 68 = $5.25 $ 85 – $102 = $6.50 $119 – $136 = $7.25 $153 – Over = $8.75			
		Michigan Sales Tax	
		Shipping & Handling	
		TOTAL ENCLOSED	

☐ Check ☐ Money Order

Michigan Residents add $1.02 sales tax per copy. Non-profit Organizations excluded.
*Ten or more copies will receive a 40% discount – $10.17 per copy.

Customer information will not be sold or given to other merchants.